EASY MONEY

EASY MONEY

Charles R. Whitlock

KENSINGTON BOOKS

KENSINGTON BOOKS are published by

Kensington Publishing Corp.
475 Park Avenue South
New York, NY 10016

Kensington Books is a trademark of Kensington Publishing Corp.

LIBRARY OF CONGRESS CARD CATALOG NUMBER: 94-075129

ISBN 0-8217-4554-9

First Printing: May, 1994

Printed in the United States of America

This book is dedicated to the millions of victims who've been swindled, conned, lied to, financially devastated, mentally brutalized, physically traumatized, and whose lives have been ruined by unscrupulous con artists whose only interest is easy money.

ACKNOWLEDGMENTS

Thanks and great appreciation to Candace Smoral for her editorial assistance and long hours at the computer. Her devotion is a constant source of encouragement, her research a constant source of enlightenment. Additional thanks to Anne Kauffman, Susan McElroy, and Bill Donahue for their respective contributions and feedback on several chapters.

Last, but certainly not least, thanks to all of the law enforcement agency personnel, the many watchdog organizations and associations, the prosecutors, prison authorities, victims and con artists who contributed to the depth and breadth of *Easy Money*. Without their cooperation, this book would not have been possible.

CONTENTS

INTRODUCTION

Whether you've been conned out of your entire life's savings or just a few bucks, you're in good company. Would you believe that water can be changed into a cheap substitute for gasoline? Henry Ford did, and so did President Woodrow Wilson. They were among the many taken in by inventor—and con man—Louis Enricht in 1916 in the midst of a severe oil crisis. Despite printed reports in the New York *Tribune* that Enricht had no background in science, had taken money for a railway he never built, sold 45,000 acres of land he didn't own, and persuaded an English syndicate to purchase a formula for making artificial stone, Ford believed Enricht's convincing demonstration. He handed over a check for $10,000 on account and a new Model T. But Enricht returned Ford's check when he was offered a million dollars from munitions manufacturer Hiram P. Maxim, who offered to build him a laboratory and to fund further research.

With the advent of World War I and the boom in munitions, the deal was called off after Maxim had invested only $100,000. A rich financier named Benjamin Yoakum then gave Enricht $100,000 in return for a sealed envelope that was supposed to contain the secret formula to the gasoline substitute. Yoakum informed President Wilson of his plans to introduce the new mixture to the American public after

Enricht found a way to patent his formula. As would be expected, President Wilson was very happy at the prospect.

But Enricht kept stalling, and his delaying tactics aroused Yoakum's suspicions. When the private investigators he hired uncovered the possibility that Enricht was a German spy, Yoakum opened the sealed envelope and found only a few Liberty Bonds. Since Yoakum had opened the envelope prematurely without Enricht's approval, their agreement was broken. Yoakum died without ever knowing the secret or seeing Enricht stand trial for fraud.

To con, as defined by *The American Heritage Dictionary,* is "to swindle or defraud (a victim) by first winning his confidence; to dupe." Whenever our hopes and ambition exceed our common sense, the con man has an open field in which to operate. We are all potential victims.

In 1993, 25 percent of the FBI's agents were working on white-collar criminal cases. And these cases are simply the ones where the crime is interstate in nature, the government is involved, or large sums of money have been lost. How often are ordinary people scammed? How many swindlers are actually arrested, indicted, and convicted? Who are the victims? It's extremely difficult to gather accurate information regarding con games because of their very nature and the general unwillingness of many victims to step forward and report the crime to the police.

According to Portland, Oregon, Police Detective John Verheul, in a recent home repairs scam there were 45 elderly victims who did not report the crime until contacted by the police. The reason that most of them gave for not coming forward? Having given money to the con artists, the individuals were afraid that their relatives would immediately consider them incapable of handling their own financial affairs. Crimes in which someone may not be aware he or she is a victim cannot be measured effectively, and attempted crimes of this nature are greatly underrecorded. Also, events in which the victim has voluntarily participated in activities that are ultimately deemed illegal are frequently excluded from police records of cons.

In 1982, there were 200,190 arrests made for fraud in the United States. In 1991, that number rose to 258,792, an increase of 29.3 percent. (This number doesn't include forgery, counterfeiting, embezzlement, larceny/theft, or gambling offenses.) Yet, the number of convictions has fallen in proportion to the increase in crime. Why? Law enforcement agencies are asking this question, but the answer is complex.

As the schemes become more sophisticated, it becomes more difficult to identify the involved parties, investigate the case, and prosecute the criminals. Once con men get wind of an impending confrontation with police or receive too many complaints, they simply fold their tents and move away. All too often, law enforcement agencies are not fully trained or are too understaffed to investigate, for instance, an intricate real estate scheme where appraisers, real estate agents, and mortgage brokers conspire to defraud lending institutions. How is a law enforcement agency supposed to differentiate between an advance payment scam and a legitimate contract providing for a materials advance? How are prosecutors supposed to be able to build a case when the victims are reluctant to come forward?

It is almost impossible to keep up with the volume and different twists being put on various schemes. Boiler rooms employ thousands of telemarketers who work the phones stealing money from unsuspecting victims twenty-four hours every day, usually calling from one state into others to help avoid detection. Millions of pieces of mail tout bogus opportunities. The newspapers are full of ads for work-at-home scams and phony investment opportunities.

A con or scam doesn't necessarily require lofty investments. There are tens of thousands of unnecessary surgeries, uncalled-for roof repairs, perfectly good transmissions being replaced, and fraudulent credit card charges. The con artist may be disguised as a caring professional such as a doctor or accountant who swears only to have his clients' best interests at heart. The swindler could be an attorney, a police officer, a nurse, a teacher, an airline pilot, an entrepreneur, or a minister of God. They assume these roles because most of us have been taught to trust people in authority.

The fleecers of the flock will sell you dreams, beauty, peace, adventure, financial freedom, success, fame, and the adoration of others. From the self-proclaimed healer who, for a small contribution, will return your sight or give a true believer the power to walk, to the likes of Jim and Tammy Faye Bakker who will offer a vacation paradise for a $1000 pledge, *hucksters are everywhere,* seducing you and promising you gold at the end of the rainbow. The fantasy may be worth the price you pay, but the pot of gold will never contain more than a few ordinary stones of little or no consequence.

Con artists look, talk, and dress like other people. There are no telltale physical signs identifying a swindler from an honest person. But make no mistake: They are not like most other people.

A con artist will sell you a baby and not deliver it. He'll sell you a home he doesn't own. Or he'll take your home from you, even if you're eighty-six years old and have nowhere else to live. He'll sell you a wonderful vacation package and never mail you the airline tickets. He'll romance you and promise you marriage, then take all that you own. He'll sell you a burglar alarm system valued at $135 for $3000 or a $700 furnace for $9000. He'll steal your credit card number and ruin your credit while enjoying the bounty he has purchased. He'll obtain your checking account number and systematically empty your account. He'll take your insurance premium or your settlement check. He'll mail you phony invoices, then harass you when you're late in paying. He'll assume your identity and ruin your life before you know what hit you. You can bet your last dollar on it—these people will steal everything you own and laugh about it at the end of their workday. Their motto is simple: If the mark is too stupid to keep what's his, it's mine.

Ralph X. Lewiston made millions plying his trade against unsuspecting apartment tenants. He would gain access to secured premises by pretending to rent an apartment, then place a notice in each tenant's mailbox or slip it under the door that read, "The owners have asked American Rental Properties, Inc., to take over the management of this apartment complex." He included directions on how to make out the rental check to the new company and the address to send it to. He always arranged for the notices to be delivered just a few days before the first of the month so that he could capture the bulk of the rent checks.

Before the true management company knew that there was a problem or the tenants realized that their rent had been paid to the wrong company, the con man was long gone. The tenants would have to pay the rent *twice* that month.

This game netted Lewiston an easy $1 million a year—tax free. He had pulled off this tidy scam in eight cities before 1991. In Brooklyn, NY, he got the surprise of his life.

How was Lewiston supposed to know that the particular five-hundred-unit apartment complex he selected in Brooklyn used to belong to a savings and loan group that had been taken over by the Federal Deposit Insurance Corporation (FDIC)? In other words, the U. S. Government was the temporary managing agent. Moreover, one of the apartments was occupied by a senior government investigations director who knew that a private management company would not have been appointed without his knowledge, because it was his job to recommend such appointments.

When Lewiston went to his post office box to collect his checks, the authorities were waiting for him. Unfortunately, it usually takes extraordinary circumstances like these before con men and women are apprehended and put in jail.

A similar mortgage scheme has been played throughout the country. A mark receives a letter that states that a new company is servicing his home mortgage loan, usually, due to a corporate merger or acquisition. The letter goes on to instruct the mark where to send all future payments and correspondence. Frequently, there is no phone number listed on the letterhead. Unfortunately, all too often people follow the instructions without first verifying the change with the mortgage lender, and the scam artist prospers.

Few con artists get caught. A very small percentage who are arrested go to trial, and even fewer actually receive prison terms. Those who are supposed to repay their victims seldom do. Those who serve time usually serve short terms. In a recent year, although there were some 290,000 arrests for fraud, less than 4 percent went to trial. Of those who went to trial, only about 30 percent went to prison.

When I wrote this book it occurred to me how often I have been conned in my fifty years of living on this planet. At seventeen, a truck came by just as I was opening my car door. Within seconds, my door was thirty yards away. In just as many seconds, a very friendly man offered to have my old 1943 Chevrolet towed two blocks away for a free repair estimate. Two days later, I went to pick up the estimate. The car was worth about $500 at the time. The repair shop wanted $150 for towing and $400 to repair my car. When I refused the estimate, they locked up my car until I had paid the $150 towing fee and informed me that I would have to pay $35 per day for storage—beginning the day the car was brought in. That was another $70.

Yes, I'm one of those who has sent money to enter a sweepstakes. I have also donated a large sum of money to a con man who pretended to be running an auction on behalf of multiple sclerosis—$6500, to be exact. I have ordered merchandise over the phone and paid for it but never received it. I've paid premiums to an insurance company that refused to pay my claims. I have paid an advance fee to a landscaper who never came back to do the job. I invested $600 in a gold mine penny stock only to learn that the gold mine didn't exist. A con man sold me a $1.5-million house that had such major structural damage that I later had to abandon it.

I have a reasonable IQ and I'm fairly well-educated. I haven't lived a sheltered life. I take pride in being able to recognize a good opportunity when I see it. However, like most of my fellow human beings, at different times in my life I was desperate for recognition, scared, anxious, greedy, or lazy. At times I needed money, was looking for help with a problem, or was simply feeling philanthropic. Any of these feelings, if expressed to the wrong person at the wrong time, can set you up to become a victim.

I've come to the conclusion that there are actually three certainties in life: death, taxes, and getting conned.

Make no mistake about it, unless you live in a very sparsely populated area and never speak to strangers, you'll be approached by at least one con artist at some time in your life. You could be in your home, on the telephone, at work, on vacation, at a funeral, driving your car, applying for a job or a loan, at church, in a restaurant, or simply walking down the street. Just a month ago while I was in Manhattan, I witnessed a con artist fleece a tourist on Broadway. In less than three minutes flat the poor mark lost $40 because he was unable to identify which shell covered a little red ball. And I'm sure it looked so easy to him because another gentleman in the crowd (a shill) was able to pick out the right shell. Of course, the unsuspecting tourist had no idea that the red ball was in the huckster's hand, not under any of the shells.

Easy Money will teach you the tricks of the con artists. If you understand how the cons work, you will know how to protect yourself, your business, your family, and your assets. In this business knowledge is critical, because it's your only protection against the con artists. If you know how they ply their trade, you will know how to spot a con game, and what to do when a con artist approaches you.

Use *Easy Money* as a reference book and refer to it often. Before making investments, read the investment chapter. Before making home repairs, read the chapter that refers to them first to refresh your memory about how repair con artists work. Use the names provided in the resources section whenever you need help or more information about protecting yourself from various scams.

While I have separated the scams and schemes by type for easy reference, you'll note that there is some crossover between categories. For example, there is a chapter on investment cons and a chapter on telephone scams, even though there are many investment cons perpetrated over the phone. You'll find the infamous Frank Abagnale discussed in the chapter on bank fraud, even though he also defrauded merchants and airlines. You may also find certain advice regarding how to protect yourself from being conned repeated in other chapters. This is done in my attempt to be very thorough, just in case you don't read every chapter, or chapters are read out of order. In some instances, a person's real name may have been changed and circumstances slightly altered without materially changing the events.

Throughout *Easy Money* I recommend various governmental agencies, watchdog agencies, and consumer groups you can contact for additional information or to report suspected fraud. The addresses and telephone numbers are listed in the section entitled "Resources" in the back of the book. Refer to the "Glossary" as necessary to look up unfamiliar terms.

I hope you enjoy reading *Easy Money* as much as I enjoyed writing it.

CHAPTER 1

The Con Artist and His Victim

And oftentimes, to win us to our harm, the instruments of darkness tell us truths, win us with honest trifles, to betray's in deepest consequence.   —*Macbeth*, William Shakespeare
Act I, Scene 3

Is the con artist a psychopath? An immature prankster? Or simply a common criminal? As I reflected on the hundreds of cons described in this book, I looked for the common denominators, common threads that would help me pinpoint what makes these people do what they do.

I realized that it wasn't enough to understand the con artist's psychological makeup alone. The picture wouldn't be complete without taking a look at his victim. If the mark won't play and pay, there's no game.

The relationship between con and mark is unique in crime because of the voluntary participation required of the victim. And some victims seem to fall into the con artist's classic traps over and over again. A good example is an elderly Minnesota woman who played the crooked sweepstakes game until she was destitute, gambling away $65,000. When she finally reported the scam law enforcement officials took twenty-five plastic garbage bags filled with phony sweepstakes mailings from her home. (See Chapter 16, "Sweepstakes Fraud.")

Is it any wonder that the con artist is so contemptuous of his victims? He considers them fools or as crooked as he is; just losers in a dog-eat-dog world. Perhaps that's why consummate cons like Bill Alderdice (whom we'll examine in Chapter 8, "Investment Cons") could take money from senior citizens for gold bullion and never deliver it. After all, he was just making a few bucks on people who thought they were taking advantage of him because he sold gold below market prices.

According to David W. Maurer in *The American Confidence Man*, the con artist is the aristocrat of the grifters, those criminals who live by their wits without using violence. The con man avoids classification as a common thief because he does not actually steal in the conventional ways. "The trusting victim literally thrusts a fat bankroll into his hands. It is a point of pride with him that he does not have to steal." The flimflam man prospers because of his vast understanding of human nature.

Maurer goes on to say that the methods employed by con men "differ more in degree than in kind from those employed by more legitimate forms of business. Madison Avenue, for instance, seems to have adopted some of their techniques." Viewed from that cynical standpoint, where do ruthless salesmanship and shady business dealings stop and fraud start? We can all think of instances in which a salesperson has misrepresented his or her product, pushing aggressively to sell us something we don't want or need until we walk away from him, angry and affronted.

Indeed, many salespeople skirt the line between misrepresentation and outright fraud. The deciding factor is the seller's *intention*. A salesperson peddling a used car that isn't quite the gem he paints it to be is certainly not to be trusted, but he does intend to deliver the car, whatever its blemishes. The true con artist will promise the moon for a few paltry dollars and deliver nothing. From the beginning his intention was to defraud his victim, without giving anything in return. For the real con "artist," the goal is to prevent the victim from realizing he or she has been conned, or at the very least prevent the victim from complaining.

The Con Artist's Motives

Profit is not the only motivating factor for the con artist, though it is certainly an important one. Con artists have a great need to feel important and powerful, acting out their fantasies with their victims. Some researchers have stated that there even seems to be a sort of psychosexual thrill associated with controlling and taking advantage of the mark. In other words, con artists perform an act of seduction as they convince their victims to give up their money.

In keeping with the con artists' need to appear important and influential, they are frequently big spenders, flashing money around, gambling heavily, and taking large financial risks that may lead to heavy losses. Many con artists demonstrate addiction problems, abusing alcohol and drugs. It is possible that the tracking and taking of the mark springs from this addictive personality profile, since the scam provides a significant high for the con artist.

Generally, con artists are predators who somehow did not learn normal social and interpersonal conventions. In short, the con artist has a conscience that allows him to justify his actions through rationalization. He believes only in the law of the jungle. The world is a competitive place in which people prey on one another, and only the strong survive. If someone loses money to the con man, it just reinforces his self-justification. The scam is really the *victim's* fault, since it was greed that led him or her to take part in the game. In the con artist's frame of reality, mark and con are the same, and there is no such thing as an innocent man.

Psychological Makeup of the Flimflam Man

In his book *Money for Nothing*, author M. Allen Henderson states: "To succeed as a confidence artist, one must have a goldbricker's heart, a silver tongue, and the brass to carry a scam through to the end, no matter how outrageous it may be." But what really makes a swindler tick? What motivates him?

Richard Blum, a distinguished criminologist and researcher, studied con artists extensively, interviewing them and their victims and observing con artists at work. In his book *Deceivers and Deceived*, he states, "Most psychiatrists and psychologists who have studied [con artists] emphasize the presence of psychopathology, either in the form of neuroses or character disorders."

He asserts that these character disorders have their roots in the con artist's childhood, in which the child learned that lies could serve as a defense mechanism against parents in a dysfunctional family. The incredible fantasies that the con artist acts out with his victims in order to gain mastery over them can be traced to these early childhood neuroses, as well. Other characteristics, such as narcissism, the inability to form close emotional bonds with others, delusions of importance, and extensive rationalization and self-justification can be seen as the extreme expression of these same childhood coping mechanisms.

Blum administered psychological tests to a group of con artists, and the results revealed they were "impulsive, amoral, uncontrolled and detached from normal relationships and thinking processes, [as well as] depressed and compulsive. There can be no question that they are an unusually sick group in terms of mental health and an unusually antisocial group in terms of lack of regard for others and the lack of control over their own impulses." They scored very low on ego strength.

Regrettably, our society has painted a different picture of the con artist, virtually deifying him as an archetype of valued social behavior. Heavy emphasis is placed on salesmanship in business, and the "sharp" salesman is viewed as a very admirable individual. It has become an expected practice for businesspeople to lie and misrepresent products in the course of normal business.

The con artist merely takes these traits to extremes. Since most con artists avoid violence and demonstrate qualities that could be mistaken for astute business practices, albeit with larcenous intent, many people have a sort of grudging admiration for them from a distance. Movies and television frequently make heroes of smooth operators who put one over on their adversaries, *The Sting* being a classic example. Up close and personal, the overwhelming charisma and manipulative power of the con artist can simply sweep away an individual's defenses and leave him easy prey for the swindle.

The Consummate Actor

Con artists come from a broad spectrum of social backgrounds, ranging from deep poverty to old money. The typical con artist is male; surprisingly few are female, although the number of female grifters seems to be growing. While many of them are well educated, others have little formal education, having picked up what they know "on the job." They present an image of friendliness and self-assuredness, with a pleasant demeanor and smooth sophistication, regardless of their roots.

The con man is a consummate actor, playing with equal facility the part of the wealthy businessman or the bumbling fool who is down on his luck. Any part he plays is designed to draw the mark into his game and, ultimately, to extract cash in exchange for the performance. This sense of theater, coupled with superb salesmanship and a nearly mystical charisma, combine to make the con artist the most dangerous of predators.

A con artist who was raised in the poorest neighborhood will make just as convincing a show of being a rich playboy or hard-nosed businessman as a swindler raised in a wealthy family. Despite economic hardship and lack of education, con artists manage to develop a superficial presentation suggestive of wealth and power. This carefully crafted image becomes the key to overwhelming their victims.

Given this extraordinary ability to rise above their circumstances, I have wondered why con artists go to the trouble of setting up complex swindles when they could simply go out and get a job. Considering their demonstrated sales abilities, they should do very well. In fact, many con artists do occasionally hold regular jobs, most frequently in sales or other high public-contact positions. The difficulty arises when the con artist becomes frustrated with his position, his boss, or his clients.

Con artists have a very low tolerance for the sort of workday annoyances that most of us take for granted, which doesn't make them good employees. Besides, a competent con artist can make far more money running scams, so why bother with a "straight" job? And there's another, more compelling reason that goes far beyond any financial gain the con artist will realize. As one con artist told Blum, "Half of being a con man is the challenge. When I score, I get more kick out of that than anything; to score is the biggest kick of my whole life."

The combination of easy income and the high gained from a successful con leads most con artists to repeat their crimes again and again. Even those who get caught and sent to jail simply con inmates or run scam operations by mail or telephone from prison.

Profile of a Victim

Victims of scams can come from any economic or social class; they may be school kids, senior citizens, or something in between. There is some evidence that women are conned more frequently than men, possibly because women—especially older women—have been socialized to be nice and sometimes have difficulty standing up for themselves under pressure.

Yet a 1992 Lou Harris and Associates poll for the Consumer Protection Network Project discovered that women and people over fifty were slightly less likely to have been cheated out of their money than men, people with household incomes less than $15,000 or over $75,000, African-Americans, and anyone who has been turned down for credit in the past year. It was noted in the poll that this finding may be because 1) women may be more conservative money managers than men, and 2) changing cultural attitudes have resulted in younger people being less likely to be cautious in their financial dealings.

The victim shows nearly as layered a personality profile as the predator, demonstrating traits that intersect with those of the con artist in a way that facilitates the success of the scam. This is not to imply that the victim is also crooked, as the con artist would have us believe. On the contrary, most victims of swindles are scrupulously honest and trusting, and many are deeply religious.

Psychological Makeup of a Typical Victim

Blum's psychological tests revealed a far different picture of the typical victim than that painted by the con artist. Blum discovered that his sample victims were "a group of simple and narrow-minded, lonely folk unable to cope with others, anxious for approval and seeking human contact; they are passive people trying hard to be nice . . . without being able to examine what they are doing, what others are proposing or what the consequences of their compliance with the bunco proposition will mean. Unhappy for the most part, they do dream dreams of a life . . . beyond their reach; some use outright magic trying to find it."

In Blum's interviews, these victims revealed that they were often depressed. Many fantasized about adventures or exciting experiences. Most wanted to be thought of as good people, and they were largely concerned with being liked, helpful, honest, practical, and a good sport. They said that while they felt people had a good deal to fear from criminals, they thought most people were basically honest. The victims also said that if they were straightforward with others, people would respond in kind.

The mark must be willing to trust, making a financial and emotional commitment to the possibilities promised by the con artist. This suspension of disbelief allows them to accept the terms of the scam, including secrecy and confusing circumstances with little or no explanation. In some cases, victims do demonstrate a willingness to conspire against another as they are drawn into scams in which the con artist is playing one person off against another (usually an accomplice). But for the most part, victims are merely on the receiving end of the scam, carried along by the con artist's assurances and fantastic promises.

Alphonse Mortier, a fifty-four-year-old convicted con artist stated it well: "Every one of my victims was smart enough to see through my scam. My job was to make sure that they didn't have any time to think."

The honest nature of many victims is what leads them to be conned in the first place. The Lou Harris poll found that nearly half the American public describe themselves as trusting or open-minded when dealing with people whom they don't know. People between the ages of fifty and sixty-four and those with post-graduate degrees were found to be somewhat more likely to see themselves as being trusting, while people sixty-five and over, those with less than a high school education, and Hispanics were somewhat less likely to view themselves as trusting or open-minded.

Interestingly enough, only 2 percent of those calling themselves trusting and 2 percent of the self-described open-minded individuals had actually been victims of telephone fraud over the past two years.

The Victim's Investment in the Con Artist

Blum stated in *Deceivers and Deceived:* "The con artist must be more than a business opportunity in the eyes of the mark. He is more than a storyteller too, for he is a magician who guides the victim into a world of pleasant dreams. Those dreams are not solely of the future, the bait of money or joy at some later time but are in the present, for it is in the present moment that there occurs the hope, the excitement, the dispelled loneliness and the sense of importance in association with prestigeful men (the con man wearing his mask), which constitute the early returns on the victim's investment in the con man."

Some writers have also characterized the con artist as having a hypnotic hold over his victims, inspiring in them a level of trust that most people would be loathe to give anyone but their closest loved ones. In fact, lonely, isolated people are far more likely to be victimized than those with close families. Elderly women and men often fall prey to the con artist's game because they are starved for attention, and there is no one close to them to advise them that the scheme seems bogus. Blum asked victims what general advice they would give to others to help them avoid being swindled. Perhaps the most telling was the response of one woman who said the best defense would be the prevention of loneliness.

Weaving the Web

Like any predator, con artists seem to have an almost innate ability to select potential victims and assess their weaknesses. Street hustlers will make a superficial evaluation of people passing by in a matter of minutes to "qualify" them as potential victims, while those who specialize in complex investment scams or marriage bunco may spend weeks selecting and researching their marks.

Qualifying the victim is one of the most important features of the scam. The con artist will make his choice based on several factors, which may include:

- A positive response to the initial contact
- An expression of interest in the con artist's proposition
- Evidence that the mark has money
- Evidence of susceptibility to control by the con artist

Let's look at a classic marriage scam. The con artist approaches his victim, usually a lonely widow, offering friendship. She is flattered by the attention and agrees to spend time with the con artist (positive response). He woos her, plying her with increasing attention and flattery, giving her gifts and taking her to expensive restaurants. In doing this, he establishes himself as a man of importance and wealth. He proposes marriage or dangles before her some other carrot she cannot resist. She consents to marry him (interest in his proposition).

Most likely, the con artist had already determined that the woman has money before the relationship began. Throughout the process of wooing and winning the woman, the con artist has demonstrated his mastery in countless subtle ways. He chooses the places they will dine, suggests she wear her hair a certain way, or any of a number of different subtle control tests (evidence of susceptibility). If he sees that she is willing to follow his suggestions, he will gradually turn up the heat, getting her to give away more and more of her control, until he has taken over her life and stolen her money. Then he disappears, leaving a bewildered, broken-hearted victim behind.

This is merely a possible scenario, but some or all of the basic elements are found in virtually every type of con. Blum interviewed con artists who shared their secrets for qualifying marks:

"To rule people you must not fear them. If you want them to do what you want, you must not show fear or weakness. The moment you show any weakness, you are done."

"When you swap money, then you know he's really in. I'm always pulling the vic inconspicuously to see what way he'll go."

"I find women who've been lied to. I like those who've been lied to and wronged many times. They don't believe the truth anymore. So if you lie they believe you."

"I look for jewelry, a thick wallet, behavior of the happy-go-lucky kind, maybe someone a little drunk, especially well-dressed people. Of course I like the foreigners—you can tell them by oddity of dress. In any event, in my business you need to know quality."

As soon as the con artist has selected and qualified his mark, he begins the process of luring the victim into his game. The first overtures are innocent, giving no hint of what is to come. After all, the con artist wants the victim to trust him, to have faith in what he says.

Once he has won the mark's confidence, he pulls a "switch," guiding the victim into a discussion of the mechanism on which the scam has been constructed. The ideal situation is one in which the con artist maneuvers the mark into bringing up the desired subject himself, effectively dispelling any possible suspicion. Before long, the mark has virtually sold himself on giving money to the con artist.

After the money has changed hands, the scam moves into the "cooling off" phase. In some of the better scams, the con artist manages to make it appear that the money is hard at work, say, in a business venture that will take a while to pay off for investors. Or the money may be lost through predictable reverses of fortune, giving the victim the idea that every person involved lost his or her investment, including the con artist.

Whatever the technique, this "cooling off" period can go on for quite some time, as long as several years, accompanied by assurances from the con artist that the dividends will be pouring in once business circumstances improve. This is all orchestrated to prevent the mark from suspecting he or she has been taken and filing a complaint with law enforcement officials.

Another technique con artists use to assure the silence of their victims is to draw them into a scam in which the victim believes he or she is implicated in some fraudulent scheme, perhaps even to the extent of participating in defrauding someone else. Usually, the other person is just the con artist's steerer, an accomplice, playing a part.

Take this con artist's description of a racetrack scam from *Deceivers and Deceived*: "Another thing is to have the steerer make an error somewhere early in the game, let's say a forgery mistake which . . . all of us catch but we go ahead anyway, but the mark thinks we're all in jeopardy of prison. So it comes out just at the end . . . that if the egg [mark] wins, [because of] that mistake we all knew about, the egg will go to prison. So when another horse wins and the egg loses his shirt, the egg is grateful as hell since he's not caught up on that felony. That's a real con, a professional job, when the egg is grateful to you for taking his money. That's the art. Anyone can take the money and get out, but blowing it off [cooling] is where the true con comes in."

Summary

Contrary to popular fiction, con artists are not suave, sophisticated good-time guys who take advantage of sleazy individuals and criminals. They are maladjusted career criminals whose activities bring pain and financial ruin to the most vulnerable people in society, many of them lonely, isolated older people who give up their life's savings for the brief attention and fantasy of importance and wealth presented by these social leeches.

There is nothing admirable about con artists. In many ways they are more detestable than the man who sticks a gun in your face and steals your money, because they pretend to be your friend, say they're there to help you, win your trust and then take away both your money and your faith in humanity.

What Can You Do to Protect Yourself?

While it is impossible to avoid becoming a victim unless you retire from society completely, there are some basic guiding principles that can protect you.

First, know yourself well. Are you at high risk of becoming a victim? Have you been a victim of a scam before? What happened and why? Do you exhibit the characteristics of the classic victim? Bear in mind that while we all possess these characteristics to some degree, it is in their most marked state that they put you at risk.

Second, be more aware in social situations. If a relative stranger begins to offer you impossible dreams, perhaps you should review the relationship and be wary of him or her. Is the person charismatic? Do you feel swept away when you are around him or her? Back off and give yourself some breathing space.

Third, always investigate before you invest. Never put your money down until you have fully evaluated a business or investment opportunity. And that includes getting the opinion of a disinterested third party, such as your lawyer or accountant.

Fourth, don't be afraid to cast a jaundiced eye on something someone is offering you, and don't be embarrassed to simply say, "No." If it's the real thing, it will stand the cold light of day. If not, you will have saved yourself a lot of misery.

Finally, never forget the truism: "If it sounds too good to be true, it probably is."

CHAPTER 2

The Con Artist's Best Friend: The Telephone

When the phone rang, Jeff Trottogott was down on his luck. An aspiring actor, Trottogott didn't have any theater or movie roles going. He was scratching by on ten-dollar-an-hour modeling jobs from the department stores near his home in tiny South Saltillo, Tennessee. And now, suddenly, there was a man on the line offering him a part in a major film. A film starring Patrick Swayze, then at the height of his popularity.

Trottogott, this caller said, would play the part of a young football player. He was to have a line of dialogue, and he might even take part in an on-screen scuffle.

How could the youth not have been overjoyed? How could he have acted calmly, and with perfect good sense, as he was being handed the break that, it seemed, would launch him into the big time?

Trottogott believed the caller, who said his name was Jack Lara. And he was only a tad suspicious when the caller's associate, Tom Lisp, an executive for a firm supposedly named Patrick Swayze Productions, phoned later that evening, to announce that Trottogott would have to pay a small fee before stepping onto the movie set.

Lisp told Trottogott that, because he would be speaking three words in the Swayze film, he would have to pay $690 to join the Screen

Actors Guild. Trottogott questioned the "executive" briefly, and even phoned the number for the union that Lisp provided for verification, but soon he was wiring his cash to Los Angeles and boarding a flight to Memphis for the alleged start of the filming.

"Jack Lara" and "Tom Lisp" were, of course, phony names; Patrick Swayze Productions was a fictitious company. And Trottogott had only one thing waiting for him when he got off the plane: an empty hotel room.

Jeff Trottogott was dejected and bitter, but he was hardly the first American ever to be scammed over the telephone. Con artists have been relying on the phone—that convenient, inexpensive tool that affords anonymity—ever since the 1920s, when south Florida salesmen hawked mosquito-infested swamps as "prime property." And now, it seems, fraudulent telemarketers are a fixture on the American scene.

Very broadly defined, telemarketing fraud is any scheme that utilizes telephone communications to cheat its victims out of their money. Most of the fraudulent schemes are cleverly designed to resemble legitimate business dealings, making detection and prosecution of the fraud very difficult.

Although 95 percent of telephone sales calls are from legitimate businesses, the telephone continues to be the easiest way for con artists to reach their marks. And since fraudulent telemarketers are experts at sounding as if they represent legitimate businesses, consumers can't assume that they'll be able to recognize a scam when they hear one.

In 1992, when New York–based Louis Harris and Associates polled American adults about fraud, it found that 3 percent of all the respondents—which translates to 5.5 million Americans—had been cheated by a phone swindler during the preceding two years.

These people, Harris learned, were not always the lonely and gullible senior citizens whom most Americans tend to believe are the stereotypical phone scam victims. The consumers who said they bought something by telephone that they now feel was fraudulent were more likely to have less than a high school education, an annual income of $15,000 or less, or be African-American or Hispanic. Some 62 percent of those people polled didn't know where to call to find out if a telephone offer is legitimate.

According to the Harris poll, more than 17 percent of Americans find it hard to resist a sales pitch over the phone. Yet, Harris reports that people who called themselves inherently "suspicious" were three times as likely to be bilked as those who said they were "trusting."

The Federal Trade Commission reports that for every written complaint they receive, there are one hundred to one hundred fifty people who should have filed a complaint but didn't. Only about half the American adults polled by Harris said they would hang up the phone when someone they didn't know presented an opportunity to make an investment; the other half are all potential targets of telephone fraud.

Telephone swindlers, according to the National Consumers League, reap over $15 billion each year in this country. They score enough illicit cash to drive Porsches and to jet to Las Vegas on luxurious gambling junkets. How do they do it?

For starters, they invoke the age-old tactic of cons: They promise to deliver to a person exactly what he or she is seeking—whether it's an acting role, a job, a bank loan, or a Visa card with a huge line of credit. Or they offer you a "free," "prepaid," or "special deal" on magazine subscriptions or exotic travel package. You may be told that a long-lost uncle has left you a fortune, or that you're his life insurance beneficiary; just send $200, and the money will be yours. And as they're making promises, phone swindlers pressure people to make hasty, foolish decisions; they offer "free" gifts and cajole their victims into giving out personal information, such as credit card and Social Security numbers. They capitalize on people's innate kindness—their reluctance to rudely slam down the phone—and they hide away in buildings that are safely distant from the scrutiny of law enforcement officials.

It's estimated that about 70 percent of all phone-scamming firms operate in Southern California, where telephone fraud laws are relatively lax. They do their business, typically, in Spartan "boiler rooms" that are crammed with simple desks bearing telephones. Solicitors—who are often unemployed actors—hunch over these desks, delivering tightly scripted pitches that their bosses have helped them to polish. Almost invariably, they phone people who live far away, in another state.

Almost invariably, in other words, they coyly seek to evade detection. Although the FTC operates a central clearinghouse database on telemarketing fraud in conjunction with the National Association of Attorneys General that's available to state and local law enforcement officials, other key federal agencies don't participate in the program. Con men and women know that if they rob honest citizens in a distant state, word of their scam probably won't make its way back to the local officials likely to nab them. And they realize, too, that historically, the

U.S. legal system has been highly ineffective when it comes to catching phone swindlers.

A 1991 U.S. House of Representatives report concluded that the U.S. Department of Justice, and particularly the Federal Bureau of Investigation (FBI), "have not given telemarketing fraud investigations and prosecutions the priority they deserve." It showed, as well, that the Internal Revenue Service—which has the power to nail the thousands of phone swindlers who evade income taxes—is too financially strapped to seriously combat telephone fraud.

All of which means that telephone swindlers can easily operate in one location for a few months and then slip into oblivion without ever facing reprimand.

There are now an estimated one thousand inactive phone fraud cases languishing in the files of law enforcement agencies across the country—and there are, no doubt, scores of con artists on the loose, scheming, cooking up new and devious ways to fleece innocent people over the phone.

How can you protect yourself? The best defense, says a group called the Alliance Against Fraud in Telemarketing, is knowledge. Read the following cases, which describe a variety of telephone cons, and you'll see the way they work.

Advance Fee Loan Scams

Factory worker Brian Haacker from Prineville, OR, was a lot like the young actor, Jeff Trottogott. He was financially struggling; he was swamped with bills. So when he saw an ad in his local paper—the one that promised "Debt Relief" and "Fast Help"—he called the 800 number for information and then, quickly, he fell for a con.

Haacker took the advice of the telemarketer to whom he spoke. He sent $239 to Associated Financial Services in Riverdale, GA, believing that, for this sum, he would be guaranteed a $10,000 loan. Then he waited for the money . . . but it never came.

Haacker had become the victim of a common scam—the advance fee loan scam. Advance fee loan schemes have been recognized by law enforcement agencies since the 1970s, when they were used to prey on farmers in the Midwest. Only recently have they become a national problem.

In this swindle, con artists seek out money-starved small business owners and consumers whose credit ratings are poor, and they assure these people that, for a "small" application fee paid up-front, their problems will be solved with a loan, perhaps even a no-interest loan.

Typically, the application fee runs from one hundred to five hundred dollars. Sometimes, when businesses are trying to borrow money, it's as high as one hundred thousand dollars. Always, certainly, the fee is more substantial than the promises the phony loan agents mouth: What advance fee scam artists do, in most cases, is forward their client's loan application to banks—to the same cautious banks that routinely deny loans to people with poor credit ratings.

Can they do this legally? That's a tough question. Companies are, of course, forbidden to fraudulently tell people they can guarantee loans. But they can legally operate as "lender referral services," and craftily dodge most allegations of fraud, which are very hard to prove to a jury. The Better Business Bureau notes that, of the tens of thousands of complaints it's received about advance fee loan firms, only a handful have been prosecuted. Law-enforcement efforts have been uneven since authorities are overworked and, despite the flood of complaints, the individual losses in most cases are too small to garner much attention. Plus, many states simply leave the terms of loans up to the lender and borrower.

Most loan scammers, indeed, incur only riches from their work. Con artists in the U.S. take in about $12 million a year in advance fees for loans, and individual firms have been known to average over one hundred thousand dollars a month in receipts and to deliver precious little in return. One Tucson, AZ, loan outfit was in business only three months but managed to take in 1702 loan applications and almost half a million dollars.

The vast majority of advance fee loan companies never secure funds for their clients. Reputable lenders can't make money lending to individuals and businesses who won't be able to repay the loans. Consider, for instance, the track record of a Staten Island firm called Greek Enterprises, which was recently targeted by federal loan prosecutors for taking in a total of $1 million in up-front fees from 1700 people. It facilitated a grand total of three loans.

And it probably didn't fail just because it was representing people with bad credit ratings. Experts note that advance fee loan firms hardly ever lobby banks on behalf of their clients. They say that these outfits are callously single-minded in their pursuit of cash—and, to illustrate their point, they point to a Redondo Beach, CA, company called Capital City Finance.

Capital City's small office, which was run by twenty-five-year-old Jerome Okeefe, was clamorous with ringing phones at all hours of the day and night. People were calling from everywhere, from Alaska to Puerto Rico, and applications, ready with checks for $75 apiece, were flowing in by the thousands.

Okeefe was so busy that he didn't even have time to eat lunch. But what was he doing? He was, it appears, merely processing the checks. Many of the loan applications, he admitted recently, never made it past a storage box.

It was an awful swindle, and apparently even Jerome Okeefe felt a bit remorseful. When an elderly woman called him one day to say that she needed cash to bury her husband, Okeefe deftly tried to talk her out of applying for a loan. "I kept trying to hint to her what was going on, [and] telling her to try a bank or something," he has said. "But we sent her an application." (Please see Chapter 4, "Robbing a Bank Without a Gun.")

Credit Card Scams

Almost everybody wants to have an infinite cash flow, or the ability to whisk out a credit card and pay for a dream vacation, a new car, or whatever he or she pleases. And almost everyone likes to be flattered.

Hubert Allen Jeffreys knew these two basic facts about human nature, and he used his knowledge for all it was worth as he directed a lucrative business called Americorp Unlimited, located in Southern California.

Americorp was a boiler room operation. Solicitors phoned unsuspecting souls and told them their credit ratings were so good, so perfect, that they deserved a new credit card. The card, the phone salespeople said, had a five-thousand-dollar credit limit, no annual fees, and an enticing 10.8 percent interest rate. But there was one catch: To receive the card, customers would have to pay a flat fee—for "processing"—of $198.

This condition should have been enough to tip people off; callers, having learned of the fee, should have phoned the credit card companies to find out the truth—that, actually, Americorp had no affiliation with either MasterCard or Visa.

But it seems that flattery has the ability to melt skepticism away and win people over. Twelve hundred people paid application fees to Americorp during the firm's brief, fly-by-night tenure. Americorp netted about two hundred thousand dollars between July 1991 and January 1992, and Jeffreys fled to Hawaii with some of the cash.

Police finally apprehended the entrepreneur at a beachfront home near Maui. They held Jeffreys on a warrant that charged him with grand theft and conspiracy, and ultimately, the twenty-five-year-old swindler was put in jail. He got just over four years and will be in prison until at least mid-1994.

But, of course, Jeffreys's imprisonment didn't slow his "colleagues"—the scores of con artists bent on bilking people hungry for credit. The FBI reports that swindlers nationwide are now, with regularity, invoking a sophisticated credit-peddling scam that is best labeled the "direct debit swindle."

Criminals, in enacting this scam, offer would-be customers low-fee, low-interest credit cards and insist that, to facilitate business, they need two things—the client's checking account number and the "routing number" printed at the bottom of his or her checks.

The request sounds reasonable, even trivial. But it's not. Con artists use the digits they've obtained to crack the electronic codes that form the nervous system of today's banks. They magnetically encode the numbers into the same sort of demand drafts—authorizations of automatic withdrawals—that are used legitimately by athletic clubs and insurance firms, and they request that large sums be transferred their way.

Their drafts are illegal, of course—technically, they must be accompanied by the written authorization of the account holder—but quite often they fly. They evade the detection of bank personnel, who are too busy to check through their files for small slips of paper bearing signatures. Although these scams are apparently on the decrease, banks and consumers should be ever-vigilant.

Swindlers have made direct debiting the cutting edge of telemarketing by reaping millions from this high-tech scam. And what are they giving people in exchange for the cash that they're raking in?

Nothing of worth.

According to Dennis Brosan of Visa International, phony credit peddlers typically mail their victims a list of banks that provide secured credit cards. These lists can be obtained for a dollar or two from state agencies, but they are nevertheless more valuable than the items sent out by the most devious of credit-peddling swindlers, such as the firms that promise their clients "gold" and "platinum" cards.

The cards turn out to be made of colored cardboard. They may only be used to make purchases from an accompanying specialized catalog—and the items in the catalog are, of course, vastly overpriced. Marketers of these "credit card" programs often promise that, by participating, an individual will be able to obtain major credit cards such as a Visa or MasterCard, lines of credit from department stores, and improved credit ratings.

These phony cards may cost up to $50, and often the merchandise catalogs cost an additional fee, despite the fact that the cards may only be used to buy catalog merchandise. And you may have to make a cash deposit (usually equal to the amount the company paid for the product) in order to charge an item from the catalog. (For more information about credit card scams, see Chapter 6, "Credit Card Fraud," and "Conclusion.")

"Handicapped" Felons

The pitch is quite simple. "I'm handicapped," the caller says, "and I'm selling light bulbs. Can you help me out?" Your gut reaction, probably, is to be sympathetic, compliant. You figure that you're going to need to buy light bulbs (or maybe it's trash bags or ironing board covers) anyway, so why not help out a good cause while you're at it?

The problem is that you very likely may be aiding a misleading cause. According to the Alliance Against Fraud in Telemarketing, most phone solicitors who claim to be handicapped are, in fact, not physically disabled. They're "handicapped" by a criminal background—and they are, the Alliance warns, usually peddling merchandise that is grossly overpriced and thoroughly inferior.

900 and 976 Line Scams

In 1991, just after the war in the Persian Gulf had come to a fiery end, images of ravaged Kuwait often flickered across American television screens. Viewers saw burning oil fields and bombed-out buildings and, spurred by the patriotic rhetoric piping out of their TV sets, wanted to help rebuild tiny Kuwait.

Thousands of Americans wanted to land jobs in the Middle East, in a society that they knew little about. It was a situation that had con artists brimming with glee.

A rash of deceptive newspaper ads surfaced in the weeks following the Gulf War. Displayed prominently in the classified pages, they beckoned readers to dial 900 or 976 numbers to learn about positions with construction projects in Kuwait. The jobs, of course, didn't exist, and callers got only one reward for responding to the ads—whopping phone bills.

Like all phone lines whose numbers start with 900 or 976, the "job lines" operated on a pay-per-call basis. Callers were charged exorbitant rates to hear prerecorded messages and, in some cases, phone swindlers invoked particularly ugly tactics to make sure that their job-seeking "clients" paid twenty dollars or more for bogus information. One firm, for instance, ran a tape that gave a phony address so quickly that one desperate caller dialed 10 times, in the hope that he could scribble all the words down. Another firm played a recording of a lengthy message followed by a seven-second silence that served as a prelude to a cruel footnote that most callers never heard: The cost of the call was twenty-four dollars. (Please refer to Chapter 15, "Fraudulent Fund Raising.")

It all may sound too depraved to be true, but in fact con artists routinely coax unemployed people to dial fraudulent 900 and 976 lines. Frequently, an advertisement will lure the consumer to call an 800 number, which is toll-free; the message on the 800 number, however, is that the party must dial a 900 number to get additional information. The Better Business Bureau in Detroit, a city hard hit by the decline of the auto industry, reported in 1991 that it was regularly fielding at least 250 complaints about job scams each day. And the New York Better Business Bureau says that it got 3345 grievances against firms that falsely promised high wages for people willing to stuff envelopes in their homes. (See Chapter 9, "Scams on the Doorstep: Home Business Opportunities.")

The swindlers who prompted most of these complaints are exploiting a means of communication that, in its short life, has earned a decidedly bad reputation.

Pay-per-call service was introduced by AT&T during the 1980 presidential debates. According to research firm Strategic TeleMedia, AT&T processed $360 million in 900-number calls in 1991, compared to $330 million in 1992. MCI processed $190 million in 1992 vs. $250 million in 1991 in 900-number calls. Sprint's 900-number volume dropped from $315 million in 1991 to just $30 million in 1992. Why the decline in revenues? The poor economy, regulatory and legislative constraints, fraud, bad debts, and the generally poor image of 900 numbers.

In 1992, according to a Harris poll, 28 percent of all American adults deemed 900 numbers "fraudulent." There's good reason for such skepticism. Though they are usually legal and often employed to deliver services ranging from sports scores to psychic counseling, 900 lines are easily abused. *DM News* (April 26, 1993) covered a report by Strategic TeleMedia that noted that the public still views the 900 exchange with mistrust. Citing fraud as a major problem from the birth of the industry, 900 numbers all were tainted by the "get in quick, get out" mentality of con artists.

Con artists can start up a 900 or 976 line with almost nothing—the only equipment they need, really, is a tape recorder—and they can often thrive in the U.S., where neither the phone companies nor the federal government wants to assume the heavy burden of regulating the huge pay-per-call industry.

They can, in other words, cash in on myriad pay-per-call scams. As well as fleecing job seekers, phone swindlers are now mailing out postcards that implore recipients to dial costly 900 or 976 numbers, to claim "free" prizes like vitamins and water purifiers. They're craftily instructing consumers to make "normal" long-distance calls, which, in actuality, are international and frightfully expensive. They're pitching "inexpensive housing," and, perhaps worst of all, they're enticing people to pick up the phone and score some sexual titillation by listening to strangers, usually sultry-voiced women, talk about sex.

The perfectly legal sex talk lines are so pernicious primarily because they can prove so costly. Lonely people see ads for them everywhere—in newspapers, in magazines and on late-night TV—and they get curious. They dial once, wondering if a sweet voice on the other end of the line will deliver the salve to their woes. And then, in many cases, they remain unfulfilled, and call again and again and again.

At the age of fourteen, Leah Moddrell, a resident of Georgia, first got intrigued by 900 numbers when she saw a scintillating TV ad about a "party line" that featured live callers chatting explicitly about their desires. She decided to dial and, by the time she hung up the phone several hours later, she was hooked.

Leah began calling 900 numbers whenever her mom was asleep or at work. She called often from her father's house—the Moddrells were divorced—and her parents didn't learn of her obsession until it was too late.

P. J. Moddrell's September 1992 phone bill was $5459. Her ex-husband was hit with a bill totaling $3176 for Leah's 900 calls. Luckily, the phone company cannot disconnect a customer's service for failing to pay a disputed 900-number charge.

The phone company decided, after four months of being pressured, to forgive Ms. Moddrell's charges. This mother meanwhile took a precautionary measure: She obtained a block on her phone. This disabled Leah from making calls to 900 lines, or at least it stopped her from running up exorbitant bills while at her mother's house.

If you are aware of exactly what you're getting when dialing a 900 number and what you'll be charged, they may be a perfectly legitimate way of obtaining information. To protect consumers, the Federal Communications Commission (FCC) recently adopted a number of rules to govern 900 and 976 numbers (along with long-distance 700 numbers). Included in the rules:

- Local telephone companies must offer one-time free blocking (to prevent all calls to 900 numbers) to all residential subscribers where feasible.
- Consumers may receive from their long-distance companies the name, address, and customer service telephone number of all companies that provide 900-number services.
- Companies providing 900-number services must provide a clearly understandable introductory message (the contents of which are specifically defined by the FCC) at the beginning of each 900 call unless the call has a flat rate of $2 or less. This preamble must disclose the cost of the call and allow the caller the opportunity to hang up in order to avoid the charges.

A variation of this rip-off is the "international toll-call swindle." The advertisement states that to obtain information about a specific subject (which can range from self-help pointers to sexually explicit messages) just call the 800 number below. Once they've done this, callers are instructed to call an exchange that is actually the area code for another country. Unfortunately, unless he or she queries the phone company prior to placing the call, the victim won't know where he or she has called until the phone bill arrives!

Another variation of this theme results in the consumer being billed *twice* even though she has answered an ad with an 800 (toll-free) number! Seeking help collecting child support payments, single mothers have been trapped when they have been told to pay $40 for the service and then receive a callback from a third-party billing system that charges $3.95 per minute.

One of the most popular phone scams is one in which the mark receives a postcard with news that he has won a terrific prize, usually a car, a vacation package, or a large amount of cash. To claim the prize, the mark must call an 800 or 900 number. When he phones he is told that he must pay a processing fee, provide a credit card number, or even buy products (usually overpriced ones) in order to actually receive the prize. Even when a consumer plays out the scam, the prize is rarely delivered. (Refer to Chapter 16, "Sweepstakes Fraud.")

Toner Phoners and Paper Pirates

The call comes, in many cases, around noon, when the boss is away at lunch, and the company purchasing agent is gone, too. The caller, excited and aggressive, pitches a great deal to the lone employee stranded in the office. He is selling "toner"—that black, inklike stuff used in photocopy machines—at a cut-rate price. The toner, he probably insists, is contained in a truck that has broken down nearby, and it's going fast—so fast, in fact, that the employee must act at once, and make a commitment to buy.

What should the solitary worker do? How should one respond to such an alarmingly good deal?

By hanging up.

Each year in the U.S. a class of swindlers known as "toner phoners" and "paper pirates" ring up over $350 million in bogus sales of photocopier supplies and cause business owners to look askance at legitimate corporations like Xerox, Kodak, or Mita, to name a few. Though there are scores of pitches, generally the callers offer considerable savings on copier supply products that have unexpectedly become available. They concentrate primarily on pitching toner and, more recently, laser cartridges. The prices are actually inflated as much as 500%. It's estimated that there are some 300,000 pitches made *every day*.

A recent press release from Xerox stated that the company reviews more than 1500 complaints annually about phony Xerox sales reps.

The toner phoners launch their scams, usually, by saying something like, "Our computer is down. Can you give me the name of your purchasing agent, and the type and serial numbers of your copiers?"

Once they've obtained this information, they can determine the type of copier supplies the "client" needs, and they can start spinning their phony tales. Sometimes the story is that there's an overshipment to a nearby company. Sometimes there's an amazing going-out-of-business sale. The caller may say that the client's supplier asked him to call, or he may say he can offer the customer a better deal since he's a warehouse supplier for the regular dealer. Always, there's pressure.

These scam artists get their victims to order the bargains on the spot, and then they deliver the goods, replete with surprises. The orders that toner phoners send out usually contain shoddy goods, or far fewer bottles of copy machine ink than were originally promised. They're often sent C.O.D., or stuffed with invoices saying that the client owes money for "taxes." According to industry experts, profits from the fraudulent sale of one bottle of toner may reach over $300.

And they tend to cause eruptions at the office. Toner phoners know that the arrival of bogus batches of copy supplies is apt to make a boss irate and a lowly employee eager to defend the mistake by heaping blame on the people who bilked him or her. These con artists have, accordingly, evolved a blackmail-like ploy to silence the poor souls they suckered: They mail gifts, such as VCRs and microwave ovens, to the homes of the employees who ordered from them. This "teleblackmail" makes the individuals feel guilty, as if they are accomplices in the purchase. (See Chapter 11, "Business Bunco.")

Toner phoners sometimes get caught. In December 1986, for instance, H. L. Marks, forty-seven, received a six-month jail term, three hundred thousand dollars in fines, and 1,250 hours of community service for running a $3-million office supply/toner scam in Culver City, CA. Likewise, in 1987, Sheldon Lawrence Block, the mastermind behind another fraudulent "office supplier" known as Park Distributing (also located in California), was sentenced to fifteen years' imprisonment. Block bilked more than $35 million from thousands of small businesses nationwide.

These convictions may be anomalous, though. Compliments of Xerox Corp., an article by Kirk V. Laughlin appeared in the June 1992 issue of *NOMDA Spokesman*, a trade magazine of the National Office Machine Dealers Association. Laughlin reported that he worked for a brief stint selling copy supplies for a fraudulent Costa Mesa, CA, toner outfit. He found the business thriving and in no pressing danger of being nabbed.

"As for the ethics or morality or legality [of running a con operation]," Laughlin said, "I never heard anything like that discussed by either the manager or the employees." Laughlin wrote that commissions ranged from 11 to 25 percent, and that one solicitor at the operation consistently took home twelve hundred dollars a week.

Some people, he wrote, worked there so they could own a BMW or live in Newport Beach or gamble whenever they pleased—and others had more frightening reasons. "One of my trainers," Laughlin recalled, "told me, 'You know, you'll learn a lot from this. You'll learn to get what you want. You'll learn to control people.' "

Restitution Scams

Suppose you've been scammed by a con artist. You feel cheated and angry and hungry for revenge. And then someone calls to tell you that law enforcement officials have caught the swindler and are now ready to reimburse victims.

Would you perhaps feel indebted to this caller and be likely to take whatever advice he or she gave you?

Quite possibly you would—and that is an unfortunate fact. Over the past several years con artists have increasingly been pulling off what are called "restitution scams." Working with "suckers lists"—lists of people who've already been conned once—they dial up their victims and make phony promises.

Restitution swindles are common, but they have probably been most heinously executed by a young con named Robert William Wenzlick.

During 1992, the then twenty-seven-year-old Wenzlick ran a Florida scam operation that offered prospective buyers novelty items for inflated prices, with the promise that they could win valuable prizes. Then, when Fort Lauderdale police caught wind of his con, he ducked them and deftly changed his tack: His employees began phoning people back to say that, for a fee ranging from eight hundred to fifteen hundred dollars, they could recover all fraudulently taken funds. (This is similar to "reload scams" in that the same consumers who fell for bogus prize offers on postcards are called again and given a second chance to win.)

Hundreds fell for Wenzlick's second scam, but police finally tracked down the criminal. They caught him at a Fort Lauderdale business called Cash Your Check and put him in jail, without bail.

Robert William Wenzlick, who'd previously been convicted on extortion and kidnapping charges, was accused this time of committing fraud and theft. But, amazingly, he has not been prosecuted on the new charges, and will almost surely get away with his lucrative scam.

The Ultimate 900-Number Scam

A recent advertisement told consumers that, to get their names off the tons of telephone and mailing lists, they could "STOP ANNOYING CALLS!" by simply calling a 900 number. In small letters at the bottom of the ad the consumer is advised that, to receive the valuable information, the call would cost $12.95!

How To Handle Calls From Phone Solicitors

No matter how many questions you ask, there is no foolproof way to determine whether a telephone salesperson is legitimate over the phone. Always check them out independently before you buy or invest in anything.

Ask the phone solicitor for his or her phone number.   If you don't get a quick, straight answer, you'll know that the caller is probably not legitimate.

Be wary of callers pitching incredibly great deals.   If an offer seems too good to be true, it probably is.

Be wary of callers promising to fulfill your heart's desire.   If you're unemployed, for instance, and someone phones to offer you a job, refuse to give the caller money for an "application fee."

If you're offered a "free gift," ask if you have to pay a registration fee, shipping and handling fees, or any other hidden fees to receive the item.

Never give your credit card, checking account, driver's license, or social security numbers to a salesperson making unsolicited calls.

Don't let yourself be pressured into a quick decision. Don't cave into any phone solicitor who grows angry and tries to force you to buy or invest.

Be wary of callers claiming to be handicapped in order to sell you something.

Ask the caller to put his or her promises in writing and mail them to you. This includes any guarantees and refund provisions.

Don't feel rude for hanging up on a phone solicitor.

Be on guard: scam artists trade what they call "suckers lists"—lists of gullible people who have already been conned once. So if you've fallen victim once, they're likely to phone you again.

How to Determine If a Phone Solicitor Is Legitimate

Check out the company or organization prior to buying anything. Always request written information and insist on having enough time to study what's sent. If you receive references, financial information, and regulatory contacts from the firm, verify them!

If the caller is trying to sell you an investment opportunity or major purchase, request that the written information also be sent to your accountant, financial adviser, banker, or attorney. Any reluctance on the part of the caller may tip you off to a swindle in the making.

Ask the caller if he or she is willing to send a courier to your doorstep immediately to pick up your check. If the answer is yes, tell them you're not interested in what they're selling.

If a caller is offering a great deal on a brand-name product, call the manufacturer of that product and ask about the phone solicitor's track record.

Investigate "charities" before donating. Call the alleged beneficiary of the fund-raising effort and find out how much of the money raised, if any, actually goes to the cause.

Get the number for the manufacturer or charity yourself. Don't rely on the phone solicitor to provide you with such numbers. He or she may give you the number of another person in on the con game.

Don't accept third-party telephone calls from anyone who says they need your help to catch a crook. According to AT&T spokesperson Sally Sherwood, the phone company doesn't ask customers to help them apprehend someone.

Call the attorney general's office or the Better Business Bureau and find out if there have been any complaints against the soliciting company.

Special Considerations For Businesses

Establish a company policy that permits only authorized individuals to order, receive, and pay for all your company's supplies.

Be wary of callers phoning to offer you cut-rate deals on office supplies such as paper and toner for photocopiers.

Never make oral purchase agreements.

Don't provide phone solicitors with any information about your company's equipment.

Accept or pay for a shipment only after confirming that the purchase was properly authorized.

Don't accept any C.O.D. shipments.

Check out all new vendors and only buy from them after their reliability has been properly verified.

How to Protect Yourself Against 900 and 976 scams

Don't confuse toll-free 800 numbers with costly 900 and 976 numbers.

Before dialing a 900 number, find out the per-minute cost of the call.

Be wary if you're told that, to get information, you need only make a "normal long-distance call." Make sure you're not calling a foreign country.

Before dialing, ask yourself if there are less expensive ways to obtain the information you're seeking.

Instruct your children never to make 900 or 976 calls without asking your permission first.

Consider having your phone lines blocked so that no one in your household is able to make 900 or 976 calls.

What to Do If You've Been Cheated by a Phone Solicitor

Don't be embarrassed. Be outraged.

Contact the company that wronged you and demand your money back. Thomas Newberry, a convicted scam artist, said recently that only about 1 percent of all the people he bilked ever demanded reimbursement—and that often he would return money to people who threatened to call the attorney general's office or the Postal Inspector. Victims of telephone fraud seldom get their money back, but always, always ask for it!

Complain to the police, the state attorney general's office, and the National Fraud Information Center Hotline. If the mails were used by the phony promoters, contact the U. S. Postal Inspector.

CHAPTER 3

Street Scams

Street scams are to some the most interesting kind of confidence games because they usually require great skill and cunning on the part of the con artist. Although street scams have been glamorized by filmmakers and the news media, they can be just as devastating as those scams pulled off by the most sophisticated of con artists who work in business and industry.

I have included the infamous Mel Weinberg of ABSCAM fame because his criminal career started with him breaking windows all night and selling window replacement services all day. Moreover, his original financial empire was founded on an advance fee scheme where his ropers brought him marks.

In addition to the well-known street cons, I've added a few police agency cons perpetrated against street thieves. Pickpockets brought in stolen credit cards while burglars brought in television sets, radios, telephones, and guns to be fenced. The fence paid well, asked few questions, and encouraged the street criminals to bring in more hot merchandise. What the street criminals didn't know was that the fence was a policeman buying goods with taxpayer money.

While we may find it truly amazing how many people "stung" by ABSCAM believed that the man in the robes was a billionaire sheik, it is equally amazing when an out-of-towner believes he can actually beat a perfect stranger at three-card monte in downtown Manhattan as he proceeds to systematically lose forty dollars.

A con artist would argue that he's not really stealing anything from his victims—they are willingly giving him their money and their trust. In fact, many marks would have to admit their own criminal intentions before they could point the finger at the con artists involved. In many of these street scams, the con men prosper largely because of the dishonesty and greed of their victims.

Police Agency Scams

Stings can be so effective that even the police use them to give the criminals a dose of their own medicine. The Los Angeles Police Department (LAPD) rented a storefront and bought stolen goods over the counter. Undercover policemen working the streets referred thieves to the phony fencing operation. Inside the store were two detectives buying everything the thieves brought in; the transactions were recorded with a hidden camera.

After several months the LAPD ran out of warehouse space for all the stolen merchandise the police had purchased. Many of the goods were bought for less than ten cents on the dollar. Many of the thieves didn't know what they had: A genuine diamond necklace was sold as costume jewelry for twenty-five dollars. Its appraised value was close to seventy-five thousand dollars.

The detectives in the store announced to their customers (the thieves) that they were throwing a party at one of their warehouses. After a few beers, chips, and dip all 106 invitees were arrested for grand larceny and selling stolen goods.

Another well-known sting—involving hundreds of irresponsible fathers who were not paying child support—was set up by the Los Angeles District Attorney's office. The district attorney's office sent a letter to the list of "deadbeat dads" inviting them to come to a state office to claim their lottery winnings. The bait worked. One by one, over half of the recipients showed up to collect their cash prizes. What they received instead was a pair of handcuffs and a trip to jail.

ABSCAM

Melvin Weinberg, a well-known con man and the owner of a window replacement company in New York, was arrested in the late 1970s for fraud. When business was slow he simply cruised around town at night breaking windows. The next day, his telephone would ring off its cradle. He eventually moved into the advance-fee-loan-scam business and made a fortune before he was finally caught.

The FBI offered him a deal he couldn't refuse. He could either go to work for them or go to jail. If he decided to go to jail, the FBI would send his accomplice (and mistress), Lady Diane, to jail, too. As you might have guessed, because of his strong feelings for Diane and his own personal desire for freedom, he decided to help the FBI.

ABSCAM was conceived with Melvin Weinberg in charge. Constantly fighting with the FBI agents assigned to him about what he considered a lack of funding, Weinberg insisted that a good sting required money for limousines, fine suits, imported champagne, and caviar. How could he convince political officials—including senators and members of the House of Representatives—to buy his rich Arabian sheik story without some serious front money?

Weinberg and an FBI agent dressed like a sheik offered large sums of money to the corrupt politicians in exchange for favors. Over and over again, the FBI's hidden video camera captured money changing hands.

It's not often that the efforts of con artists result in *capturing* criminals. Many powerful men were convicted of accepting bribes, including Congressman Frank Thompson, Jr. (NJ), Congressman Raymond F. Lederer (PA), Congressman John M. Murphy (NY), Congressman Richard Kelly (FL), Congressman John W. Jenrette (SD), and two phony art dealers.

The Payoff

The payoff is classified as a "big con," because the mark is sent away to withdraw money from a bank account to invest in the con game. Like other classic big cons such as the wire and the rag, large amounts of money usually change hands in an effort to beat the system.

Very popular during the Great Depression, when many were desperate for money, this "inside information" scam has been used effectively for hundreds of years.

Basically, the mark is led to believe that a very successful-looking person can predict the outcome of a horse race, boxing match, or other competitive event. Con artists have used every story imaginable to convince the mark that the information is very reliable. A few variations include:

- "The fix is in—I know because my brother works in the stables."
- "My brother works for the Mafia, and if their fighter doesn't throw the fight, his entire family will be killed."
- "We get the results one minute before they are broadcast to the off-track bookie joints."

The mark gives the con man his bet. Usually the con man only bets half of the money and keeps the rest. If the mark ever questions this, the con artist will explain that the other half was bet on another horse to throw off any suspicion. If the horse wins, the con man gives the mark half of the purse, keeping the other half as further profit. Now that the mark has seen firsthand that the con man was telling him the truth, he may mortgage his home in order to ante-up a significant bet in hopes of hitting the jackpot. If the mark wins a second time, the same procedure follows.

Of course, even if the mark loses, the con man disappears with the half of the bet he retained. The payoff is conceived so that the con man cannot lose; it's simply a matter of how much he'll win.

Insider Stock Scam

This scam can be as simple as a con artist representing to a mark that he or she has inside information about a stock going up. The mark invests his money and, if the stock goes up, he gives the con man half of his earnings in exchange for the hot tip. If the stock goes down, the con artist merely apologizes for having been given bad information.

In its more complicated form, a group of con artists set up what is known as a "big store." A big store is a place of business that's been created to fool potential victims into thinking it's a legitimate establishment. In more elaborate cons where the mark needs reassurance, the offices may be stocked with lavish furniture and expensive-looking artwork in order to suggest success and wealth. Contacts are made in a community, and one of the con artists is set up as someone who consistently makes profitable buys.

The mark is introduced to the stock market guru and allowed to make small investments just to test the genius's abilities. Of course, the mark doubles his money two or three times. He is then allowed to invest a substantial amount of money. When he comes back to collect his fortune the big con shop is gone.

Some of these scams are well acted and can involve millions of dollars. Shills may pretend to misread buy and sell instructions to effect a solid "blow-off" of the mark so that he will leave after he's been conned, never the wiser. Or before the mark can withdraw his money at the cashier's window, phony detectives will storm in and arrest the stock market guru and the mark for insider trading. The con-artist-posing-as-office-manager and the guru will plead with the detective to release the mark, saying that he knew nothing of the scam. The detective agrees, and the mark is sent scurrying as fast as he can go, grateful for not being arrested. This is known as a solid blow-off because the mark seldom complains to anyone, especially the police, about his losses.

Such elaborate stings require a con mob, which consists of brokers, customers, and employees typically found in a stock broker's office. A roper is used to bring the marks into the office, and an inside man actually works the marks into the scheme. The con mob is usually made up of down-on-their-luck con men who have not made recent hits and floating grifters in need of money. Some big con stores have as many as fifty ropers and work twenty cons a week. (See Chapter 8, "Investment Cons.")

Short Cons

The short con is one that only takes what the mark has on him at the time he is scammed. For example, in three-card monte the victim is asked to guess which of three cards is a queen. At first, a mark is able to pick the queen because of its bent corner. But as the betting gets heavier and the mark is sucked in deeper, his luck disappears. Any good magician can put the queen in any position by covering up a corner of the selected card with his finger.

The shell game, where participants try to guess which shell the peanut (ball, pea, or whatever) is under, is another short con, as are carnival games and short-changing cashiers.

What is known as the block hustle is considered a short con and is often perpetrated by younger, inexperienced hustlers. These young cons hawk merchandise on the street, giving the impression that they are able to offer the mark remarkable prices because the goods for sale are stolen. Usually, the merchandise is simply counterfeit or below par in quality.

Carnival Cons

Keep your money in your pockets at the carnival because your chances of winning the games are probably one in a million. One of the easiest ways to lose your money is to play the baseball toss game. The player must toss two baseballs into a basket to win a prize. All the concession operator has to do is increase the angle of the basket upward and you'll be unable to win. If he loosens the wooden slats on the sides of the baskets or gives you harder balls instead of soft ones, a player simply cannot win. If the operator does all three of these things, there is no force on this earth that will enable you to win.

Every now and then a concession operator will want you to succeed in order to drum up business. In most cases, that's the only time you'll win. Throwing darts at balloons is probably the best legitimate chance a player has of winning a carnival game. However, think of the cost of winning if:

> It costs $1 for two darts.
> You earn two points for each balloon you break.
> You break a balloon with each throw.
> It takes 100 points to win a major prize.

You'll probably end up paying twenty-five dollars or more for a prize worth no more than five dollars.

The Pigeon Drop

This classic street scam has been around for decades. In the presence of the mark, the con artist contrives to discover a bag containing lots of money. He or she tells the mark that they'll split the found money, but that they should give the money to a disinterested third party (another con in on the game) for safekeeping while waiting to see if anyone comes looking for the money. Or, the swindler may let the victim keep the bundle said to contain the cash. But first the con artist persuades the victim to put up a sizable sum of money as a "good faith" deposit. Of course, there is no money, except for the cash deposit the mark gave to the con man, who disappears.

"Illegal Immigrant" Capers

A woman becomes violently ill on a busy street corner. Pleading for help, she gasps for breath. Wilma Soloman stops. The sick woman, saying she is an illegal alien who can neither read nor write, needs someone to help her get the cash for her winning lottery ticket so that she can pay her medical bills. She promises Soloman ten thousand dollars for being one of her two witnesses, but needs assurance that Soloman won't steal the ticket proceeds.

Excited about the prospects of receiving ten thousand dollars, Soloman rushes home and retrieves three thousand dollars in "good faith" money. The other witness has already gone to the bank to withdraw the "proof" of his trustworthiness. Soloman gives her money to the woman, who promptly disappears without a trace.

In this recurring scam, the con artist purchases a lottery ticket with the winning numbers from the previous day's drawing. Then, he or she changes the date on the ticket to match the previous date. To the untrained eye, the ticket now appears to exactly match the winning ticket from an earlier date. Working with an accomplice who poses as the second witness, the stage is set.

This con can be fairly lucrative, as evidenced by three Hispanic bunco artists who bilked over $47,000 in cash and jewelry in just one month's time in Chicago.

Grifters who pose as illegal aliens flimflam their marks in many other ways. As long as ships have been pulling into port, sailors have been jumping ship. Some were fugitives from the law in their homelands, others were seeking political asylum. Often the living conditions on board ship were deplorable, or the work too hard. And sometimes the uniformed sailor was not a sailor at all, but simply a con artist looking for his next mark.

A sailor with a Russian accent enters a local merchant's store and tells his mark that he has just jumped ship and is heading for the American Embassy for asylum. The sailor explains that he has smuggled over twenty thousand dollars in gold out of Russia and pulls out an ingot of pure gold. It's engraved with a Russian hallmark, proof of its authenticity. If the merchant will hold the money belt for safekeeping, the sailor will turn himself in.

There's only one small snag: The sailor could use a few thousand dollars to hire an attorney, so he asks the merchant for a loan, with the gold to be used as collateral. If the merchant is hesitant or reluctant to go along with the deal, the sailor offers to let the merchant keep half the gold for his troubles.

For many people, the opportunity to make ten thousand dollars from a transaction costing only several thousand is too great a temptation to pass up. By the time the merchant opens the belt and closely examines his collateral, he finds gold-plated copper bars that are worth only a fraction of real gold.

One con artist who specialized in this game reported that each and every merchant he approached over a three-year period fell for the con—except one who had been similarly duped the previous year by another grifter. This time, he accepted the belt, then pulled out a gun and held his prisoner at gunpoint while he called the police.

The Federal Express Caper

One of the newest street cons is the Federal Express Scam. A uniformed driver appears at your door with a package sent C.O.D. for $96.25. The mark pays the driver cash for the package and the driver disappears down the road. When the recipient opens the package he discovers it contains either worthless stolen merchandise or it's empty.

A single driver has been known to make as many as fifty drops per day. At nearly five thousand dollars per day, an industrious con man can easily earn one hundred fifty thousand dollars per month tax-free.

The Bail Scam

One enterprising con man who purchased a policeman's uniform visited residences and asked for bail money for the neighbor next door, an uninsured driver who'd been involved in a traffic accident. Looking official as he held a clipboard in his hand, the con artist had simply taken the next door neighbor's name from his or her mailbox.

Another slant on the bail bond con: Posing as a neighbor's friend, the con artist telephones his victim late at night. He tells his victim that the neighbor is in jail and wants the victim to post bail. If the victim agrees, the con artist drives over and picks up the money.

A surprising number of people come to their neighbor's (or shall I say the con artist's) rescue.

The Taxi Cab Caper

Visitors from around the world pour into New York's JFK Airport. One cold wintry day, a woman dressed in an official-looking uniform asked travelers if they were in need of a taxi. If the answer was yes, she asked them their destination, and then told them that, in order to take a cab from JFK, they had to pay the fare in advance. After receiving payment based upon the mark's destination, she'd open the cab door for the visitor to hop in.

How Can You Protect Yourself?

There are some really basic rules of thumb that should be remembered if you're going to protect yourself from being conned on the street:

Don't participate in anything illegal because you've been promised a good return on your money.

If someone claims to have insider trading information, don't participate or invest in the opportunity.   Instead, call the Securities Exchange Commission.

Know that no one can accurately predict the outcome of anything.   If someone can, the police should know about it.

Make it a policy never to buy anything from street merchants.   The merchandise is often counterfeit, stolen, or has a value far less than what you'd pay for comparable merchandise elsewhere.

Don't participate in carnival games unless you understand that your chances of winning are, as the old saying goes, slim to none.

Don't play a game of chance or gamble with someone whom you don't know.

Never hand a stranger any money, not even just to "hold" for you.

Never give a stranger—or anyone whom you haven't properly investigated—a deposit for the promise of a payoff.

Don't make spontaneous decisions when large sums of money are involved. Sleep on every proposition and thoroughly investigate every angle before you give anyone your hard-earned dollars.

If you invite strangers or new-found friends into your hotel room or even your home, hide your wallet, checkbook, jewelry, and other valuables. Con artists have been known to turn into common thieves when given the opportunity. A safe deposit box is an excellent place to store stock certificates, family heirlooms, etc. Perhaps the best policy is simply not to let strangers in.

Always keep in mind the old adage, "If it sounds too good to be true, it probably is."

What Should You Do If You've Been Conned?

If you've been conned, call the police and file a criminal complaint.

Never physically confront the con artist by yourself or try to back him or her into a corner. Remember: Under the confident facade of the grifter lurks an antisocial, amoral individual.

CHAPTER 4

Robbing a Bank Without a Gun

There's an old adage: "The man with the gold makes the rules." I suspect that this is normally true, except when the systems of those making the rules are infiltrated and violated. Like other businesses, banks are competing—for depositors and credit-worthy borrowers. Despite the checks-and-balances systems in place in most established banks, every depositor is not what he or she appears to be, and the person who may be very credit-worthy on paper isn't always telling the truth.

Banks fall victim to borrowers with phony credit reports, fake identifications, and erroneous financial statements. Some depositors open multiple checking accounts and float checks between them, sometimes running a hundred dollar deposit into ten thousand dollars worth of withdrawals. Banks may be tricked into automatically debiting a customer's account and sending the money to an illegal account set up by a con man.

Banks are susceptible to computer hackers, credit card misuse, employee theft, loan fraud, conspiracy, and embezzlement. If you store your money in or borrow money from banks, do business with banks, or work in a bank, you should find this chapter of great interest.

Frank Abagnale earns the distinction of being the most flamboyant con artist in this century. Between the ages of sixteen and twenty-one, he became a millionaire by writing over $2.5 million in bad checks. His story is at once tragic and fascinating.

Raised in Bronxville, NY, in a family of wealth and influence, Abagnale had an IQ close to 140 and a photographic memory. At sixteen, however, Frank found himself in the middle of a custody battle as a result of his parents' divorce. The judge asked Frank to choose between living with his mother or his father. Frank loved both of them very much, and rather than making such a choice he ran away to the streets of Manhattan.

Although he had worked part-time for his father, Frank found that he couldn't support himself on the minimum wages paid to someone his age. Already sporting a small amount of gray hair, Frank realized that if he could convince others that he was older than his sixteen years, he could earn more money. Necessity being the mother of invention, he added ten years to his age by changing his date of birth from 1948 to 1938 on his driver's license.

Watching an Eastern Airlines crew on the street in Manhattan, Frank imagined that impersonating an airline pilot would be a perfect front and phoned Pan Am's corporate offices. Posing as John Black, a San Francisco–based co-pilot whose uniform had been lost by a hotel dry cleaning service, Frank asked for the Purchasing Department. Pan Am sent him to a uniform company, who quickly outfitted him. Refusing to take a check or cash, the uniform company told him to fill out a form so that Pan Am could reduce his next paycheck by the cost of the uniform.

To make his disguise complete, Frank needed an identification card. After phoning many companies he discovered that 3M produced the cards for Pan Am. Ever adaptable, an impeccably dressed Frank posed as a purchasing officer for a major manufacturing firm and secured a sample card with his picture on it. Yet there was nothing on the card that identified him as a Pan Am employee, so he purchased a Pan Am 707 cargo jet model from a hobby shop and used the wing decals on his new ID.

Looking like the real McCoy, Frank was on his way. Early in this scam, Abagnale learned several very important things. As long as there was room he could fly on other airlines at no cost to him by wearing his uniform and showing his identification badge. By walking up to United Airlines Operations, for instance, Frank would merely ask, "Is the jump seat open?'' If they answered affirmatively, Frank would board the plan and off he'd go.

Frank also learned that he could stay for free at Pan Am's assigned hotels for as long as he wanted and cash personal checks of up to $100 at the airline hotels. He soon discovered that he could write checks for up to one hundred dollars at all of the other airlines' counters under a reciprocal agreement, so he would begin at one end of an airport and write a bad check at every counter. At the end of each eight-hour shift, he would return to each counter and cash more bad checks.

Abagnale observed airport merchants depositing their day's receipts in a night depository. He returned one evening in a rented security guard's uniform and placed a sign over the depository slot: ''Out of order. Please give deposits to security guard.'' One by one, the unsuspecting merchants hand-delivered their money to Abagnale, who merely sat in his chair by the sign.

Unsure of Abagnale's identity, the FBI issued a ''John Doe'' warrant for Frank's arrest. Before he quit his scam at the age of eighteen, Frank had flown approximately 2 million miles for free in over 83 countries. Interestingly enough, he never flew on Pan Am; he was afraid he might have been caught if anyone began asking questions he couldn't answer.

Next, Frank settled in Atlanta. When renting an apartment in a singles complex, he was forced to list an occupation, but he obviously didn't want anyone trying to verify the information. He felt he would be pretty safe claiming that he was Dr. Frank Williams, a nonpracticing pediatrician from Los Angeles. Things were moving along nicely until a real pediatrician moved into the complex and sought out Frank's friendship. Soon, a Marietta, GA, hospital administrator asked Frank to fill in on an emergency basis, and he accepted. At eighteen years old, Frank Abagnale was practicing medicine! Although he couldn't stand the sight of blood and never diagnosed an illness or prescribed drugs, Abagnale practiced medicine in Georgia for a year. One of the eeriest aspects of Frank's cons: his scribblings of jibberish on patients' charts—intended to be illegible—were never questioned by any of the hospital staff.

Frank next took up residence in Baton Rouge, LA. At the time, Louisiana didn't require a person to have a law degree prior to taking the state bar exam. As Assistant Attorney General Bob Conrad, Frank tried civil cases for the state. All of Frank's cases have been upheld despite attempts to have the rulings overturned due to claims that he was not a qualified attorney. Frank then became a sociology professor at Brigham Young University, teaching while staying just one chapter ahead of his students. The hardest part of the scam, Frank would later admit, was being a Catholic trying to impersonate a Mormon.

In one city, with only a hundred dollars in his pocket, Abagnale went into a bank with the intention of opening a checking account. The teller gave him temporary checks to use until his personalized checks arrived, but he received no deposit slips. She instructed him to use the blanks provided on the table. Taking a stack of the blanks back to his hotel room, Abagnale had trouble sleeping. The next day he purchased some magnetic ink like that used by the bank, encoded his account number, and placed his stack back on the table in the bank. In one day, Abagnale received almost $40,000 in deposits. Needless to say, he made several large withdrawals in short order.

Wanted in twenty-six countries, Frank Abagnale was caught by the French police when he was twenty-one. Tried and convicted of forgery, Abagnale spent six months in a maximum security cell in southern France. Stripped naked and locked in the pitch black of a cell measuring five feet by five feet by five feet, with only a bucket for urinating and defecating, Abagnale subsisted in solitude on a diet of bread and water, soup, and coffee. There was no heat, electricity, or plumbing, and no light entered his small cell. He lost eighty-nine pounds and nearly lost his life.

After six months Frank was turned over to the Swedish police, but he was too ill to stand trial. After two months of recuperation, Abagnale was tried and sentenced to one year for forgery. After serving six months, he was expelled and sent to the United States to stand trial for interstate transportation of fraudulent checks. Due to the extent of his crimes, Abagnale was treated as an adult and sentenced to twelve years. He was paroled after serving half of his term. With only seventy-two hours to find work, Frank was hired by a pizza restaurant, where he performed so admirably that he was given a promotion. The promotion proved to be his downfall, because when the company found out who he really was, they fired him. Unfortunately, every subsequent promotion led to Frank's dismissal.

Realizing that he would never be able to hide from what he had done, Abagnale took what was negative and turned it into a positive. He had already received numerous letters from insurance companies asking for his advice, so Abagnale began to write risk management programs for banks, savings and loan associations, and credit unions. Living with his family in Tulsa, OK, Abagnale specializes in secure document management and makes millions of dollars every year teaching others how to thwart the efforts of con artists, forgers, and swindlers. His Washington, D.C.-based firm serves companies in twenty-three countries.

One final note: Abagnale returned the $2.5 million he had illegally obtained, paying an additional seventy-five thousand dollars in legal fees. He never saw his life in crime as glamorous. He had been alone and missed his family very much. His father died while he was in the French prison, and Frank never had the chance to tell him how much he loved him or to say good-bye. Today, his family is the most important thing in his life.

Automatic Withdrawal Caper

Just under 79 percent of American adults have checking accounts. Over 28 percent of these individuals have payments for loans automatically deducted from their checking accounts. Most likely to have automatic deductions are people with a college education and those in households with an annual income of over seventy-five thousand dollars. At one time or other, 2 percent of people with checking accounts have had funds withdrawn from their checking accounts without their permission in a situation where someone misused their account.

Ever sign an automatic withdrawal card with your bank? It's very convenient to have your mortgage payments, car payments, and other monthly obligations automatically debited from your bank account each month. And as long as you reconcile your checkbook with the monthly statements you receive from the bank, it's not hard to keep your account balanced and everything under control, right?

Not necessarily. Con artists have been known to infiltrate lending organizations by taking a job, by developing a relationship with an existing employee, or by accessing the institution's computer files illegally. If an unscrupulous individual gets his or her hands on your request for automatic payment, your funds could be up for grabs. All he or she would have to do is submit a new request for a larger amount, payable to a sham company with a similar name that would make it appear to be an affiliate company. By increasing the amount, it appears as though you have increased your original purchase and generally goes through the bank system without raising any red flags. Picking up a few thousand payments from various victims over a period of several months is easy money.

Unauthorized Use

There are many ways a con artist can get your money out of your account and into his pocket. He can call you, for example, and pretend to be a bank employee—often a bank security director—at another branch attempting to track an unauthorized withdrawal from your checking account. He would, of course, ask you to prove that you are the person with the account; he asks you to give your account number, date of birth, Social Security number, mother's maiden name, automatic teller machine number, and "PIN" (personal identification number). Of course, the PIN code gives him access to your account at the automatic teller machine with your card. He may ask you to mail in your ATM card so that a new one can be issued. One con man in Columbus, OH, removed over $110,000 from a number of accounts in a three-month period using this method.

Track your ATM transactions carefully. According to Gerri Detweiler of BankCard Holders of America, if you discover an unauthorized transfer and notify the bank within two business days, you'll only be liable for up to $50 of the stolen amount. After two days, your liability goes up to $500 if the bank can prove you had prior notice but didn't report it. Everything in your account is liable if your monthly statement is mailed and 60 days pass before you notify the bank of any unauthorized transactions.

One Dollar Will Get You Five Scam

Give a swindler a check for any amount and your checking account balance may be in jeopardy. Imagine that you write a check to purchase something: It could be at a grocery store, dry cleaners, department store, florist, anything. If someone without scruples handles the check, he or she could order replacement checks for your account with his or her own address and phone number, saying that you've moved. He simply needs your account number or numbers, name, address, and, in some cases, Social Security number; all of this information is available on your check, deposit slip, credit report, and/or any credit applications you may have completed.

In Virginia as well as other states, a person's driver's license number is the same as his or her Social Security number. Many people in Virginia put their driver's license number on their checks to expedite check writing, but this means that con artists have all the information they need on one document. Many banks have computerized balance information available twenty-four hours a day. All the swindler has to do is phone an 800-number and request your bank balance. When the new checks arrive at his home, he simply makes a check payable to himself, forges your signature, walks over to the bank, empties your account, and disappears with the money.

One con man in Dallas, TX, had the nerve to steal from the same woman twice in one year. She lost $61,305, and it cost her another $15,000 in legal fees to force the bank to reimburse the stolen funds to her.

The Texas Land Flip

Robert D. Kimura III, an attorney in Idaho, Duane Mondragon, a physician in Washington, and Stephen Michael Olivettie are the same man. Over the past ten years, Olivettie has bought property any way he could, often using the Kimura and Mondragon aliases. Although he denies any wrongdoing, Olivettie has been involved in real estate transactions that led to bank fraud. He formed bogus companies and paid employees to sign loan and property documents in their names even though the deals were his. He continues to negotiate real estate purchases.

Here is how the scam works: The con man buys a piece of cheap property in a low-income area. He immediately sells the property to an accomplice, who gets a bank loan based on the artificially inflated price. Thus, the bank has lent more money on the property than it is worth. If a single bank accepts too many of these deals, it could go bankrupt.

A key to the success of a land-flip scam is the appraiser, who must be in the con man's pocket. Most real estate agents who need a high appraisal to sell a property know which appraisers go high on their appraisals. Olivettie certainly did: Before a house sold to one of his associates for $18,000, its value was appraised at $41,500. Another home was appraised for $47,000 just six weeks after it sold to the same associate for $12,000.

Based upon the sales history and appraisal, the banks and savings and loans institutions lent 80 to 90 percent of the fictitious value. The financial institutions that have been victimized are highly respected institutions that have come to rely on a system based on trust. Of course, a well-established system of trust is extraordinarily important to a successful scam.

In the Olivettie case, records indicated that real estate dealers concealed or outright lied about property values, the identity and qualifications of buyers, and the relationships between some buyers and sellers. Some of the property tripled in price almost overnight—on paper, anyway.

This is a scam that can go undetected for years and in an up-market may never be detected. It becomes known when the con artist fails to repay the loan and the bank attempts to sell the property to recapture its money. Imagine the embarrassment when the bank forecloses on a house to whose owners it lent a hundred thousand dollars and the top offer is twenty-five or thirty-five thousand dollars! When banks lend more money than properties are worth not just the banks but their depositors and even the taxpayers are placed at risk. Similar scams contributed to the horrible losses sustained by the savings and loan associations.

The Portland, OR–based newspaper, *The Oregonian,* outlined how Olivettie allegedly conned major lenders out of real estate loans:

- First accomplice buys house in low-income area for $14,000.
- One month later, first accomplice sells house to second accomplice for $48,000.
- Second accomplice obtains a loan in the amount of $38,400.
- Second accomplice defaults on loan.
- Bank forecloses and loses $43,548 (original loan of $38,400 plus legal costs).
- Bank later sells house for $17,000, losing more than $26,500.

In the house in the example above, neither the appraiser's nor Olivettie's names appeared on the title, but the appraiser later claimed a 50-percent interest in a financial statement.

Artificially inflating real estate prices by accomplices buying and selling to each other is not a new con. After World War II the practice went on all over the United States. The con works well and for a long time because, typically, law enforcement and industry regulators find the deals too difficult to track, too complicated to unwind, and too time-consuming to investigate. District attorneys hesitate to prosecute because these kinds of white-collar crimes are costly to prosecute.

Sometimes swindlers work with other swindlers on a double-sting operation. As an example, a con man could turn over a group of houses with high paper value to another con man, who offers investors the opportunity to own a financial interest in the entire portfolio. If one con gave another con artist properties worth $2 million on paper, the other swindler would show a four hundred thousand dollar net worth based upon 20 percent equity to obtain an asset value. Remember: Banks only lend 80 percent on most real estate loans, rarely 90 percent. The second con man sells the portfolio to the mark for two hundred thousand dollars and the mark is left with worthless deeds. The result: The bank loses its loans, the investor loses his buy-in price in the portfolio, the accomplices lose their credit, and the con artists are on their way to Tahiti, or their next land-flip deal, cash in hand.

The buyer who purchases the property at the top price in the con may not have any idea what is going on. Frederick R. McKoy, convicted of defrauding four Atlanta, GA, banks of $10 million, persuaded three Atlanta Falcon teammates to buy houses at inflated prices for a fee. Atlanta Falcons Aundray Bruce, Jessie Tuggle, and Tim Gordon were all duped into buying properties under their own names for McKoy. McKoy pocketed $2.5 million after he paid off the original mortgage on the homes; then he left the banks with the overvalued homes.

The destitute McKoy stood somberly as U. S. District Judge J. Owen Forrester sentenced him to seven years in prison and ordered him to pay up to $5.3 million for defrauding the banks of $10 million. He could have been sentenced to 117 years in prison and $6.25 million in fines. Witness after witness described McKoy as a charismatic, flashy, smooth-talking, very friendly guy. Aundray Bruce has been sued for $2 million by two mortgage companies that want their money back.

During the trial, Assistant U. S. Attorney David E. McClernan said McKoy falsified bank documents in order to purchase at least twenty new homes in Atlanta. McKoy then sold the houses for highly inflated prices—sometimes almost double the price—on the same day to people who never intended to live in them or pay for them. McKoy claimed that he was simply following his attorneys' advice. His attorneys, brothers Robert and David Martin, have served prison terms for closing fraudulent sales.

The Inside Job

A federal indictment charged a New York loan originator, already charged with masterminding a mortgage scam, with defrauding more than one hundred thousand dollars from his employer. Michael Margicen allegedly submitted mortgage applications for nonexistent customers and then paid friends to be "straw men," acting as the customers and picking up the money for him. He was also charged with falsifying information for applicants for a fee. Margicen also employed a man to verify false employment information when the bank called for the verification.

According to authorities, Margicen originated forty-three mortgages for more than $6 million. Twenty-two of these were foreclosed, costing the bank over $3 million.

Margicen had already been indicted for conning a mortgage bank out of five hundred thousand dollars for orchestrating a phony house sale scam. Allegedly using forged documents, men paid by Margicen posed as a buyer and seller at the closing of a house sale. The men had apparently forged the deed and filed it in the county clerk's office to show ownership.

Cash-in-Advance Loans

FBI agents raided a boiler room operation in Hollywood, FL, in December 1991 and arrested Saul Semininko of Coral Springs, along with Salvatore H. McCuistion of North Lauderdale, whom investigators said were netting over fifty thousand dollars per day. During fourteen-hour, two-shift workdays, telemarketers worked the telephones answering calls made by people looking for a low-interest loan.

Semininko and McCuistion ran newspaper ads across the United States in which they advertised loans up to one hundred thousand dollars for an up-front fee. The ad, which included an 800 number, targeted those with poor or no credit, people who would be really desperate during a downturn in the economy. And it came just in time for the holidays.

The FBI also suspects the men of running a lottery scam, offering large prizes for cash deposits, and of producing fake drivers' licenses. The tougher the economy and higher the unemployment rate, the more successful these boiler rooms are. According to FBI sources, the boiler room took in over $10 million a year.

A recent Florida law makes it a felony to take money before arranging a loan. As a result, many boiler room operations have moved to other states.

Loan Application Scams

Most of us have borrowed money at one time or another. We go to the bank, the credit union at work, or a storefront lender and complete an application. The lender runs a credit check, verifies employment, and approves or denies the loan request. A loan that is denied is often where the real trouble begins. Frustrated borrowers frequently will do just about anything to get desperately needed cash. Despondency creates a fertile breeding ground for swindlers.

The rejected borrower may receive a phone call, a letter in the mail, or see an advertisement in the local newspaper. The following ad appeared in a Milwaukee, WI, newspaper:

> We have money to lend.
> Bad credit—no credit
> Turned down elsewhere
> Talk to one of our loan
> officers today. We under-
> stand and we care at
> Money to Lend, Inc. Almost
> no one is turned down.
> Come in today, call or
> write but do not give up
> until you talk to us.
> Call LENDERS

Pretty enticing to someone who needs money to pay for surgery, to post bail, to stop a foreclosure, or to buy an airline ticket to his or her father's funeral in Memphis. So the unsuspecting victim takes the plunge and calls for an appointment.

When the hopeful victim arrives at Money To Lend, Inc., which looks like any other lenders' offices, he is offered a cup of coffee and asked to fill out a credit application. He is also asked to pay a fifty-dollar credit report charge in advance.

The loan officer comes back in five minutes with the good news that the mark's loan request has been approved for the full amount! The loan origination fee is just 10 percent of the loan amount. Determined to come up with the fee, the applicant pawns his video camera or skis, figuring that when he gets the cash he can reclaim his property.

When he takes the money back to the loan office he's surprised to meet twenty other people sitting in the lobby waiting to pay their fees. The loan officer retrieves the man's file and again offers congratulations on his loan approval. After handing over the loan origination fee, the excited man is told to expect his loan check in two or three days; it takes that long to process the paperwork.

Three days pass, and sure enough he receives a piece of mail from the lender. But the envelope doesn't contain a check. You guessed it: It contains a rejection letter. According to the letter, the lender detected a failure to disclose certain information on the original application just prior to issuing the loan check. Unfortunately, the loan origination fee was used to process the loan. This can be avoided next time if he simply tells the truth and fully completes the application. More depressed than ever, he realizes he's been scammed.

These types of operations exist in every major city in the country. A dead giveaway is the required up-front payment. Legitimate lenders generally take their fees from loan proceeds. Other than a small fee for a credit check, there should be no up-front fees required to process loan paperwork.

Bait-and-Switch Loans

Unlike cash loans, real estate loans usually require fees to pay for a credit check, appraisal of the property, and loan paper preparation. But there are many mortgage bankers who are not what they appear to be. They can "lowball" customers by quoting an interest rate that is lower than anyone else's. Based upon this terrific rate, you pay your fees and wait for the loan. When you return to sign the final loan documents, the interest rate is substantially more than the going rate. People refinancing their homes are particularly at risk because federal law allows lenders to withhold truth-in-lending disclosures until settlement.

The loan officer informs the disbelieving, horrified victim that the interest rate that was originally quoted was good only for ten days. He says they found a blemish in the victim's credit history—something about a car payment that was missed five years ago—thus eliminating him from qualifying for the lower rate. The victim feels sick to his stomach as he thinks about having already given notice to his landlord, the new furniture that's on order, the drapes his wife has already selected. The lender steers the borrower into a higher-cost loan package than what was originally pitched. Like most people who get caught in this bait-and-switch scam, the victim shrugs his shoulders and signs the loan papers. Often the process is so slickly performed that the victim suspects nothing.

Mortgage Payment Scam

This is one of the top-ten scams in the United States today. Typically, the mark receives a phone call from a telemarketing company. The mark is asked if she would like to save tens of thousands of dollars on her mortgage. During his presentation, the telemarketer will ask the mark to make a half mortgage payment every two weeks. By paying half her usual monthly fee twenty-six times per year, she basically adds one full month's payment at the end of the year.

One extra payment a year reduces the principal owed by that amount, unlike the other payments, which include interest. If she continues to reduce her principal year after year by just one payment per year, it will have a dramatic effect on the mark's total loan costs. For example, on a mortgage of one hundred thousand dollars with a 10-percent interest rate, one additional payment a year reduces a thirty-year mortgage to eighteen years, saving approximately sixty-seven thousand dollars in interest.

The scam has two twists. The first is that the victim pays an up-front fee of one thousand to three thousand dollars and monthly maintenance charges. She ends up losing more than she is saving.

The second twist is that, although the woman makes her biweekly payments to the people who brought her the opportunity to save money, that firm is not paying her original lender biweekly. Their pattern is to either pay monthly and send an additional check at the end of the year, or perhaps keep a few months' worth of their clients' payments and then head down the road to strike again.

The irony is that all these unsuspecting individuals had to do in the first place was to check with their lender and directly send them a half payment every two weeks to achieve the same goal without having to give any swindlers a red cent. In short, it doesn't require a middleman to pay off one's mortgage early. Of course, you must first make sure that you don't have any prepayment penalties or ceiling on the amount you can pay your lender each year.

Foreclosure Scam

In most states the law requires a lender to announce foreclosure proceedings in the newspaper. Greggory S. Longsdorf studied the notices carefully and then sent an urgent letter to each homeowner, asking if he wanted to save his equity. If so, Longsdorf insisted that he could help. Even after Longsdorf was charged with felony swindling and ordered to pay a $21,250 judgment, he continued to send his letters and offer his services.

Longsdorf told his financially beleaguered victims that he would help them sell their homes and recover their equity before lenders foreclosed. He persuaded his victims to move out; then he rented their property to others and pocketed the money.

Court documents suggest that Longsdorf has victimized homeowners all over the country. One tenant of Longsdorf's said the man showed him a computerized list of his properties in Minnesota, Kansas, and Colorado.

In one case, Longsdorf is accused of conning a couple into paying him $641 a month so they could stay in their own home while he tried to sell it. Still, the lender foreclosed. In another case, Longsdorf promised to help a seriously ill, unemployed fifty-one-year-old Minneapolis woman sell her home. Then he forced her out, rented the home, and kept the rent.

Longsdorf was collecting between $425 and $675 per month per house from six houses in Hennepin County alone. These were houses that he was supposedly selling for their owners.

A grand jury in Ramsey County, MN, found that Longsdorf and an associate, David M. Wilson, operated under the name Homesavers of Minnesota. For defrauding George Y. Pomerantz and Jane Pomerantz of St. Paul in a foreclosure scheme, the jury was quoted as saying that Longsdorf and Wilson each should pay the couple $1,250 in general damages and $20,000 in punitive damages. The jury award has not been paid; Wilson left the state and Longsdorf filed for personal bankruptcy.

More than a year before Longsdorf was arrested for felony swindling, several state governmental agencies had received complaints about Longsdorf and Homesavers. The state attorney general's office did not feel that it had jurisdiction; the Minnesota commerce department decided it did not have jurisdiction; the Housing and Urban Development officials felt it was a state matter since it didn't appear that Longsdorf had broken any federal laws. And the attorney general's office was informed that the practices had stopped as a result of Longsdorf and Wilson leaving the state.

If authorities had acted more quickly, many desperate families might have saved their homes by other means. While his victims were depending on Longsdorf to "save" them, they were not exploring other possibilities. The results are analogous to those of medical quackery: While the patient is depending upon some phony scheme or fancy gadget with bells and whistles to correct a medical condition, he is not receiving proper, responsible health care.

Longsdorf pursued his home foreclosure scam after the civil county jury verdict in March 1991 and continued to operate even after the first criminal charge was filed against him two months later. Other swindlers only stop their operations when they are hauled off to prison.

If you find yourself facing foreclosure, consider moving in with relatives or friends temporarily. Rent your home and pay the mortgage with the rental payments, which may stall the foreclosure long enough for you to get on your feet again. Rent it yourself or turn to a well-known, well-established realtor with references. (Also refer to Chapter 10, "Confidence Games Against the Elderly.")

Financial Statement Scam

There are countless cases of loan applicants falsifying financial records and tax returns. Banks rely heavily on balance sheets and profit-and-loss statements for credit worthiness. One of the biggest bank scams in U. S. history was perpetrated by Bruce Helgason, a Connecticut oil executive.

Crimes against banks were up 45 percent in New York in 1992, according to FBI statistics. In May 1992, Helgason was charged with

cheating five banks out of $150 million. He is alleged to have given
Chase Manhattan Bank and four foreign banks false financial reports
and fictitious invoices and receipts that showed that he had oil or oil
contracts to use as collateral for a $250-million line of credit. Accord-
ing to one such set of false documents, Helgason's corporation had
$60-million worth of Tapis crude oil stored in Malaysia and $48-million
worth of petroleum condensate in Puerto Rico. But, according to the
indictment, Helgason did not own the oil.

The majority owner of two Advanchem companies, Helgason reportedly had a third solely owned company in the Cayman Islands,
which he used to hide oil futures contracts larger than his banks would
allow. With a 10 percent cash deposit, an investor can control high
amounts of a given commodity. If the price goes up, the buyer gets to
take the oil at a low price. Thus, if Helgason got lucky, he might have
earned enough money to repay the banks and put a lot of money in his
own bank account. Unfortunately, Helgason was not lucky, and he
could not repay the loans. Helgason's chief financial officer pleaded
guilty to conspiracy and bank fraud.

As long as there are depositories for other people's money, there
will be bold, daring criminals prepared to walk in with gun in hand
and attempt to help themselves. Less obvious but no less bold are the
white-collar criminals who plot to rob the bank in quieter, yet often
more effective ways. (See Chapter 11, "Business Bunco.")

Check Kiting

The Federal Reserve reports that approximately 1.2 million bad
checks are written each day in the United States. There are a number
of ways for con artists to commit fraud in this area, including creating
phony checking accounts and ordering checks for other people's existing accounts. According to Frank Abagnale, the former swindler who
wrote more than seventeen thousand bad checks totaling around $2.5
million, swindling banks is ten times easier today than it was twenty
years ago. "The ability to order checks by mail has made it simpler for
criminals to commit fraud. Deposit slips also are more valuable to a
criminal than blank checks. The slips often are reproduced and deposited with a worthless check, minus a healthy portion for less cash received."

Check kiting, a very common crime, occurs when a con artist opens two or three bank accounts. The con artist opens a checking account at Bank A using a check written on an empty bank account at Bank B. The next day she deposits a check written against her Bank A account into her Bank B account. She floats, or "kites," checks among her various accounts.

The Saturday Check Caper

A con man of unknown origin moved to Minneapolis. After establishing an identity with a Minnesota driver's license and opening an account at a local bank he rented an office in a building where many jewelry manufacturers were located. Looking the part of the successful jeweler, he spent two weeks cultivating friendships with the merchants in the building. He told them that he had emigrated from Israel to open a jewelry manufacturing operation.

One Saturday morning he proceeded from one merchant to the next, buying diamonds and precious stones including rubies, pearls, sapphires, and expensive opals from Australia. He bought gold bars, silver bars, and expensive watches, paying for all of his purchases with checks.

By the end of the day he had purchased over one hundred thousand dollars worth of valuable products with worthless checks. His two-week investment of time had paid off. Every merchant in the building he approached had been duped. By making his buys on a Saturday afternoon, the con man was confident that the merchants could not readily verify the funds in his checking account. The merchants certainly needed the sales. Besides, he was located in their building, seemed to be a very trustworthy individual, and didn't dicker over the prices like their other customers. And they probably reasoned that they could simply go to his shop on Monday if there were any problems with his check. Or so they thought.

Greed and desperation often play key roles in providing a swindler with an edge. Sergeant Jack Gorczyca, the Minneapolis detective who handled the case, assured me that the confidence man had pulled the same scam before in other cities—often around Christmas—and would most likely continue "purchasing" jewelry from unsuspecting merchants in the future.

Accounts Receivable Scam

Companies may find it necessary to borrow money on their accounts receivable. In other words, a company produces a product, ships it to their customers, and waits for payment. If they need cash while waiting for payment, the company might go to the bank and assign the customer payments to the bank in exchange for a loan. The bank then lends the company money (usually up to 85 percent of the face value of the total accounts receivable) so that the company may meet its financial obligations.

A group of con artists may set up three or more phony corporations in a given state. Then they invoice each other for hundreds of thousands of dollars. Each corporation then goes to a different bank and borrows against the accounts receivable amounts. The con men close up shop and move to the next town with significant amounts of ill-gotten cash.

Another twist on the accounts receivable con game is for the con artist to buy a small but established company using little cash down and a large promissory note. Once in control, the new owner cons the company's bank by preparing phony invoices in order to borrow against them. Once he has the cash in hand he disappears, leaving the bank and the seller with large losses to explain. (See Chapter 11, "Business Bunco.")

What Can You Do To Protect Yourself?

Use good judgment in managing your money and credit cards.   A good rule of thumb: Never risk more than you can afford to lose.

Reconcile your bank account statements every month using your check ledger and deposit receipts.   If there is a discrepancy, contact your bank immediately.

Never give your account number, PIN, Social Security number, or other personal information to anyone unless you know the individual and have verified that he or she really has a need to know.

Never lend your ATM card or any credit cards to anyone.

Track your ATM transactions very carefully.   If you're able to notify the bank of any unauthorized transfers within two business days, you'll only be liable for $50 of what's taken. The longer you wait to report any questionable transactions, the greater your liability.

Verify any automatic withdrawals on your statement against what you have authorized.

Never authorize money to be withdrawn from an account except for automatic installment payments, and never give such authorization over the phone.

Avoid any lending institutions that require you to pay an advance fee other than a small fee to check your credit history (except when you are buying a home and appraisal fees and other loan preparation fees may be necessary).

Ask any provider of loan quotes how long the rate is actually "protected."

Be suspicious of anyone who offers to stop a foreclosure on your property by closing your existing mortgage and issuing another mortgage. Only licensed mortgage brokers are allowed to do that, and any new agreement must be in contract form. If the person making the offer isn't properly licensed, forget it.

Don't believe anyone who makes promises to "take care of everything" with a bank or other lending institution that's threatening to foreclose.

Always pay your lender with a check or money order, never cash.

Never allow yourself to be involved in a bogus real estate deal. Don't accept payment in exchange for your signature or appearance as a "straw man" in any real estate transaction.

Be concerned if you learn that a property in which you're interested has been sold very recently for a much lower price. Always ask for a title search and investigate any questionable transactions.

If you're considered a poor credit risk, be concerned if someone guarantees to give you a loan without a credit check or for cash in advance. Ask yourself, "What are they getting out of it?"

Ask lots of questions whenever you're seeking a loan, and make sure your questions are thoroughly answered. Don't assume anything! Always get any promises in writing.

If someone who works for a bank or lending institution offers to help you obtain a loan by falsifying records or paying others to lie to "help" you, respond with a hearty, "No, thanks."

Don't accept a check from someone you don't know or for an amount that you can't live without unless you have seen his or her check guarantee card or otherwise verified that the check is good.

Always do your homework when it comes to people with whom you do business. Don't accept anyone at face value unless you've thoroughly investigated first.

What Should You Do If You Think You're A Victim of Bank Fraud?

First, contact the bank or lending institution in question and attempt to resolve the problem with one of the executives. If you are unable to resolve your concerns, contact the state banking department.

CHAPTER 5

Repair Scams

The prison interview room is stark, elemental. There are two chairs, a phone, a table, and, on that table right now, a high, disarranged stack of legal documents.

Inmate Jack Richard Kowalski has been endeavoring, over the past two hours, to explain these papers, to show how they prove irrefutably that he was unjustly tossed into jail. Kowalski, a tall, thin man with a bristly black-and-white beard, aims to make clear that the home repair business he once ran was honorable; that it did not, as his criminal record indicates, defraud senior citizens.

And, in a way, he is very convincing. Though he's a high school dropout, Kowalski can discuss the nuances of antitrust law with some facility. He seems to believe his own defense, and he is affable, too; he leans over the table, from time to time, to whisper confidences in your ear.

The only snare, it seems, on this scorching spring afternoon at the Eastern Oregon Correctional Institute, is Kowalski's voice. The voice is gravelly and insistent, and you hear more than cigarettes in its scratchy sibilants. You hear years of hard living in that voice. You hear half a decade of prison and you hear, if you listen long enough, a deep wellspring of hatred.

Jack Kowalski, beneath his charming veneer, is at war with the world. He's at war with the lawyers who prosecuted him. He hates the judge who watched over his case; he's enraged at his ex-wife and the girlfriend whom he sought to throw out of his home. And in his forty-six tumultuous years he has wrought anguish on most of these people, and on scores of others as well.

A 1992 Oregon jury convicted Kowalski, the former owner of several Portland-based home repair enterprises, of racketeering, and of thirty-one separate counts of theft or attempted theft committed between 1989 and 1991. Police and Better Business Bureau reports show, furthermore, that this con man has been scamming old people for well over a decade. He has sold them furnaces they never needed, pressured them into installing vastly overpriced water pipes, and stuffed drains with tissue so he could later return and fix them for an exorbitant fee.

His deeds, certainly, have been ugly, but all along he's presented himself to everyone—the law, his customers, and even his staff—as reasonable and upstanding. Oregon court records show that Kowalski kept meticulous tabs on all of his company's transactions, and even circulated a strict "code of conduct" to his employees. Kowalski admits that he didn't always take the necessary precautions in screening the people who worked for him because he was always willing to give someone a break: "I've got a big heart."

Likewise, Steve Todd, the Portland deputy district attorney who prosecuted Kowalski, says that the con oozed apparent goodwill. He'd have his work crews cut customers' lawns for free, Todd says; he'd exalt the sparkle in an old woman's eyes and tell her he wished he were older so he could take her out on a date.

In short, Kowalski behaved like a typical home repair scammer. These swindlers almost invariably victimize the elderly by preying upon their desperation and bewilderment. They show up, like long-lost sons, on the doorstep, and then proceed to "discover" holes in fine, sturdy roofs, or canyons in driveways that are, in truth, riddled with just a few cracks. They take down payments for work that they never quite finish, or they sneak into houses to rob their old victims blind. Often they intimidate by threatening a lawsuit or by merely demanding payment of the sick and the frail.

How do they bring themselves to such cruelty? The most ruthless con artists are, it seems, the sad characters who have conned themselves—the ones who have led such horrid lives, and made so many enemies, that they begin to see the world as hostile and chock full of liars, and to lose all sense of what innocence is.

Jack Kowalski grew up dreaming the American Dream. A poor kid, he and his seven siblings wore what he called "horrible clothes" to their Catholic school and spent summers as salespeople.

"When I was eight or nine years old we'd go to the farmers' market in the morning and buy bags of corn. We'd put up a little stand by the road," he recalls, "and sell corn to supplement the family income. It was three dozen ears for a dollar." Once the people stopped at his stand, made from cinder blocks and a couple of planks, "I'd tell 'em, 'While you're buying some corn, buy some tomatoes, too.'"

Kowalski's father, a welder, rewarded his son for his work. He'd give him an extra quarter after good sales days—and the boy would take the cash down to a nearby market and invest in tomatoes, which he'd sell for a profit.

Kowalski was a natural, so when he came to Portland in the early 1970s, after a brief stint in the Marines, he took a job peddling furnaces door to door, and relished the work.

"Selling was fun," he says, "and people were buying from me because they liked me; they didn't care about the company."

And the company, Kowalski assures, was hogging the profits. It was paying its salesmen a mere 8-percent commission . . . so Kowalski started to think. *These people are charging eighteen hundred dollars for a furnace,* he thought to himself, *and their wholesale cost is only a hundred dollars."*

The salesman knew that if he could undersell his old boss, he could strike it rich; he could, as he puts it, "make money hand over fist." The prospects were dazzling to this youth who'd grown up in poverty. The temptation, it seems, was too much.

Kowalski opened up a furnace firm. Larry Carmen, a seasoned Portland con man and a longtime associate of Kowalski's, has said that his friend was bilking seniors in the mid-1970s.

Kowalski was raking it in, and darkness was swirling about him. The con man says that, almost from the start, he had awful fights with the woman he married when he was seventeen. Kowalski wanted to leave the marriage, but he stayed, he says, out of honor, out of a desire to emulate his father who, despite frequent layoffs at New York's steel mills, kept his family together. "I knew that if I left," he says, "it would be turmoil and chaos [for my three kids]."

When he finally did leave his wife in 1982 he let loose. He moved to California and lived, he concedes, as a "hell raiser. I'd go out and bring home different women every night," he says. "I got mixed up with a few shady characters."

Characters who, it seems, were criminals. California court records show that in 1985 Kowalski and a cohort, William Oster, visited seventy-six-year-old Ruth Jadwisiak, rang her doorbell, and then assured her that if she did not install a steel beam in her basement, the house she had inhabited for fifty years would come crashing down.

The two men hustled Jadwisiak out of her house—the victim says she was dragged away—and checked her into a motel. Oster gave her food which, she says, made her feel drowsy, and both cons began removing Jadwisiak's belongings, under the pretense that her home needed "fumigation." They also plundered the old woman's savings.

When Ruth Jadwisiak awoke after three days she was hungry, dehydrated, and bedridden in a motel room, and she had lost $36,500. Her signature had been forged on a check; she was so traumatized that she had to be hospitalized for seventeen days.

Kowalski remembers his interlude with Ruth Jadwisiak, certainly; he served three years' time for it. But he won't discuss the incident. He prefers to regard his stint in California as a black hole, a nightmare from which he has wholly escaped. "I'm not sitting here trying to tell you that I'm an angel," is all he hoarsely admits, "because I haven't been an angel and, in the past, I've pulled some, some . . . I know the difference between good and bad."

When Jack Kowalski got out of prison in 1989 he wanted what so many people hope for—a fresh start. He wanted to move back to Portland and fish along the Deschutes, a cool, twisting river that pours out of the mountains and into the Oregon desert. He wanted to start a business that could employ his kids, now in their early twenties, and afford them a good living.

He had a real yearning to be an honorable businessman, but he was, it seems, too far gone by this point: Public Heating and Home Improvement was a racket right from the start.

Kowalski ran this business out of a battered trailer, with his old friend Larry Carmen. The two men focused on selling overpriced, low-grade furnaces to older folks whose existing machines were actually in fine repair, and their flimflam was systematic. Kowalski claimed to "have a good rapport with senior citizens."

Jack's daughter would phone prospective victims and offer a free furnace inspection. When asked how he got his list of names Kowalski said that a good businessperson doesn't disclose his trade secrets: "Trade secrets remain trade secrets." Then, if the senior desired the service, a Public Heating employee would pay this person a visit, and proceed to spin a tale of doom.

Typically, according to voluminous records kept by Portland's Better Business Bureau, the swindler would say the furnace was on the brink of a breakdown.

Sometimes a hole in the basement floor boded danger.

Similarly, when Kowalski went to examine the furnace of eighty-six-year-old Goldie Liptak, he deemed it okay, then exclaimed with nervous alarm that her perfectly functioning water pipes were "ruined," and that it would cost her $1,850 to replace them. Then he demanded $2,475 from her when the job was done. According to Kowalski, there was no problem with the job and no fraud.

When seniors consented to such "repairs" Public Heating usually sent out work crews right away, *before* the victim had a chance to change his or her mind. The crews—which were headed by Kowalski's son, Jack, Jr., and Carmen's son, Dan—would do work that was, in most cases, deemed sub-par by the Oregon State Builder's Board, and then the senior Kowalski would coldly contend with his outraged, overcharged clients.

Kowalski said of his relationship with his old friend Larry Carmen, "The combination between us was unbeatable." Mark Coffey, a detective with the Portland police, says that, while Carmen was Public Heating's exuberant blue-collar huckster, Kowalski styled himself the firm's erudite corporate exec. The con man, whose weekly income sometimes reached $3,300, ran Public Heating with an iron hand. He treated his employees as petty underlings—his daughter, for instance, was paid four dollars an hour—and he regarded angry customers as so many mosquitoes he needed to swat.

Kowalski's smug, steely manner was evident, certainly, when he visited a retired Portland hardware merchant and his wife and tricked these old people into thinking that their water pipes were worn out.

The con man insisted on a $1,425 down payment from Mr. and

Mrs. Marion Reslefski to replace their water supply lines and then, when the Reslefskis' son, John, disputed the charge three days later, Kowalski was outraged and patronizing. He refused to return the Reslefskis' deposit, and he mailed the Better Business Bureau a grandiose explanatory letter that began, "In this commercial age contracts are daily entered into between parties who expect to profit or benefit from them."

What's more, a Better Business Bureau complaint form alleges that Kowalski phoned John Reslefski's boss and threatened to sue the man for letting young Reslefski use a work phone to "harass" Public Heating.

Kowalski was ruthless toward the Reslefskis, but he had zero remorse.

"I'd known Mr. Reslefski for the last fifteen to twenty years," Kowalski said of the hardware store owner. He explains loudly, so once again his deep, scratchy voice fills the small prison room, "He didn't have any qualms about taking my money every time I'd go there for parts. I figured he'd made money off me for the last fifteen years. I figured it's time I made a few bucks off him. Is there anything wrong with that?"

The police finally caught Kowalski in 1991. Steve Todd was able to get the swindler sentenced to seventeen years. Larry Carmen was sentenced to five-and-a-half years in prison for his involvement, while the two sons were sentenced to short jail terms with work release for cooperating with the authorities to prosecute their fathers. Nonetheless, Todd says home repair cons are hard to prosecute. "Their victims," he explains, "are much like abused children in that they have a built-in inclination to hide their losses from their families. They're just a few steps away from the nursing home, and they realize that if they let their relatives know they got ripped off, they'll get put right in a home."

Mark Coffey, the Portland detective, agrees with Todd, and adds that there's one more obstacle to prosecuting home repair cons. "To prove someone is racketeering," he says, "you can't just point to one or two incidences of fraud, even if they're blatant. You have to prove that the guy repeatedly ripped people off, and that's hard to do when most of your witnesses are elderly—because old people are generally weak witnesses. They tend to forget things, and to be unassertive when they're up on the stand."

Coffey says many home repair scammers never get caught, and that scores of Kowalskiesque swindlers still approach elderly people daily. The Better Business Bureau of Oregon/SW Washington reported in 1992 that Oregon homeowners and businesses were losing approximately eleven thousand dollars *a day* to scammers selling asphalt "left over from a nearby construction site." Since the asphalt was left over the con artists could offer terrific savings on the job; but following acceptance of the quote and completion of the work, they'd present a bill for sometimes triple the price they'd quoted. Victims who didn't want to pay often were threatened into compliance. The work was not only overpriced but usually shoddy, lasting only a few months.

I believe that seniors and other consumers can best defend themselves from these cons by being aware of how they operate. Accordingly, in the following pages I explicitly describe a now-prominent contingent of cons and several of the home repair scams that are currently common.

The Travelers

Jack Kowalski, whose business number was at times unlisted, knew how to steal a victim's money and run from the consequences. But he never quite mastered the scramble in the way one group of Deep South residents has. The so-called "Travelers" have made escaping with illicit funds a tradition, an integral part of their singular culture.

The Travelers are Scottish-, Irish-, and English-Americans who live as clans, typically dwelling close by one another in opulent homes in Georgia and Florida. They speak Gaelic and English, tend to withdraw their kids from school after eighth grade, and wander for months at a time. Hundreds of male Travelers spend the spring and summer crisscrossing the eastern half of the nation, doing home repairs.

Sometimes these handymen do legitimate work. But all too often they rip off old people. Law enforcement officials from Long Island to Chicago say that, each spring, they issue warnings to homeowners to be wary of large work crews who rap on doors, offering their services in distinctive southern accents.

The Travelers often work in pairs, and once they've stolen a victim's cash—or pulled whatever hustle they're invoking that day—they slip out of town.

Travelers are hard to track because they pay neither Social Security nor income taxes, and because their clans are so insular. "They've intermingled so much," Ron Knapp, a Georgia bunco investigator explained recently to the Atlanta *Constitution,* "that you might have one hundred fifty Matt Murphys in one place, so even if you arrest somebody, they won't show up" in court.

When Travelers do show it is frequently with a high-powered attorney. Knapp has called the Travelers "organized," and a Mississippi lawyer proved him right when he said in 1991 that he gets more than six hundred calls each year from Travelers seeking representation.

The Travelers are, it seems, scarcely easy legal targets, and trying to settle out of court with a Travelin' con can be harrowing, too.

Look, for example, at what happened when one of these swindlers ripped off an elderly man named Odell Tollackson. Tollackson contacted the police and got them to locate the home of the suspect. Then, just as the seventy-one-year-old victim was about to press charges, the suspect's mother beseeched him tearfully. She begged Thompson until he agreed, finally, to take his money back and let the young man who bilked him off the hook.

Pay Up-front Scams

When Jack Kowalski cajoled Marion Reslefski, the retired hardware man, into paying $1,425 up front for plumbing work, he was invoking an age-old tactic. Repair cons have long had a yen for taking money up front for a job and then skipping away with the cash. They capitalize on people's admirable belief that all deals are cut in good faith, and they can make filthy piles of cash.

Consider, as a case in point, a Southern California swindler named John Rocky Yanis.

Yanis ran a phony outfit called A-I Consolidated Roofing that routinely collected down payments for roofing work and then never completed the work it promised to do. He bilked at least six homeowners before he was sentenced, in 1992, to a wrist slap of sixty days on a labor crew and one hundred hours of community service. And his ploys may not even have been as lucrative as those of a Georgia man who took, recently, to calling himself a "mobile auto mechanic."

This hustler would travel to a "client's" workplace, ostensibly to repair his or her car. Then, after a while, he'd shamble into the office to say he needed some money for parts. He'd get the money—in one case he gleaned $180—and never return.

Shoddy Job Scams

When the con men came to the door and told Dorothy Pomajevich her roof needed work she was in no position to doubt them. Seventy-eight and wheelchair-bound, she could hardly climb up a ladder to see if James Wayne Carnochan and his two cohorts were telling the truth.

So she trusted the men. She let two of them up on her roof and let the other wait inside with her; she even let them write out a check for her to sign when they finished. A big check: Pomajevich paid the trio of "roofers" $1,250, and all they did during their two hours of labor was dab a quart of tar onto the roof and foundation of her Minneapolis home.

Carnochan and his accomplices had enacted a shoddy job scam—a prevalent swindle that sees repair crooks charging outrageous fees for lackluster work done with dirt-cheap materials.

Ron Knapp, the Georgia investigator, has noted several variations of this sort of rip-off. Sometimes, he told the Atlanta *Constitution* recently, the crooks use watered-down paint to coat houses; other times, they pave driveways by laying down coal tar and flimsy Styrofoam packing peanuts—a mixture that looks shiny and sharp when applied but washes away with the first rain.

Con artists use shoddy supplies, of course, because they aim selfishly to keep their costs down. Consider, for instance, the swindlers who recently visited an elderly Georgia man in the dead of winter. These cons (whose names are unknown) told their victim he needed to repair the crack in his driveway quickly, before ice seeped into it and made it expand. Once they "did the job" and demanded more than one thousand dollars in payment, they told the old man they'd coated his crack with sealant. What they'd used, actually, was water.

Home Diversion Capers

The man said he was an electrical inspector, and he needed some help. He needed his "client," an eighty-four-year old Illinois widow, to monitor a handheld electrical tester.

He seemed a trustworthy fellow so the woman complied; she clutched the device—and watched to see if it blinked—as the man ostensibly checked the circuits in the next room.

The tester never lit up, and the "inspector" never checked anything except the old woman's cache of large bills. After he left the woman discovered he'd taken over nine hundred dollars. It was a classic example of a home diversion con.

Such acts of burglary, Nassau (New York) District Attorney Dennis Dillon has argued, are now commonly perpetrated by con artists, who've become too brazen to stay outside the house as they enact their repair scams. Indeed, in 1991 the state of Illinois alone received thirty reports of repair con games that resulted in thefts of cash or jewelry, and it's estimated that those reports represent only 10 percent of the repair crimes committed.

Losses from these scams totaled over $226,000, and 90 percent of the victims were over age sixty.

The victims, in other words, were mostly people who remember the Depression, and the rash of bank closures that swept the nation. Such seniors are apt to stow their money under beds and in closets "to be safe," and, unfortunately, they play right into the hands of con artists. The tricksters have evolved an array of methods to connive their ways into seniors' homes, and to distract their hosts once they're there.

Their scams begin, almost invariably, with an unsolicited visit and a complex tale. The swindler might say that he's been sent by the landlord to check the light fixtures inside. He might say that he's thirsty and needs a glass of water before mowing the lawn.

In one popular scam, for instance, the con says he represents the local water company and needs to give the victim a rebate. Once he gets a warm reception he cracks out a one-hundred-dollar bill and asks for change. He watches as the homeowner steps toward his or her money stash and later, as an accomplice distracts the victim, he pilfers the cash.

In another scam, enacted in the Portland, OR, area in 1992, a woman phoned victims to announce an alluring home service bargain. Work crews, she promised homeowners, could clean carpets for cheap.

Several seniors and handicapped people fell for this pitch and let a pair of men carrying cleaning tools go to work in their homes. The men, Portland's Better Business Bureau reports, talked one woman into leaving her house as they "cleaned"; they walked off with her television.

The men told another set of victims, an elderly couple, that they needed to wander through their home to "inspect the carpets." The couple found, once the crooks had snuck away over the still-dirty rugs, that their cash and valuables had been taken. They felt violated, no doubt, but their experience was perhaps not as devastating as that of an elderly New York couple who, in 1991, was vastly overcharged for a roof repair.

These seniors paid a pair of scam artists more than three thousand dollars for a job that, according to the cons' initial estimate, was supposed to cost only six hundred fifty dollars. Then, ten months later, they encountered the swindlers again, on their doorstep.

The cons wanted to waterproof their work this time and, for some reason, the homeowners let them in. The elderly woman escorted one con to the basement as he clutched his walkie-talkie and waited to hear from his partner.

After a while a voice crackled over the radio. The con man said, "Everything's okay up here, Bill."

And everything was okay . . . for the con men: They'd stolen ten thousand dollars in cash and jewelry.

Bogus Car Repairs

Manhattan executive Howard Einarshon took his silver Porsche to Leonard Sabatella's Grand Prix Auto Salon for a "slant nose conversion." He was quoted a price of seventeen thousand dollars. Five months and over twenty-eight thousand dollars later, the Porsche was missing its engine, tires, fenders, and seats, and the work on the car's nose job was still incomplete. Einarshon decided to hire a flatbed to take away his car. He spent an additional twenty-one thousand dollars for another shop to fix what Grand Prix Auto Salon had done to it.

In February 1991, Sabatella pleaded guilty to charges of bilking customers and insurance companies for bogus repairs on luxury cars, padding bills, and forging checks. According to authorities, Sabatella bribed an insurance adjustor to report that he had repaired a customized 1986 BMW M3 racing car valued at thirty-two thousand dollars. In fact, the car he worked on was worth only fifteen thousand dollars. By increasing the value of the car Sabatella also was able to inflate the cost of the replacement parts. He had the insurance company send a check for $9,464 for the repairs to him instead of the BMW's owner, forged the owner's signature, cashed the check, and pocketed the money. Then, instead of giving the insurance adjustor the six hundred dollars he'd been promised, Sabatella only gave him twenty dollars.

Sabatella was expected to serve a year in prison and pay five thousand dollars in restitution, even though he had almost $1 million in debts and filed for bankruptcy in 1990. The banks that cashed the forged insurance checks would have to reimburse the victims.

This was not Sabatella's first brush with the law. In 1988 he pleaded guilty to fifth-degree criminal possession of stolen property after an undercover agent caught him chopping up a stolen Ferrari. He paid a two-thousand-five-hundred-dollar fine.

The Recreational Vehicle Caper

Imagine driving into a small town in South Carolina in your RV on a long-awaited vacation. Suddenly the car you just spotted in your rearview mirror is alongside you, the driver beeping the horn and the passengers waving to you to pull over. The friendly driver warns you that your RV is swaying in the back and needs emergency repair.

You thank the concerned citizen for his efforts and, fortunately, you spot a repair shop just up the road. You pull in and speak with the mechanic, who's willing to set aside his other work so he can look at your problem. Sure enough, he finds a major differential problem and quotes $1,612 for repairs. The good news is that, if he can get the parts, he can have you and your RV back on the road again in a few hours. You think to yourself, *Thank goodness I found a qualified mechanic.*

The bad news is that, while you are killing time in the coffee shop down the block, the mechanic and his accomplice are having a good laugh on you for being such a sucker. The mechanic will gladly accept your check for the invisible repairs and give the "steerer" his cut.

Sometimes these swindlers never get caught. When they do, if they are found guilty, their sentences and fines are rarely enough to discourage them from starting another similar con as soon as they can.

How to Avoid Falling for a Repair Scam

Realize that if the price of a repair sounds too good to be true it probably is.

Be wary of repairmen and women who knock on your door, offering to work for you. Most legitimate businesses let clients come to them.

Be wary of repair outfits peddling special "one-day-only" deals.

Remain coolheaded when a repair person warns you of an "emergency" and says that you'll need to fix your furnace, roof, car, or whatever, right away.

Get a second opinion. If someone comes to your door telling you you need a repair job done, don't take his or her word for it.

Know your warranties. Realize that household equipment such as furnaces and dishwashers are often covered by long-term warranties—and that you may be able to get the manufacturer to fix your broken item for free. Keep all warranties, guarantees, etc., handy, and know what they include.

Insist on new, quality materials. Make sure the repair business does not use shoddy materials such as diluted driveway sealant or paint thinned with water. Ask the car mechanic what parts he plans on using and ask to have the old parts returned to you.

Slam the door or hang up the phone on any solicitor who becomes overly insistent in pitching his or her repair services.

How to Determine if a Repair Business Is Legitimate

Ask for local references and call them.

Ask if the repair workers slated to come to your home are licensed and bonded and demand to see proof.

Call the Better Business Bureau to see if any complaints have been filed against the company. Contact the contractor's state license board to check up on a contractor's license and reputation.

How to Avoid Being Swindled by the Repair People You Hire

Never pay in advance for repair work.

Ask your local district attorney's office for details about building contracts. Realize that, in many states, people have a right to rescind written contracts if they do so in writing shortly after the contract's initial signing.

Get repair people to put their quotes in writing before they start working. Always insist that they tell you exactly how much their services will cost, and make sure that the amount quoted includes all of the necessary materials and labor to complete a quality job. Most states have legal requirements regarding written estimates and bids. Find out what your state's are.

Get at least two estimates for the work to be done.

Insist that the repair person return to your home one month after he's finished working to ensure that he did the job properly if applicable, and add it to the contract.

Don't leave your home while repair people are working there.

Always use checks to pay for repair work. It is nearly impossible to catch repair swindlers who get paid in cash.

If You've Been Swindled by a Phony or Unethical Repair Outfit

Contact the repair firm and demand your money back immediately.

Cancel your check if possible.

Complain to the Better Business Bureau, your local police and the district attorney's office.

CHAPTER 6

Credit Card Fraud

Imagine that you are twenty-seven-year-old Susan Caltabianos, a beautiful blond woman working in London, England. Suddenly you learn that you're no longer able to open a bank account, obtain credit or get a passport. Imagine what you would do when you requested your medical records only to find that they had been transferred to another physician who refused to send them back on the grounds that he had Susan Caltabianos sitting right in front of him. Can you imagine how you would feel if this nightmare lasted for three and a half years?

Susan's nightmare began shortly after Loveth Udoji, a thirty-year-old Nigerian woman, obtained a copy of Susan's birth certificate in a scheme to avoid detection in a drug-trafficking ring. She used it to get a passport and National Insurance Number (similar to our Social Security number) as Susan Elizabeth Caltabianos. She arranged for the real Susan Caltabianos's medical records to be transferred, and opened bank and credit card accounts in her new assumed name. She rented an apartment in London under Susan's name and began charging items on credit cards with Susan's name.

"Susan Caltabianos" was arrested after eight air mail letters from Nigeria containing 113 grams of cocaine were intercepted by a London customs officer. Richard Caltabianos, Susan's fifty-year-old father, told the Snaresbrook Crown Court in London how he learned of his "daughter's" arrest for drug smuggling: "I came home one day to find a policeman waiting outside my home. He told me my daughter had been arrested on drug charges and was in custody. I was stunned and my wife thought it was a joke, especially when we were told that our daughter was Nigerian. When the policeman produced my daughter's birth certificate and explained the black woman claimed we were her parents, we knew she was lying."

Until the imposter's arrest the real Susan Caltabianos had no idea why her life had become such a misery. Following the unraveling of the sinister scheme, she said: "This whole thing has been a terrible ordeal. She ruined my life for three and a half years. I have never met or heard of her before, but she swindled every document I needed to prove who I am."

Loveth Udoji collapsed screaming as Judge Robert Southan passed a six-year sentence, describing her as a "compulsive liar and swindler." How many fellow convicts will she teach how to use other people's identities during her incarceration?

Although impostors generally steal the identities of dead people, an ever-increasing number of con artists are using the identities of people who are still living because these individuals still have active bank accounts, jobs, and established credit. A con artist may assume anyone's identity, move to any city, and live on someone else's good name, credit, and bank accounts. While the victim in such a hoax may have to spend a lifetime proving that he or she did not withdraw the money from bank accounts, charge the goods, and run up the bills, the con artist is off to the next city to assume another identity. When a victim finally gets things worked out—if he *can* get things worked out—the con artist could resume using the false identity once again.

I interviewed several swindlers who gave other people's names to police officers when they were arrested. In several instances they were released on their own recognizance because they were perceived to be upstanding citizens. Police usually take fingerprints, which will, of course, eventually uncover an impostor. But on busy nights when jail cells are full and the volume of bookings is high, it is not uncommon for those detained to be released without having their fingerprints checked. Imagine the horror felt by the unfortunate victims whose names were used when the police come to their homes or places of employment and take them away in handcuffs for crimes they did not commit.

In the United States today, your identity to society consists of your Social Security number, driver's license number, bank account numbers, credit card numbers, and passport number. If a criminal obtains this information, he or she can assume your identity. From that point forward everything he or she does while posing as you will be taken as your behavior and actions by the rest of the world.

There are few defenses against these types of con artists. Unfortunately, "the system" and computer networks allow those who pretend to be others to use good credit, good character profiles, and flush bank accounts. Access to information ushered in by the computer age has been a blessing to banks, credit card companies, police departments, merchants, and, unfortunately, to con artists who know how to take advantage of the system. (See Chapter 19, "Computer Scams.")

You are completely defenseless if a con artist (or any desperate individual looking for easy money) gets a job as a loan officer, credit manager, personnel manager, or secretary to any of the above because access to important information such as your Social Security number, bank account numbers, credit card numbers, and driver's license number is instantaneous. Not a very comforting feeling to be so exposed, is it?

The Almost Perfect Crime

There is a crime wave going on in this country that staggers the imagination, cutting across the strata of society from the average man on the street all the way to the boardrooms of multinational corporations. The criminals responsible for this crime wave range from cheap pickpockets to highly placed members of the fraternity of organized crime. They all share one thing: the understanding that credit cards aren't made of plastic. In the hands of thieves and con artists, they are solid gold.

Credit card fraud is big business, often netting individual practitioners hundreds of thousands of dollars in cash and merchandise. According to a 1992 Louis Harris and Associates, Inc., poll, 5 percent of all American adults—which is over 9 million people—reported that they had experienced fraudulent misuse of a credit card such as American Express, Visa, or MasterCard. Anyone can do it, and does: from the petty thief who uses a credit card found in a victim's purse to big operations run by organized crime that buy and sell credit card numbers on the black market. It's so profitable that even otherwise "honest" merchants sometimes indulge in the practice, ripping off their own customers to generate additional cash flow.

Take the case of Michael Angelo Stramboni, a convicted con artist who was scheduled to report for a prison term in connection with a bank fraud scheme. He didn't show up. According to federal documents, he was registered at a luxury hotel in San Francisco, where he ran up an eight-day bill of over five thousand dollars on room service and gift shop purchases.

Stramboni had used an alias and the Social Security number of a Kentucky woman to secure the credit cards. He then ran up unpaid bills totaling over five hundred thousand dollars at department stores, luxury hotels and a host of other businesses in several states before authorities caught up with him.

Stramboni's antics are simply the tip of a very large iceberg, as countless numbers of thieves and con artists make use of credit cards that don't belong to them to rack up millions of dollars in charges annually. Credit card companies take the fraud business very seriously, devoting ever-increasing resources to try to stay one step ahead of criminals. Security measures like watermarks and holograms on cards helped cut down on counterfeiting in the middle of the 1980s. Recently, Citibank inaugurated a program to put the photo of the card holder on its credit cards, so merchants can easily match the buyer's face to the card. Some banks now send a notice along with new credit cards requiring card holders to "activate" their cards by calling an 800 number and punching in their Social Security numbers to verify receipt of the card.

Visa USA and MasterCard announced in mid-1993 that they would be offering a new technology to place a secret, encrypted code on its cards. "Smart cards" will be encoded with microchips that contain identification and security information aimed at derailing con artists. But this won't necessarily protect against "skimming" devices, which crooks use to record information on the card's magnetic strip.

The companies are also looking into biometrics, which uses fingerprints or eye-retina prints to verify that the actual cardholder is who he or she says he is. The problems associated with the programs are twofold. The cost of such security measures increases the cost of producing a credit card from one dollar to almost five dollars. And getting a customer in to pose for the photograph is difficult; some may feel that fingerprinting or other biometrics are simply too intrusive.

Many banks are using courier services to deliver credit cards to people in areas where "never received issue" fraud (the theft of newly issued credit cards before they are delivered to the correct party) is high.

It is shocking that fewer than 1 percent of credit card con artists are caught, leaving most of them free to strike again and again. The primary reason for their success is the sheer volume of credit cards and immense numbers of transactions that make tracking nearly impossible.

More than six thousand different banks issue Visa and Master-Cards, and there are over 130 million credit card holders nationwide. And most of them have multiple credit cards. That adds up to tens of millions of transactions and billions of dollars in sales over the course of each year. It's no wonder credit card watchdogs have trouble tracking down criminals.

Who are the targets of these crimes? The card holder is the primary target, since his or her number is what the thieves really want. It is the key to the kingdom, providing the thief with the means to acquire merchandise, cash, even collateral for loans and large purchases, such as automobiles and homes.

Fortunately, if your card (or card number) is stolen, you are only legally liable for the first fifty dollars charged on each card, and many issuers will not hold you liable for even that amount. In addition, if you report the theft to the issuer before the thief uses the card, you are protected against any loss.

Financial institutions that issue the cards have shouldered a great deal of the responsibility for fraudulent card use, but they require merchants to follow increasingly demanding security procedures. For example, most card issuers require that merchants get an authorization code for each sale.

If the merchant has failed to observe the security requirements, the bank can refuse the payment and even suspend the merchant account that allows them to take credit cards. And merchants discover that they have little recourse in collecting on bad debts run up on credit cards, since the thieves are usually long gone or impossible to trace.

Some innocent merchants find themselves caught in the machinery of a bank's security system, with no way out. Michael Silvers and Patricia Silvers, owners of a New York boutique specializing in women's formal and evening wear, felt they were doubly victimized, first by a ring of credit card thieves and then by the bank that froze their merchant account.

Silvers said he is reconciled to swallowing a loss of at least seven thousand dollars on a fraudulent telephone order. But he couldn't understand why his bank froze eighteen thousand dollars in deposits to his account and suspended the use of the desk-top machine that authorizes credit card purchases.

Silvers and his sister cooperated fully with authorities. In fact, he notified the bank of his suspicions concerning the order in question when a second large order came from the same woman the next day. Secret Service agents subsequently informed him that his buyer was probably part of a national credit card scam being run by a group of transvestites who stole credit card numbers and racked up huge charges for women's clothing all over the country.

Eighteen people were indicted in connection with the case, but several months later Silvers was still unable to convince his bank to put him back on line with MasterCard and Visa. His experience underscores the vulnerability of merchants in dealing with con artists wielding phony credit cards.

While it is unfair for a bank to penalize an honest businessperson, it can happen, and the merchant may spend months trying to unravel the mess. It is far better to attack the problem at the point of sale. Retailers must be diligent in training clerks to recognize potential frauds and must set policies and procedures that help prevent criminals from passing bad credit cards.

Extensive security measures instituted by credit card companies, banks, and merchants add significantly to the cost of doing business. Ultimately, the overwhelming cost of credit card fraud comes back to haunt the consumer in the form of higher prices at the cash register, and higher fees and interest rates charged by banks on credit cards.

There are two basic types of credit card frauds:

- Crimes against consumers in which their cards or card numbers are stolen and used illegally.
- Crimes against merchants in which thieves use stolen or counterfeit cards to purchase goods or services.

Knowing what to watch out for and how to protect yourself can give individual card holders and the small businessperson the edge in dealing with this plastic crime wave.

Going for the Gold

Stolen cards account for the majority of credit card fraud. Con artists get cards and card numbers in a variety of ways. The most popular method is simply to steal a card from its rightful owner. Pickpockets, car thieves, burglars, and even prostitutes get into the act, pumping stolen cards into a black market pipeline that fences them for anywhere from fifty to two hundred dollars apiece. Premium cards with high limits, like Gold and Platinum cards, are in big demand and bring the most on the street.

Thieves use the stolen cards to get cash advances as well as to charge items such as jewelry, computers, and other items that can be easily resold.

Mail Theft

"Never received issue" credit card fraud (or NRI) is the fastest-growing method for acquiring cards. Visa lost $91 million and Master-Card $83 million in 1992 to NRI fraud. Basically, thieves steal newly issued credit cards from mailboxes; some thieves have even been known to go back to steal the verification letter that notifies the card holder that a new card was recently forwarded to them. Since most people don't pay attention to the expiration dates on their credit cards, they may not realize they haven't received the card until their expired card is refused by a merchant.

Stemming the tide of NRI fraud is the Postal Service's number-one priority. Thefts are most common where bulk shipments of cards are easily spotted, such as mailbox facilities and airports. Working with the credit card companies, postal investigators are using sophisticated computer tracking techniques to catch thieves. Unfortunately, organized rings of post office workers and contract mail handlers, such as air freight services, have been caught in the act themselves. There have even been cases of thieves hijacking mail trucks just to get the credit cards, then dumping the rest. All that easy money is just too tempting for some people to pass up.

Other thieves specialize in stealing catalogs that often contain the person's credit card number in addition to the name and address from household garbage and mailboxes. Or they will take your credit card statement and get all the information they need from it. In either case, they contact the credit card issuer and request a change of address or an extra card in another name. When they receive a reply letter showing the account number, they have all they need to begin placing orders.

A ring of thieves on Long Island received fifty cents to a dollar for each catalog they stole, five dollars for getting a reply letter that listed the credit card number, and one hundred dollars for every one thousand dollars worth of merchandise they got fraudulently. Police arrested one man when he accepted a package charged to a deceased man's credit card by signing the dead man's name. He had thirty stolen catalogs in his possession at the time of his arrest.

Trash Treasures

One of the most popular methods of getting credit card numbers and information involves theft of the transaction slip carbons from trash cans. Mail order companies and large retailers use order forms on which the card holder's information is recorded, and these order forms frequently end up in trash bins that are easily accessible.

The carbons contain all the information the thieves need to order merchandise by phone: the card holder's name, card number, and expiration date. In California, rings of thieves using this method ordered large quantities of merchandise by phone for delivery to a mail drop or phony office, then disappeared before authorities could catch up with them.

The easy accessibility of carbons resulted in a deluge of credit card carbon fraud. In an effort to counteract it, credit card companies advised merchants to return carbons to card holders along with copies of the transaction slips. It also spurred the credit card companies to develop carbonless slips, which leave no telltale treasures in the trash.

Place Your Order

There are a variety of other ways that criminals can gain access to this information. The inside job involves a person working in a bank or retail store, who takes down credit card information and sells it. Or crackers can break into computers and extract the information.

Thomas Hope Vincent found this an irresistible way to enhance his income as a computer analyst for *Time* magazine. Undercover police in Florida arrested him after he tried to sell them the credit card numbers and card holder information of three thousand *Time* subscribers for one dollar apiece. A bargain price, to be sure, but potentially very profitable for Vincent, who had eighty thousand additional card numbers on computer disks at home.

Many people are duped by phony telemarketers, who call to tell them they are eligible to receive some desirable item as part of a promotion. All the customer has to do is give his credit card information to cover a small handling charge. Needless to say, the consumer never receives the item and the con artists begin racking up large charges on the ill-gotten credit card number.

There is a mail-order version of this scam in which the victim receives a catalog or flyer offering a free item for a minimal handling charge. While many people will send checks, thieves receive large numbers of credit card orders as well.

The Invisible Man Schemes

The simplest way to get a credit card is to apply for it. The con artist steals someone's identity or creates a phony identity and begins applying for credit cards. The information may come from a personal check, credit card transaction slips, credit card company records, or even personnel files.

Sophisticated criminals turn to credit "doctors" who sell good credit records that they acquire by breaking into a credit bureau's files or tapping into the computers of retail stores' credit departments. These skilled computer crackers can create new files built on someone's credit history, then market them to con artists or people with bad credit histories. (See Chapter 18, "Credit Repair Scams.")

A thief who acquires a consumer's credit card and driver's license may use them to open instant credit accounts at retail stores, charge a large number of purchases to the new account, and disappear. The advantage of this technique is that the original card holder won't cancel these accounts because they won't even know they exist!

Consumers aren't even safe when they die. One man working in northern California and Oregon bought cars and merchandise and took out loans using the names taken from obituaries. He would apply for credit cards in the dead man's name, run up bills, and skip town.

Criminals using phony identities can create a complete credit history for themselves, including great employment records and a sterling credit background. Con artists running these scams build entire lives around their fraudulent activities, lives that on the surface seem to be entirely legitimate.

Bruce C. Carrington lived such a life, until his world crumbled around him. He was arrested in connection with charges that he had bilked two companies, including General Electric, out of a hundred-thousand-dollars' worth of computer equipment using a phony credit card. He then sold the equipment to doctors, using the profits to support his lavish lifestyle. General Electric hired private investigators, who tracked Carrington down and tipped off Illinois state police officials. Carrington's big mistake was having the computer equipment delivered to his own home instead of a mail drop.

The Crime of the '90s: Encoding Fraud

Encoding fraud is considered an advanced form of credit card fraud because of the equipment and computer expertise required. But investigators are finding out it isn't really that difficult. Even teenagers can do it. Investigators in Los Angeles arrested nineteen-year-old Alija Modammjani for orchestrating an encoding fraud scheme in which he and a group of other teenagers working in a San Fernando Valley mall stole credit card information and then coded it onto their own credit cards.

Modammjani picked up his computer skills in a college class, bought an encoder at a computer store for a few hundred dollars, hooked it up to his home PC, and was ready to go. He simply recorded the name, account number and expiration date of a stolen, valid card and then transferred the information to the magnetic strip on the back of another credit card. It's estimated that the fraud cost credit card companies as much as one hundred thousand dollars. Modammjani used the re-encoded cards himself in addition to selling them to others for up to four hundred dollars each.

When the altered card was run through the computer at a store, it authorized the purchase, printed the transaction slip, and charged the sale to the other person's account. The con man usually signs the name illegibly. And, surprisingly, clerks almost never notice that the name and number on the card differ from the printed slip.

"If it comes up clear, you are clear. Most of these folks don't check the number while making the sale," said Special Agent Jim Miller of the U.S. Secret Service. More sophisticated criminals emboss the cards with matching names and numbers.

Incidences of encoding fraud exploded in the early '90s, growing from zero to $39 million in losses for Visa International alone over a three-year period. But the credit card companies have been slow to respond to the problem because the losses, estimated to run from hundreds of millions to billions of dollars throughout the credit card industry, are small compared to the amount they take in overall and the prohibitive costs of updating their equipment.

"You have a big conflict between marketing and security in the industry," Miller said. "Meantime, the criminals are having a field day. Once losses hit a percentage the credit card companies can't live with, they will change things."

Visa has moved most aggressively, developing complex coding systems and sophisticated terminals that will verify sales using algorithmic codes that thieves will be unable to manipulate. But other credit card companies are lagging behind in dealing with the problem, so encoding fraud will probably be around for a while.

An interesting footnote: The magnetic strips used by encoders were added to credit cards in the mid-1970s as a security feature.

Counterfeit Credit

Visa USA lost approximately $120 million to counterfeiters in 1991. In the past, some criminals bypassed the need for a stolen card by simply printing their own. Any crook with a little ingenuity and the cash to buy an offset press (or the services of a crooked printer) and a laminating machine could create pretty convincing imitations of real credit cards.

California was the capital of counterfeit credit card manufacturers, cranking them out for sale to whomever was ready to pay. But the credit card companies developed security measures, such as holograms and watermarks, in the middle of the '80s that made it more difficult and expensive to counterfeit cards.

These days, the Golden State has dropped to third place behind Hong Kong and Spain. Sophisticated international criminals in those countries now manufacture the finest fake credit cards in the world, distributing them in the U.S. to criminals who rip off department stores, restaurants, airlines, hotels, car dealers, and a host of other businesses that accept plastic in lieu of cash.

Advance-Fee Credit Cards

Another scam that credit-hungry consumers are falling for in record numbers are phony "gold" cards that turn out to be good only for buying items in a company's catalog. Typically, the offer comes by way of a postcard or other direct-mail piece often bearing Visa or MasterCard logos, even though the card is not affiliated with either company.

All the consumer has to do is call a 900 number to get easy credit. Of course, the call costs an arm and a leg, and frequently, the consumer still has to send in a check to obtain the card. Often the card never arrives. But even if the consumer finally receives the credit card, purchases, which may be made only from the company's catalog, often require a deposit, too.

One Chicago-area man was recently sentenced to a year in prison for advertising that his firm could guarantee that anyone could obtain a major credit card. All applicants had to do was pay fifty dollars, which went into the pockets of the man and his partner. It's estimated that the scammers took in over $145,000 from hundreds of people looking for instant credit. (See "Conclusion.")

Putting Plastic to Work

Once the criminal has acquired a card or the vital information, there are virtually no limits to the damage that can be done. Inventive criminals constantly create new schemes to bilk retailers and other businesses. The best of them may work for months or years before perpetrators are caught, if they are ever apprehended at all. The following are just a few of the most popular types of scams run on businesses by credit card con artists.

Exceeding the Limit

Experienced users of stolen cards make large purchases immediately, running the card up to its limit. When the card is refused because the credit limit has been reached, the criminal will try to make small purchases that do not exceed the card's "floor limit." This is the amount—usually fifty dollars—that a merchant will accept before running a verification on a card. The thief can greatly extend the limit of a stolen credit card using this technique.

In an effort to cut down on this type of game-playing with credit limits, credit card companies have provided merchants with machines that read the magnetic strips on the cards, verify them with the central computer, and issue an authorization number. The newest equipment even prints the transaction slips.

Merchandise Return Scams

This has caused thieves to become more inventive in enhancing the life spans of stolen cards. One way of adding to a stolen credit card's balance involves returning stolen merchandise or counterfeit merchandise to a retailer. Sometimes criminals simply pick up merchandise off the shelf in the store and take it to the desk for a refund, claiming to have lost the receipt.

A variation on this trick is the counterfeit goods scam. This is quite common in major cities, where crooks have access to phony high-ticket items, like imitation Rolex watches. The criminal presents the phony products to the unsuspecting retailer, requesting a cash refund or credit against a stolen credit card. (See Chapter 11, "Business Bunco.")

Another version of the merchandise return scam involves double charge backs. The con artist orders something by phone or mail for delivery, then contacts the merchant claiming it never arrived and requesting a refund. The merchant issues a charge back, or credit, against the account. Then the criminal contacts the bank that issued the card and tells them the item was billed to his card in error because he had never ordered the item. A second credit is issued and the merchandise is sold, netting an even greater profit for the con artist. This trick is less effective these days, since credit card companies and smart merchants are growing wise to it.

Traveling on Someone Else's Money

Some con artists specialize in travel scams, in which they visit foreign countries using stolen credit cards to pay for their travel expenses, get cash advances at banks, and purchase merchandise that can be shipped to the U.S. for resale. The difficulty of verifying the validity of credit cards once they are outside the country makes it relatively easy to rip off our neighbors abroad. Even banks will skip the verification and simply advance the funds to someone who appears to have the right papers and identification. These international thieves then proceed to steal or purchase foreign credit cards, which they bring back to this country for use or sale to other criminals. (For other con games involving travel, see Chapter 7, "Travel Scams.")

Crooked Merchant Scams

Even dishonest merchants get into the act, helping con artists by running crude counterfeit cards through their imprinting machines for nonexistent purchases and pocketing a percentage of the take. Since the merchant is in on the deal, the cards don't have to be particularly convincing in appearance. They just have to produce an imprint on a transaction slip that will pass cursory inspection at the credit card company.

Some crooked merchants realize huge profits by selling products twice. Mohammad Masood used his two travel agencies as fronts to bilk airlines for more than a million dollars. He sold discount airline tickets to customers for cash, but he pocketed the cash and never paid the airlines. He claimed that the tickets had been paid for with American Express card numbers that proved to be bogus. Needless to say, investigators found out he was behind the scheme and a federal judge sentenced him to nine years in prison.

The most obvious merchant scam is commonly run by telemarketing firms and mail-order firms that take credit card orders, pocket the cash, and disappear without shipping the merchandise. Or the phony merchant files for bankruptcy and leaves the buyer with little recourse. (Refer to Chapter 11, "Business Bunco," for similar business scams.)

One group of telemarketing con artists used a prominent charitable organization that helped locate missing children as a front. It used the organization's merchant account to quickly process fraudulent credit card orders for rare coins from Metropolitan Rare Coins, a telemarketing firm that sold bogus coins. Merchant accounts are extremely difficult for telemarketing firms to get because they allow the seller to receive cash almost immediately from the bank, often a month or more before the customer is billed.

The crooks were running the telemarketing business right out of the charity's offices, billing customers for coins they never ordered and for orders the firm never filled. Money was passed from the charity's account to the con artists' pockets. By the time police caught up with them, they had pulled in over two hundred fifty thousand dollars in cash. (For other charity-related cons, see Chapter 15, "Fraudulent Fund Raising.")

Another common merchant rip-off that is very rarely uncovered is the double billing scam. The merchant simply runs the card through the imprinter twice and submits two slips to the bank for payment. If the card holder doesn't catch the additional charge, the merchant gets to keep the money. If the card holder complains, the merchant claims it was a computer or clerical error and issues a credit. In the meantime, the merchant has had an interest-free loan from the credit card company for several months.

Crooked clerks can take advantage of their employers and customers in a similar way. The clerk runs two slips and holds the second one until a cash transaction comes along. The clerk pockets the cash and fills out the charge slip for the amount of the bill. The merchant will probably not catch it because the cash register totals will balance. And, unless the consumer is matching charge slips against card statements, the entire transaction will go undiscovered.

Fencing the Goods

Cash is much better than credit when con artists use stolen cards at banks, casinos, and ATMs to get cash advances. Thieves also use stolen credit cards to wire money to an accomplice, converting plastic to cash quickly and easily. Of course, this requires an identification number that the cash machines will recognize, which reduces the amount of credit-to-cash fraud significantly. Most credit card criminals must rely on purchase and sale of merchandise for the larger part of their incomes.

Professional con artists have little use for the goods they purchase and try to convert them to cash as quickly as possible. There are fences who will take the merchandise off their hands, returning far less than face value for the products they receive.

Some con artists seeking to maximize their profits have formed discount buying clubs that sell memberships to ordinary people and send catalogs of name-brand merchandise available at very attractive prices. When customers order products the crooks order the same products from legitimate mail-order firms, using stolen credit card numbers. Then they sell the products to their members, who are unaware that the products they receive are "hot." Sometimes they send counterfeit products.

Car rental agencies have been victimized by thieves who use stolen credit cards to rent automobiles, which are then either sold to an unsuspecting third party or stripped and sold for parts. Other types of rent-and-sell scams run the gamut from furniture to sailboats. Rental agencies of all types usually hold a signed credit card slip against return of the items rented.

Dialing for Dollars

A category of credit card fraud that is frequently overlooked is telephone calling card fraud, but annual losses to calling card fraud are running around $600 million. That's probably because most people don't think of their calling cards as credit cards, but that's what they are. You have an account with the phone company (your phone number is your account number), and all you can buy with your credit card is phone calls. But anyone who has winced upon opening his phone bill knows how quickly those calls can add up to significant amounts of money.

More than half the households in the U.S. report having a calling card, and a third of those households said that more than one family member used the card. Some even reported that people outside the immediate family had used the card with their permission. This easy sharing of calling card numbers can make it possible for thieves to gain access to the numbers, with obvious results.

The phone company will generally accept an individual's word in disputes over phone charges, especially if the customer immediately reports the loss of a calling card. (This doesn't necessarily hold true for toll fraud, which is addressed in Chapter 19, "Computer Scams.")

However, the phone company must absorb the loss, and it is eventually passed back to the consumer in the form of higher long-distance fees.

There are numerous ways for thieves to get phone access codes, but the most direct is to simply call the card holder and ask for the number. The Harris poll referred to earlier indicated that 15 percent of consumers who had calling cards would willingly give the numbers to someone who called and said they worked for the phone company. It should be obvious that the phone company doesn't need to call and ask for a calling card number—they issued it in the first place—but many consumers don't think that quickly or clearly when queried.

This naïveté makes life easy for criminals like the Arsenau brothers. At the time of their arrest, the two men and a woman had over four hundred stolen phone card access codes in their possession, along with a piece of paper detailing over seven thousand dollars in sales of the numbers.

Investigators believed the threesome eavesdropped on people using pay phones at airports and other locations where banks of phones are common. Known as "shoulder surfers," such scammers frequently peer over the shoulders of people using credit calling cards. As customers gave their card numbers to operators or punched them into the keypads, the Arsenau brothers dutifully recorded them for later sale.

Summary

Credit card companies and the banking institutions that sponsor the cards adapt as quickly as possible to meet the challenges presented by creative con artists, but they are working against impossible odds. Ultimately, it is just too costly to change security safeguards as frequently as would be needed to keep the crooks out of the credit system, so the old rule of "every man for himself" must apply.

Merchants and consumers must do all they can to keep the con artists away from their doorsteps. While there is no 'sure way for individuals and businesspeople to protect themselves from becoming the targets of credit card fraud, there are a number of steps that can be taken to greatly reduce the odds of being victimized.

What Can You Do To Protect Yourself?

Tips for Consumers

Keep track of your cards.   Make a list of your cards, including the name of the bank, account number and the phone number for reporting a lost or stolen card. Keep the list in a safe place.

Keep copies of your credit card applications and follow up with the issuer if you have not received the card or a rejection notice within four weeks.

Keep track of the expiration dates of your credit cards.   New cards are generally sent out a month or so before the expiration date. If you haven't received one two weeks before the expiration date, call the issuer to let them know.

Watch for notification that a credit card has been mailed to you.   If you receive the letter but have not received the card, call the company immediately.

Always verify charges on your monthly billing statements to insure that you are not paying for illicit use of your account.

Check your credit file annually for inquiries or entries that you do not recognize.   You can request a copy of your file from a credit bureau for a nominal fee; order one and compare it with your own records.

Don't carry more credit cards than you absolutely need.   It makes it easy for thieves to lift one or two without making you aware they have been stolen.

Never leave credit cards in your glove compartment or other easily accessible places.

Don't give your credit card number to anyone over the phone, unless you placed the call and know the firm to be reputable.

Never give your credit card to a store clerk as identification when writing a check.

Never give a clerk your address or phone number when paying with a credit card.

Beware of sleight-of-hand artists, who switch expired or stolen credit cards for your card during a transaction.   Most people just put the cards in their wallets, only to discover later that their card has been stolen, right before their eyes. Always look at your card before you put it away to make sure it's your card.

Get mail out of your mailbox as quickly as possible. If you are going away for a few days, either have your mail held at the post office or have someone pick it up daily.

Check catalogs to make sure your account number is not listed on the order form. Contact any company that lists your number and request that it be removed from future mailings.

Never put your credit card number on a postcard order form for a magazine subscription. Anyone can read the number and use it.

Never let anyone outside your immediate family use your phone calling card.

Look around when using your phone calling card at a public phone. If you see anyone suspicious hanging around the phones, go somewhere else to make the call. It's always preferable to make your call from a touch-tone phone so that you don't have to tell an operator your card number. Always protect your calling card number from the view of others; if necessary, cover the numbers with your other hand when punching in your calling card number.

Call your card issuer if you don't receive a statement one month. Thieves sometimes steal statements to get the account numbers.

Tips for Merchants

Merchants try to protect themselves from fraud by checking credit card numbers against a hot list provided by credit card companies. Unfortunately, the list is generally outdated by the time it is printed because thieves will only use stolen cards for a few weeks. There are other measures that are more effective in the battle against credit card fraud.

Invest in a BIN book, if possible. The first four digits of a MasterCard or Visa number are called the Bank Identification Number (BIN). Despite the high cost, many mail-order companies feel it is worthwhile to invest in a BIN book, which lists bank names, addresses, and telephone numbers. Depending on the rate of loss, retail merchants may want to invest in this directory.

The procedure is simple. The clerk asks the customer for the bank name and the billing address of the credit card. If the buyer knows the name of the bank, chances are good that the card is valid. Some retailers even call the bank and verify that the billing address given by the buyer is accurate. Although this method is not foolproof—anyone can buy a BIN book—it goes a long way in protecting the merchant from fraudulent credit card users.

Run all cards, regardless of the amount of purchase, through an electronic terminal that reads the credit card's magnetic strip, calls the central computer, and verifies that the card is good. This is the current best bet as a countermeasure against fraud at point of sale.

Train employees to check the numbers and information on the face of the credit card against the printed transaction slip. This is a quick way to catch people using cards encoded with stolen information.

Establish an internal "hot" file of fraudulent credit cards, names, and addresses, and require clerks to check against the list before making credit card sales.

Always require a receipt for return of merchandise. Post a sign that states this is store policy. Contact the credit card company to verify the original sale before issuing a credit slip, especially on expensive items.

What To Do If You're Defrauded

If your credit cards are stolen or you've been defrauded:

If your cards have been stolen, notify the credit card companies immediately. Most have toll-free hotlines that will take the information and cancel your cards for you. Follow this up in writing, keeping a copy of the letter for your files, to prove that you did file a report. Don't overlook your phone calling card. Call the phone company and have the card canceled.

If you notice an error on your statement, you should report the matter immediately in writing. Even though some credit card issuers will accept a report by phone, your rights under the Federal Billing Rights Act are preserved only if you notify the company in writing. The Federal Billing Act gives you up to 60 days to report an error.

It's important to file a crime report, even if you've lost your cards. The report will be needed to prove to creditors that you were no longer in possession of the cards when they were defrauded. Keep the records for seven years, the maximum length of time negative information may remain on your credit report, in case the problem arises again.

Contact the following agencies in your local area if your cards have been stolen or you've been defrauded: the police, and the Secret Service/FBI which have jurisdiction over credit card fraud, which is a federal crime. Be aware that these agencies may refuse to investigate cases that do not involve several victims or several thousands of dollars. Also contact the attorney general's office. Some local offices have units that investigate credit card fraud.

Notify the credit bureaus and ask them to place a fraud alert on your file. Financial institutions will contact you to confirm future applications for credit before approving them.

Chapter 7

Travel Scams

Mascarenas Giguere was not the kind of person who could be easily swindled. Educated and articulate, this Lake George, NY, mother of two taught art and had visited places like Japan and Hong Kong. She knew that when you hear of a dazzling deal on a travel package you need to be wary.

She was skeptical when she found in her mailbox a "certificate of award guarantee" touting a seven-day "fabulous luxury vacation" in Florida and the Bahamas.

Giguere figured that, probably, the certificate was a worthless gimmick. But she called the travel firm, Boca Raton–based "National Customer Research," anyway, on a whim. And then she learned of the marvelous package NCR was pitching: For $399, two people could fly from New York to Florida, then cruise in style to the Bahamas and jet back home; they could stay in hotels and use a rental car every day.

It seemed too good to pass up, so Giguere began doing some research. She poured over the photocopied sheets NCR mailed her. She contacted the Better Business Bureau in Boca Raton, and phoned the Holiday, FL, wholesaler that sold batches of travel packages to NCR. And everything she read or heard indicated the same thing: NCR was an upstanding company.

Giguere decided that she had lucked out. On October 25, 1991, as she awaited the dreary chill of a New York winter, she wrote a check for $399, payable to NCR. She gave it to a messenger sent by the company, and then she dreamed of basking in the Florida sun.

And dreamed, and dreamed. The airline tickets she'd ordered never came. Mascarenas Giguere had, despite all her caution, been conned by a fly-by-night travel firm—an outfit that was so invisible just one month later that it lacked even a working phone number.

She'd become another victim of a booming industry. The American Society of Travel Agents (ASTA) estimates that con artists swindle prospective travelers out of $40 billion each year—and it suggests, too, that travel scams are proliferating. Sixty-three percent of all travel agents, a 1992 ASTA poll reveals, feel that fraud is increasing in their field, and 45 percent encounter scams frequently. Even travel agents are falling victim.

Con artists, the poll shows, typically send their victims the same sort of phony, sensational literature that Mascarenas Giguere got in the mail. But they invoke myriad other scams, too. They place newspaper ads, beckoning people to call costly 900 lines that deliver bogus information. They rent shoddy, overpriced cars, and pitch "tranquil weekend getaways" that, in reality, are anything but.

And they're able to swindle victims, it seems, because they deftly appeal to a modern urge: Almost everyone these days wants to travel, to enjoy a stress-free holiday in one of the exotic places that we all see, over and over, on TV and in the movies. And almost everyone realizes that you no longer have to be rich to journey far away, to places like Tahiti and Guam. Travelers are always on the lookout for a good deal.

America's middle-class citizens have been flying frequently since the early 1980s, when the airlines were deregulated and fares plummeted. They've made a habit of vigorously hunting for travel bargains.

And though they get what they're seeking sometimes, they also contribute quite often to an industry that is seemingly beyond reproach, as well as downright fraudulent.

Consumer experts say that most people who fall for travel cons never fight for restitution. These victims reckon that it's not worth their while to wage a costly court battle, and often they're right. Travel scammers typically operate out of "boiler rooms." They can easily close down and evade detection once they're accused, and a victim cannot count on beating them in court.

Indeed, there is only one sure way to beat travel swindlers: You need to know their tricks.

"Phone Now for a Cheap Vacation" Scams

At the very same time Mascarenas Giguere was contacting the Federal Trade Commission to complain about the outfit that bilked her, people all over the country were getting postcards from a bogus Maryland travel firm—now defunct—called Jet Set. Postcards that trumpeted to recipients that they had won a trip to the Bahamas, or, in some cases, even free cash or a brand-new car. (See Chapter 16, "Sweepstakes Fraud.")

Jet Set sent out thousands of such cards. And when suckers responded by dialing an 800 number they were told that there was a small fee for the "free luxury vacation." It would cost $329 to $399 per couple; there was a tax of $99, and callers had to furnish their credit card numbers, "just for verification."

Once they uttered these numbers, callers heard the real catch: Flights, they were told, were not immediately available, and they would need to provide a choice of three trip dates—usually two to three months in advance—and then wait.

For a long time.

Jet Set typically kept "discovering" that the flights on chosen trip dates were booked; it kept asking victims to change their travel dates, and by the time people realized they were being conned, the sixty-day period permitted by most banks to dispute credit card charges was past.

Jet Set—which was recently nailed by the Federal Trade Commission after reaping $4.2 million in its short, one-year life—treated a few of its victims to vaguely luxurious getaways. It sent them on "cruises" (actually six-hour boat rides) and put them up in seedy hotels.

Which is more than most phony travel "bargain" hawkers do. Some, such as the Georgia-based telemarketer Feelin' Great International, resort to vicious bait-and-switch tactics.

During 1991 and 1992, Feelin' Great regularly placed newspaper ads hyping cut-rate vacations, and sometimes changed the terms of its deals once it had collected customers' cash. In early 1992, for instance, the agency sold Brent Lognetti two Bahamas vacation packages for $698, then delayed his departure for months and suggested, finally, that he upgrade to a VIP package (for an additional $698), or exchange his package for another vacation. "You are not entitled to a refund," a letter from Feelin' Great informed Lognetti.

Art Weiss, a Missouri assistant attorney general, insists that scams like the one that hit Brent Lognetti are complex because they're facilitated by a host of illicit collaborators—travel agents, postcard printers, mail houses, credit card factories, and travel certificate wholesalers. He believes that all outfits involved in a scam are guilty, and thus he and other law enforcement officials are now going after what he calls the "roots" of major scams.

They've had some luck. In October 1992, for instance, the Federal Trade Commission obtained a preliminary injunction against Passport Internationale Inc., a Daytona Beach, FL, wholesaler that sold travel packages to at least thirty-seven U.S. boiler room outfits nationwide. Likewise, the state of Wisconsin recently shut down TravelPorts Unlimited, the phony agency that peddled trip packages to Feelin' Great.

Resort Swindles

There are some destination resorts that actually do give away free— or very low-cost—travel packages. But visiting them is, quite often, hardly a vacation. The American Society of Travel Agents reports that, usually, free or cut-rate resort vacation offers are made by companies trying to sell time-share options on condominiums.

Such companies offer a sweet deal at first; their postcard might say something like, "Come visit us. Come spend a weekend golfing and horseback riding and lounging in the sauna right by your room." But they tend to subject their poor "guests" to nonstop huckstering.

People who consent to visit a resort that is hawking condos, ASTA reports, are apt to be badgered into taking a tour of for-sale properties; they're also likely to be visited several times during their vacation by salespeople and to get a few follow-up phone pitches once they've returned to their homes.

Probably the best thing to do with a postcard offering a "free resort stay" is tear it up.

Travel Club Memberships

One of the most popular ploys of late is "travel club" memberships, which offer nothing but overpriced vacations, according to the Federal Trade Commission.

The first contact may be a telephone call that offers a fabulous vacation for a bargain-basement price. The catch: To be eligible for the package, the consumer must pay a club membership fee of anywhere from fifty dollars to four hundred dollars. Or the offer may arrive in the mail in the form of a postcard that provides a toll-free number to call in order to get all the details.

If a person unsuspectingly falls for the ploy and pays the membership fee, he or she will probably find out—sooner rather than later—that another fee is required to cover the cost of making the actual reservations. It's a no-win situation for the trusting consumer.

Car Rental Scams

Say you've reached your vacation spot safely, on an airline that treated you fairly. Now you're eager to explore. You want to see the beaches or the mountains, so you phone a car rental agency and get a quote of nineteen dollars a day.

It doesn't sound half bad, you think, so you venture down to the rental car lot and find, subsequently, that there are extra charges. Travel is twenty cents a mile, and insurance is thirteen dollars a day. The clerk doesn't tell you that if you have car insurance for your own car, it probably covers damage to any rental car that you drive. He or she says only that, to be safe, you'll need to spend over thirty dollars a day.

And you probably just pay this sum. You might reason, "What's a few extra bucks when I'm on a thousand-dollar vacation?" Many people think this way. Brian Kennedy, executive vice president of marketing for Hertz Corp., says there are some rental firms that thrive on selling "extras" to consumers anxious to get on with their vacations or business trips. And a spokesman for a national agency called Rent-A-Wreck says that many clerks get healthy commissions for "upgrading" their clients from inexpensive small cars to spacious—and more costly—midsize vehicles.

The car rental industry is by no means thoroughly corrupt, but it is so competitive and so volatile—standard rates change daily—that many operators feel that, to survive, they must constantly nickel-and-dime the people to whom they rent.

It's hard to put a dollar figure on all the swindling, but James Baumhart of Chicago's Better Business Bureau says that the scams hardly stop once a client drives out of the rental car lot.

Often, says Baumhart, car renters are charged with unexpected penalty fees when they bring autos back either early or late. At times they're hit with exorbitant per-mile or tow truck charges they didn't know were coming.

And perhaps worst of all, they are occasionally confronted with a nasty dilemma when it comes time to drop off their cars. Some rental firms, explains one industry expert, instruct their clients to "bring the car back empty"—and, at the same time, charge for mileage.

A vacationer must thus decide: Either she drives around until the car is completely empty and incurs mileage costs as she does so, or she beelines back to the rental lot and donates several gallons of gas to the company that thrust her into a no-win situation.

How Can You Protect Yourself?

Be wary each time you see an ad touting a "great deal" on a flight, cruise, or vacation package.   Realize that if a price sounds too good to be true, it probably is.

Be skeptical of any special travel "deals" that come looking for you through postcards or letters in the mail or by telephone.

Be wary of any travel firm that asks you to wait sixty days before traveling or denies your reservation dates even though you booked far in advance.

Beware of any false sense of urgency presented by the salesperson.

Be wary of 900-number travel sales.   If you do decide to call and investigate the travel information, at least find out the cost-per-minute for the call before dialing.

Don't give your credit card number over the phone unless you initiate the transaction and are confident about the company with which you're dealing. Don't confirm the number or expiration date of your credit card to anyone who calls inquiring about such information.

Check with your friends and relatives for the names of established, legitimate firms and travel agents in your area.

Know exactly what you're getting for your money. If a travel outfit promises you a ticket that is good for "all major airlines," or a voucher good for "all major hotels," ask specific questions. Find out exactly which airlines or hotels the company is referring to.

Make sure you receive all details in writing before paying for your vacation. Check your contract and schedule carefully to make sure it agrees with your understanding of the travel arrangements.

Ask about any surcharges (such as ground transportation, hotel taxes) that may be "hidden," and ask if there are any special restrictions.

If the company is promising a cut-rate resort vacation, ask if you will have to spend any of your holiday time inspecting the condos or houses at the resort.

Comparison shop. Once you've gotten specific travel package information, call a travel agent in your community to determine how much the ticket (or trip) would cost if booked locally.

Consider obtaining travel insurance to protect your investment. Although not inexpensive, it may be worth the price if something goes wrong and you can't take your trip as planned. It's best to secure such insurance from a second party, and make sure it covers your costs in case the tour operator fails to deliver what you paid for.

If you're getting shuffled around from person to person, if conditions and requirements for your trip keep changing, and you find that your frustration level is reaching astronomical heights, simply find another agency or forget the so-called "bargain" trip.

How To Determine If a Travel Outfit Is Legitimate

Stay away from any travel package that requires a nonrefundable processing fee, a deposit that exceeds the advertised price of the trip, or a fee for "travel club" membership.

Be concerned if the travel operator or salesperson won't provide you with any information until you pay a fee. Legitimate travel agencies don't operate that way.

Find out if the travel outfit is willing to send a messenger to your doorstep to pick up a check.   If it is, you can be almost certain you're dealing with a swindler.

Ask the salesperson if his or her company does its own booking. If it doesn't, get the name, address and phone number of the agency that does the booking and check it out personally.

Find out if the company and its booking agency are members of a professional group such as the American Society of Travel Agents.   Call the group to make sure you were told the truth.

Ask the Better Business Bureau and the attorney general's office in the state where the travel outfit is based if any complaints have been filed against the company.

How To Pay for a Vacation

Always pay for trips with your credit card.   That way, you can cancel the charges if the company turns out to be shady. Then call your credit card company to make sure the travel outfit has canceled the charge.

If the promised materials don't show up on time, call the company to cancel your purchase.   And don't worry about offending anyone by doing so.

Special Considerations for Travelers Renting Cars

Ask for the specific make and model of the car you will be getting.   Don't let an agent promise you something vague like a "midsize" car.

Verify that the car will be there and that it will be available for the agreed-upon price before you go to the rental lot.

Find out if you will have to pay a per-mile charge for driving the car.

Realize that if you own an insured car, your insurance policy will probably pay for damage to a rental car.   Contact your insurance agent to confirm this.

Find out if you will have to pay a penalty if you return the car before or after the due date, or if there are any drop-off charges for returning the car to another location.

Read the rental contract carefully.

Thoroughly check out the car to make sure all systems are in good working order before you drive off the lot. For example, does the air conditioning work? What about the radio? Are there any dents or scratches that you could be charged for upon returning the car?

What To Do If You've Fallen for a Travel Scam

Don't pour good money after bad. Don't let a phony travel agent tell you that if you just pay $349 more you'll get the dream vacation you were promised in the first place.

Demand that the con artist give you your money back, and be persistent.

Complain, complain, complain. Call the state attorney general's office, the local police, the Better Business Bureau, the Federal Trade Commission, the Postal Inspector (if the offer came through the mails), and the consumer affairs division of the American Society of Travel Agents. Don't be embarrassed to get some help!

CHAPTER 8

Investment Cons

America is a nation of investors. We purchase stocks, bonds, municipal bonds, mutual funds; contribute to savings and retirement programs; own real estate; participate in futures and options markets; and provide venture capital for new business ventures. We buy franchises, invest in oil exploration, foreign stocks, penny stocks, public and private stocks, and acquire collectibles including art, gold coins, and precious and semiprecious stones. The strength of our total economy is, in large measure, the product of our combined investments.

The most basic relationship in investing is the one between risk and reward. Usually, the higher the potential for great returns, the higher the risk factors. Generally, it's wise to avoid risky investments unless you have a very reliable income, adequate insurance, and readily accessible cash that can be used in emergencies.

Over half of all American adults have some kind of financial investments, but just over a quarter of American adults read the financial news regularly, while only 37 percent of American adults are at least somewhat familiar with the specialized language used to describe investment and financial matters (Louis Harris and Associates Poll, May 1992). This gap between making investments and having enough knowledge about investments highlights the window of opportunity open to swindlers.

Other findings that reveal the high potential for investment fraud include these startling facts:

- Nearly 63 million American adults have been contacted by phone about purchasing a financial investment.
- Nearly half of American adults are reluctant to simply hang up on such callers.
- Only 7 percent of those receiving calls about purchasing a financial investment had previously done business with the firm.
- One out of twenty phone call recipients actually purchased financial investments from strangers.

Investment fraud in the United States is estimated to be a $10-billion-dollar business per annum. That's more money than the combined annual profits of the nation's three major automakers. The North American Securities Administrators Association, which is made up of state securities regulators, estimates that phony international investments, bogus oil and gas partnerships, and precious metal scams cost the American public $3 billion each year.

The most common fraudulent investment schemes in the 1990s have involved franchises, vending machine businesses, mail-order businesses, multilevel marketing, land development deals, marketing of inventions, and work-at-home businesses. Investment swindlers find their victims through the telephone, mail, advertisements, and referrals. Daily, unscrupulous promoters abuse investors' desires to choose a winning investment by concocting schemes that have no possibility of making money for anyone other than the con artists themselves. They cannot possibly deliver what they promise.

Successful investment con artists use every trick in the proverbial book to relieve their customers of the burden of worrying about their money. Some of their methods of gaining trust are truly ingenious. They may tell their unsuspecting victim that he or she has been specially selected to participate in a once-in-a-lifetime opportunity, or that a friend referred him. Rather than come on like a glib, aggressive, fast-talking salesperson, the con artist may appear shy and retiring. They may perform financial surgery on a victim's pocketbook from a boiler room operation or from an opulent suite in a new high-rise. They'll use whatever it takes to separate you from your money.

The first rule for protecting yourself from an investment swindle is to rid yourself of any preexisting notions about what an investment con artist looks or sounds like. In fact, many swindlers do not start out to con you. There are countless cases of a trusted individual—a lawyer, investment broker, accountant, or banker—who suddenly sacrifices his morals and disregards the code of ethics so vital to his position.

A wise investor is one who carefully investigates the person and firm with whom he or she will be dealing. Take a close, cautious look at the investment offer itself and analyze it thoroughly. After deciding to invest, monitor your investments continually. While none of these precautions alone may be sufficient to prevent you from being swindled, they will help minimize your risk of becoming a victim to investment fraud.

Although victims of investment fraud obviously differ in many ways, they often share two common traits: a willingness to believe in what they want to happen and greed. Swindlers can be very convincing in their mimicry of the sales approaches of legitimate investment firms, and their techniques are as varied as their methods of establishing contact with a potential victim. The skills that make a swindler convincing are essentially the same skills that enable a legitimate salesperson to be successful. Yet swindlers have one major advantage: They don't have to make good on their promises. In the absence of this responsibility, they don't hesitate to promise whatever it takes to persuade you to part with your money. Beware if you notice any of the following characteristics:

- They promise huge profits and fast gains.
- The low-risk, "safe" investment is highly collateralized.
- There is an urgency to the transaction, a compelling reason to buy immediately.
- They gain your trust and confidence. (There's a reason they're called "con artists.")

International Gold Bullion Exchange (IGBE)

In the 1980s American investors made billions of dollars by investing in gold and silver. The price of gold went from one hundred thirty dollars to eight hundred fifty dollars per ounce, while silver went from five dollars to over fifty dollars per ounce. To put these price swings into perspective, individuals who bought ten thousand dollars worth of silver found that it was worth one hundred thousand dollars just one year later. People who purchased silver futures by investing ten thousand dollars on a 10 percent margin would have earned $1 million a year later. No wonder Bunker Hunt wanted to control the precious metals market.

Everyone who could was buying gold and silver. Bars, coins, ingots . . . if it had gold or silver in it, people wanted it. As the prices for gold and silver kept going up, people were even selling family heirlooms. The temptation to convert grandmother's good silver into cash was too great for some to bear. People were mortgaging their homes, selling their cars, using their charge cards despite the high interest rates, and emptying savings accounts in order to buy these hot commodities.

As everyone kept buying, the prices kept going up. It looked like there was no end in sight. As the feeding frenzy increased, the honest brokers and dealers did the best they could to deliver genuine precious metals to their customers. Major banks issued certificates of deposit so that bullion customers did not actually have to take delivery of eighty-three pounds (one thousand ounces) of silver bars.

Wherever there is a feeding frenzy you'll find sharks, those fascinating predators that possess terrific timing. Phony gold mines began popping up everywhere. Costume jewelry stamped with 14K was unwittingly sold by some of the finest jewelry stores in the country.

From his small Fort Lauderdale retail jewelry store, William Alderdice began selling one-ounce gold bars to his customers. It was easy for Alderdice to sell his customers gold. He was charming, personable, and fun to be around. At six-foot-two, he had a neatly trimmed moustache and a handsome physique. He was the son every mother dreamed of and a friend to all. Or so it seemed.

Alderdice, who was legally blind and never finished high school, was someone an unsuspecting person could easily pity. Once, while he was hosting a large dinner party, he accidentally jabbed his fork into a slice of lemon instead of fish because of his poor vision. Rather than embarrass himself, he proceeded to eat the whole thing—seeds, rind, and pulp.

Despite his attractive appearance and gentle demeanor, Alderdice was one of the most dangerous con men in America. Before he was through, thousands of investors would lose hundreds of millions of dollars. Many life savings would disappear and individuals would file for bankruptcy or lose their homes and businesses. Others were confined to mental institutions because the pressure of losing their savings was more than they could bear. Some even decided to end their lives.

Alderdice placed a small advertisement offering gold bars for sale at spot price (the actual intrinsic value of the gold) in a Miami newspaper, a move unheard of in the gold trade. His competitors charged customers the spot price *plus* a bar minting charge and a sales commission, but Alderdice's customers would not have to pay these additional fees. As expected, Alderdice's single phone line became jammed with calls from people wanting to buy gold from him.

Alderdice would take an order for ten gold bars and buy them at one hundred thirty dollars per bar. By the time the customer expected to receive them the price of gold would be up to one hundred fifty dollars. Alderdice would tell the customer that he bought it at one hundred fifty dollars and pocket the difference. The spot price was skyrocketing so fast that Alderdice could virtually pick the buy price and the sell price.

Before Alderdice knew it, he was routinely selling a few thousand ounces of gold and pocketing about twenty thousand dollars each week. With his newfound riches he was able to rent one of the most prestigious office spaces in Fort Lauderdale and staff it with some fifty telephone salespeople skilled in the boiler room tactics of making quick money.

International Gold Bullion Exchange (IGBE) had been born, and with its birth some truly creative marketing schemes were hatched. For example, IGBE offered a discount on the spot price if a customer took delivery in ninety days and an even greater discount for delivery in one hundred eighty days. What a deal for the customer, who could buy an ounce of gold with a published spot price of two hundred fifty dollars for just two hundred dollars or one hundred seventy-five dollars if he simply waited three to six months. More importantly, if gold went up to three hundred dollars or four hundred dollars per ounce, the investor would really make a killing.

Knowledgeable brokers in the precious metals business were highly suspicious of these offers, for they knew that honest businesspeople simply didn't give a customer two hundred fifty dollars in exchange for one hundred seventy-five dollars and stay in business very long. Fortunately for Alderdice and his boiler room sellers, thousands of investors who weren't as knowledgeable bought the discount plan hook, line, and sinker. Alderdice reasoned that if he could hold on to the customer's money for three to six months and not buy the gold, he could earn interest on literally millions of dollars. Then, with the money that came in during the subsequent three months, he would buy and ship gold to those customers who had made purchases during the previous three months. Alderdice reasoned that by continually floating three months' worth of money, he could earn interest on millions of dollars forever. This was a classic Ponzi, or pyramid, scheme in which clients are led to believe they're making lucrative investments when, in fact, any returns they receive are coming from newly recruited investors. The following chart illustrates Alderdice's plan:

Month	$ Gold Purchased	$ Gold Delivered	$ Interest Earned	$ Principal Retained
Jan.	6,000,000		50,000	6,000,000
Feb.	9,000,000		70,000	9,000,000
Mar.	12,000,000		100,000	12,000,000
April	14,000,000	6,000,000	116,000	8,000,000
May	12,800,000	9,000,000	124,000	3,800,000
June	16,200,000	12,000,000	133,000	4,200,000
				$43,000,000

Alderdice had $43 million in the bank, plus almost six hundred thousand dollars in interest money. Not bad for just six months' work. There was no turning back with the inauguration of the next marketing scheme, which directed the boiler room telephone sellers to call all of the existing customers with a great offer: "Leave your gold purchase on deposit in our safe, secure vaults and we will pay you one percent interest per month. There are no storage fees and you won't have to worry about someone stealing your precious metal coins or bars. Imagine earning over 12 percent per year on your investment. Even better, if gold or silver goes up, you can enjoy the increase in your precious metals deposit. When was the last time the interest earned on your savings account exceeded the principal?"

It seemed that Alderdice could do no wrong. The investors once again bought the proposition. When the majority of IGBE's customers took advantage of this extraordinary offer, Alderdice could then earn interest on hundreds of millions of dollars. But where would he get the gold?

By the perfectly legal means of depositing a 10-percent option buy on margin, Bill Alderdice invested millions in the futures markets, hoping to acquire large quantities of precious metals at a fraction of their cost. For example:

January 1, 1982:	Purchase 100,000 ounces of silver @ $10 per ounce for delivery on June 1, 1982.
	Deposit $100,000 or 10 percent of spot price to hold 100,000 ounces. Balance of $900,000 on June 1.
June 1, 1982:	Sell 100,000 ounces of silver @$20 per ounce, or $2 million (spot price has doubled since the futures contracts were purchased). Pay balance due of $900,000.

Even though he must pay the balance due on delivery of nine hundred thousand dollars, the transaction still netted him a $1 million return on a one hundred thousand dollar investment if the market went up.

There was a downside, of course. If Alderdice agreed to buy silver at ten dollars per ounce six months into the future and the market went down instead of up, he could end up paying one hundred thousand dollars for silver worth fifty thousand dollars or less, depending on the spot price at the end of the contract period.

As fate would have it, the prices of precious metals kept falling while Alderdice played the futures market. He turned to investments in gold mines, but other con artists swindled him by planting gold nuggets on the hillsides of southern Nevada. Alderdice invested several hundred thousand dollars only to have the miners and mines disappear. He funded a major gold exploration project in the ocean just off Alaska's northern coast. Although some gold was found, the crew stole it, sunk the ship, and disappeared into the tundra.

While all of this insanity was running rampant, Alderdice painted Styrofoam bars gold and placed the phony bars in clear view inside his walk-in vault, but he left the vault door open with the inside gate locked so that no one could physically examine the bars. Not even the top officers knew about the fake gold bars; only Bill Alderdice and his brother Jim were aware of the deception.

IGBE had become one of the biggest gold and silver dealers in the United States, with sales of over $80 million in 1982. As fast as the millions poured into IGBE, however, millions poured out. Alderdice bought an auto rental company, a yacht brokerage firm, a sporting goods store, and various pieces of real estate, and flew around the country in private Lear jets.

IGBE had two serious "partners" without whose help Bill Alderdice could never have pulled off his extraordinary caper: *The Wall Street Journal* and the U.S. Government.

IGBE advertised every business day in *The Wall Street Journal,* and nearly 90 percent of IGBE's customers came to them as a result of the ads. One day IGBE missed the deadline to place its advertisement and IGBE's sales dropped 94 percent. In spite of the fact that complaints were pouring into *The Wall Street Journal* from concerned and unhappy IGBE customers throughout the country, the paper continued to run the advertisements.

The other unwitting "partner" was the Securities and Exchange Commission, which regulates precious metal sales in the United States. Its Commodities Futures Commission also received numerous complaints from IGBE customers and yet never acted upon them. If its staff members had performed a few simple mathematical calculations, they would have known that IGBE could not have been a legitimate business. Gold would have to *double in price* before IGBE could hope to break even, much less make a profit. Surely the SEC and its Commodities Futures Commission at the very least suspected that a national scam of tremendous proportions was taking place.

When one of Alderdice's many girlfriends finally went to the FBI in 1983, a grand jury was convened and William Alderdice and James Alderdice were indicted for grand larceny and securities fraud, among other charges. Bill Alderdice was murdered at his home in July 1984 shortly after posting bail, by James Doyle, a county jail inmate he had befriended, following an argument over the use of Alderdice's car.

With good behavior, James Alderdice could be released from prison soon. Over $10 million has never been located, although the Alderdices were known to frequently travel to a number of islands in the Caribbean, usually carrying a number of large suitcases.

Not one of Bill Alderdice's businesses truly succeeded, because he hired people like himself to run them. Like him, they lied, cheated, and stole money to support their outrageous lifestyles. The biggest problem the two Alderdices had was that they themselves also made very good marks.

The Golden Goose Egg Scam—Yet Another Ponzi Scheme

U.S. District Judge James M. Ideman handed a pretty tough prison sentence to the man he dubbed "the king of swindlers," Gilbert Traylor, Jr., in Los Angeles. Traylor was given thirty years in prison and his partner/sales manager, Lester Thompson, was given ten years. His company, First American Currency of Laguna Hills, solicited investors by telephone to invest in silver and other precious metals. Investors mailed, wired, and hand-delivered $16 million to buy precious metals that were never delivered. Instead, Traylor bought a six hundred fifty thousand dollar house, gave himself a salary of $1 million a year, lived luxuriously, and apparently hid about a quarter of the funds he received in the Panamanian branch of Bank of Credit and Commerce International (BCCI), the Luxembourg-based bank so notorious for its reputation as a haven for money launderers and drug dealers that it has been called the Bank of Crooks and Criminals International.

Lists of known investors in legitimate programs were purchased from mailing list suppliers. A boiler room was set up and the best phone salespeople in the business were hired. First American Currency could afford to pay top commissions because they had no product costs. The average precious metals dealer buys the gold bars or coins for the spot price plus a bar or coin fabrication fee and delivery charge. He will then mark up his total cost by 1 to 5 percent per ounce, depending upon the number of ounces purchased and the form of bullion delivered. For example, a one-ounce bar costs more per ounce than a ten-ounce bar.

When investigators confiscated First American's records they found commissions of one hundred dollars per ounce had been paid out. The commissions paid the phone operators, coupled with the overrides paid to the sales management and executive salaries, meant that there was nothing left with which to buy the customers' gold.

Another key element of the scam was the product discounting. The phone solicitors offered discounts that brought the price below the spot price. Why should anyone believe that they could buy gold for less money than anyone else in the world? They believed it because the salespeople said they mined it and, therefore, could eliminate the middlemen. Although that concept may hold water with radios, pies, or certain other products, it doesn't work with gold. People simply do not sell a buyer something for three hundred dollars per ounce when every market in the world will gladly pay four hundred dollars per ounce. But the boiler room sellers were good at what they did, and their persuasive capabilities netted everyone a lot of money—except, of course, the mark.

The Ponzi Game is Everywhere

Investment scams are not unique to the United States. In March 1993, St. Petersburg, Russia, police charged three firms, Amaris, Revanche, and Business Navigator, with fraud and began investigating nine other companies. The St. Petersburg firms systematically liberated four hundred fifty thousand people of their savings. Taking advantage of the widespread confusion about Russia's privatization program and the citizens' lack of business experience, the company offered to accept deposits and promised to increase the deposits 250 percent in ninety days.

The businesses told the investors that their money and vouchers were being invested in stock and currency exchanges. Russia had issued the property vouchers in 1992 as part of a program to divest itself of state property.

Unlike the modern, well-furnished office often found in the U.S. to give the mark the impression of success, the scam artists ran their businesses out of run-down one-room offices guarded by men wearing police uniforms. Following an impressive advertising blitz, the investors traded their money and vouchers for a simple one-page contract that guaranteed 250 percent profits.

The first investors received the promised profits, which they promptly reinvested. As in all Ponzi schemes, the initial payoffs resulted in a greedy feeding frenzy as more investors were attracted.

According to Vladimir Barashnikov, an official of the St. Petersburg mayor's privatization committee, the Amaris company disappeared with about $1.3 million in rubles and two hundred thousand vouchers (each with a face value of seventeen dollars). Revanche took approximately two hundred thousand vouchers and five hundred thousand dollars in rubles, while the third company charged, Business Navigator, took an estimated fifty thousand vouchers and an unknown amount of money.

According to Farid Safeyev, a police spokesman, the estimate of

450,000 victims is probably low since several thousand people a day began turning to the police for help recovering their money. This scam can have a sobering effect on Russia's attempt to privatize its industries and compete in the world markets. Imagine con artists being so effective that they could literally change the course of a nation.

Upon unification, many East Germans came into large amounts of money as their savings were converted to West German currency. New to capitalism and inexperienced at sorting sound, legitimate business offers from shady deals, 16 million people became ideal targets for frauds such as chain letters and pyramid schemes.

Advertised as "self-help" groups in newspapers in eastern Germany, these pyramid or "snowball" scams offer membership from six to two thousand dollars. Members are told to send their fees to one or more bank accounts and to recruit others as participants. As their names reach the top of the pyramid and new members are recruited, their own bank accounts will grow.

Back home, Thomas R. Mullens, a convicted swindler, set up Omni Capital Group Ltd. in Boca Raton, FL, and was able to evade federal regulators for more than two years while he collected over $25 million from over 150 clients by promising them returns on their investments of 24 percent. Mullens used his clients' money to buy a home worth almost $1 million, a $2.2-million private jet, a Rolls Royce, a Mercedes Benz, country club memberships, jewelry, and artwork.

The Securities and Exchange Commission shut down Mullens's four offices across the country. If Mullens's clients had routinely checked into his background, they would have found that he was not an SEC-registered broker/dealer. They could have learned that Mullens pleaded guilty in 1976 to defrauding ninety investors of more than $3.6 million in another pyramid scheme. In 1981 he admitted to defrauding the U.S. Customs Service of more than nine hundred thousand dollars.

The Condom Crusade

Some investment scams are pretty clever, while others defy logic. A federal jury convicted Timothy M. Mucciante, a thirty-two-year-old Detroit man for bilking millions of dollars from investors. His proposal was to purchase condoms in England, barter them in Russia for chickens, and then sell the chickens to Saudi Arabia. Among those taken in by the scheme was a very famous New York diet doctor.

South-of-the-Border Scam

A group of investment scam artists in Mexico got their hands on a Mexican government invitation to a political event. By covering up the invitation copy and exposing only the official agency letterhead, they were able to make copies of what now looked like a piece of governmental agency stationery. Then the swindlers typed up a very official-looking grant from the Mexican government to buy up to 5 million barrels of oil at ten dollars per barrel.

After purchasing a list of Americans who had invested in oil partnerships from a list broker in Dallas, the men drafted a cover letter that explained to their unsuspecting marks that the president of their company had negotiated a very favorable contract to purchase oil from the Mexican government at unbelievably low prices. The government granted the deal because the company president was a relative of the Minister of Natural Resources.

Oil was selling for twenty-six dollars per barrel at the time. Thus, a profit of sixteen dollars per barrel would be realized simply by buying it from the Mexican government and selling it to the Texas oil companies or to a Costa Rican consortium. A simple multiplication of sixteen dollars times 5 million barrels meant that $80 million could be made quickly. However, $50 million was needed to buy the oil, and the Mexican government insisted on U.S. currency.

The cover letter and a copy of the official-looking document were mailed to 61,312 potential investors. A boiler room was set up in Houston and two months later the $50 million was in a Mexican bank. Of course, no oil was ever delivered to the investors, and the perpetrators of the fraud have not been apprehended. All that remains are thousands of people with fewer investment dollars for their children's education funds and their retirement accounts, emergency medical expenses, and legitimate investment opportunities.

Conning City Governments

People are not the only targets of investment fraud. Government agencies caught up in their own bureaucracy are also prime targets. Entire cities can be swindled, as evidenced by the work of Steven F. Warner, a forty-three-year-old Irvine, CA, investment adviser. A federal judge froze $1.2 billion of investments managed by Treasury Management Institute (TMI) and Denmany Corporation, companies run by Warner.

TMI promised returns as high as 30 percent even though U.S. Treasury securities yielded less than 10 percent. Rather than helping the residents of eighty-six small communities, counties, and school districts, and city governments including Dubuque, Warner allegedly took $65 million in Treasury securities from the Iowa Fund without paying for them and used the money, according to the Securities and Exchange Commission. California, Colorado, and other states were also defrauded by Warner. Prosecutors claim he made fictitious trades with his clients' money and is personally liable for $113 million in misappropriated funds.

Iowa communities invested up to $29 million each in the Iowa Fund. Times are tough for city governments, creating greater stress to make money so that they don't have to raise taxes. Yet, frequently, investment officers of small cities and government agencies are not wise to the tricks of con men. (See Chapter 17, "Scams Against the Government: Biting the Hand of Uncle Sam.")

Oil Hoax

Not all con artists receive light sentences. Some have been killed for their deeds. John J. Colgate of Agoura Hills, CA, was shot at point-blank range outside a delicatessen in broad daylight. The California Department of Corporations had named Colgate and five others in a civil suit for defrauding eight thousand investors of $140 million over a five-year period while he was involved in the Los Angeles–based firm of Barker, Inc.

The firm sold limited partnership interests, mostly in oil drilling programs. Investors in Zenith 90A were told that only 15 percent of the money raised would go toward commissions, overhead, and syndication fees. The other 85 percent would go toward drilling expenses. In fact, an audit of their books revealed that only 3 percent of the money raised actually was used to drill wells. Commissions of 30 to 40 percent, management fees, consulting fees, and almost any deductions the firm could dream up were taken off the top.

Many of Colgate's investors were retirees who invested their retirement money or savings in these partnerships. Oil and gas partnerships can be pretty attractive to the uninformed investor who does not understand the risks. Usually, the actual partnership document will warn the investor that he or she may lose the entire investment. Of course, the salesperson may merely assure his or her victim that the state securities commission insists that all partnership documents say that, but it really doesn't mean anything. They'll say confidently that their investors never lose.

The state usually requires an investor to have a minimum net worth and a high net worth exclusive of home and automobile. If the salesperson does a good job, the victim gladly signs an affidavit attesting to his worthiness to buy into such a good thing because he doesn't want his current status to stand in the way of a great, once-in-a-lifetime investment.

Just imagine hearing a sales pitch that sounds something like this: By investing twenty-five thousand dollars today you can reap enormous government tax breaks. The IRS will allow you to deduct intangible drilling costs (the cost to drill the hole) and depletion allowances. As you pump oil out of the ground, the IRS will allow you to write off the depletion of your oil or gas asset. In addition, you can take depreciation on the well equipment. Almost twenty-thousand dollars of your twenty-five thousand dollar investment comes right from your taxes. Isn't it about time the government does something for you? As for the other five thousand dollars, you'll get that back in the first ninety days, as soon as we hit oil, which we always do. And, of course, these are offset wells, which are drilled in a known field of discovered oil or gas.

So you send in your check and the con artists split $23,750 and use $1,250 to drill a hole. In the unlikely event that they actually hit oil or gas, they'll charge production fees equal to the output. These partnerships are known for "front-end loading" in the industry.

One outstanding characteristic of all investment scams is that they seem too good to be true. Unfortunately, most people realize too late that they've been scammed. In this case, one of the six people named in the suit lost his life before the judicial system had the chance to weigh his guilt. A twenty-nine-year-old man named Mark Daryl was charged by the Los Angeles Police Department with killing John J. Colgate. Police detectives planned to search the investor files to see if Daryl was one of John's clients.

Friends of John J. Colgate described him as a nice guy, a pleasant human being who was simply relying on the information his firm provided. Of course, the court records indicated that he was personally responsible for $11 million in transactions and was listed as president or general manager of several of the partnerships.

Many con artists are pleasant people. Their ability to win you over, to instantly earn your trust, is their stock in trade. People like buying from people they trust, who are concerned about their customers' welfare, their financial security, their peace of mind. A con artist assures his or her mark that the only reason he sells a particular program is that it enables him to help people become financially independent.

Con artists will fabricate any number of stories to persuade a prospective buyer to buy right away. A favorite story goes something like this: "One of our thirty-five investors died yesterday, leaving an opening in our highest-yield drilling project. This is your lucky day. Just wire us your money right away and we'll hold that position for you. This particular program promises returns in excess of 3000 percent. I am not supposed to say anything, but I know that I can trust you. I am actually taking a position in this one myself. That's how good it is." Investment cons generally only work if the victim can be convinced to drop his or her guard by acting immediately.

The Collateral Caper

Con artists often infiltrate a trusted institution so they can trade on that institution's credibility and long standing in the financial community. Or they may set up an insider by catching him in a compromising situation and then blackmail him to prepare valuable financial instruments. That's why checks-and-balances systems are so critical in financial institutions.

One group of con artists opened a bank in the Cayman Islands. They printed certificate of deposit forms and made them out to themselves. They then borrowed money from U.S. banks using the CDs as collateral. Tommi Makani, a branch manager at Osaka's Toyo Shinkin Credit Union, issued thirteen fake certificates of deposit for $2.5 billion to a friend, Hideko K. Masako, in 1991. With the certificates

Masako was able to borrow $2.2 billion from ten other financial institutions. Japan's top long-term credit bank, the Industrial Bank of Japan, was among the banks that supplied loans to Masako.

Bank officials were dumbfounded when they learned that Masako, widely known as a semiprofessional stock investor who negotiated large deals and held shares of more than ten top companies, passed the certificates as collateral. No one bothered to check them out because the certificates bore proper signatures and seals.

Chief Wise Wolf Strikes Out

If you own a company and you need to prove that you have established significant credit in order to get a loan, provide a bond, or give a customer a good feeling about your company's financial stability, all you have to do is call Chief Wise Wolf, Little Fox, or Screaming Wild Dog of the Cherokee Nation Tejas in Dallas, TX. (*Tejas* is Spanish for Texas.)

This Indian tribe is not listed with the Bureau of Indian Affairs, so its legitimacy is highly suspect. Wise Wolf speaks with a British accent, which also raises one's suspicions. But Wise Wolf's customers have no need to inquire about his ancestry as long as he provides them with what they want. It appears that the tribe was created to provide businesspeople with legitimate-looking financial instruments to aid them in "credit enhancement." It advertised for business clients in financial hard times and issued letters of credit backed by what it said were valuable gold reserves. In fact, it was a scheme to make a fast buck in the financial and insurance industries.

Insurance companies need to prove that they have minimal reserves to cover predictable losses based upon actuarial analyses. The tribe provided insurance companies with treasury certificates that, of course, were worthless. The tribe's gold holdings, which supported the face amounts of the letters of credit and treasury certificates, were really tailings from the old Glory Hole Mine in Central City, CO. Apparently barren of gold, the area is considered by the Environmental Protection Agency to be a Superfund pollution site.

When businesspeople cannot pay back their loans to the bank and the bank attempts to draw down on their collateral the bankers and their depositors are in for a shock. When an insurance company defaults on its claims and people who thought they were insured for accidents or hospitalization find out they have no coverage, this scheme may not appear as harmless or amusing as the chief's name implies. (Refer to Chapter 14, "Insurance Cons.")

Interestingly enough, the ability of the state of Texas to prosecute the Cherokee Nation Tejas is limited because anyone can legally issue letters of credit. According to authorities, it would have to prove that the tribe never intended to honor their letters of credit.

Self-cooling Beer Cans

It appears that Marshall Zolp's mission in life was to concoct grandiose money-making scams. In 1989 federal authorities convicted Zolp and sentenced him to twelve years for promoting a phantom product: "self-chilling" beer. He had raised $2.5 million for his Laser Arms Corporation, which had developed a beer can that cooled itself. When the tab was pulled back a cooling agent cooled the can and its contents.

After placing a half-page advertisement in *The Wall Street Journal* announcing his company and its new wonder product, money literally poured into his penny stock company. The price of his stock went from ten cents per share to over three dollars per share. In 1986 Zolp, his attorney, and eight co-conspirators were indicted. Before he was caught federal prosecutors stated that Zolp had been enjoined at least seven times by federal and state regulators under his real name and two aliases. With time served and by cooperating with authorities, Zolp was paroled in April 1990.

Earlier in the 1980s Zolp had raised four hundred thousand dollars to bring a ladder device to market. Designed to help hotel guests escape fires, it was marketed to hotels, who were urged to equip each room with one.

To promote the device, Zolp hired William Frederickson, a retired firefighter from San Diego, to demonstrate it by going over the side of a twenty-story building. As the man approached the seventh floor, the device snapped; Frederickson fell and was seriously injured. Zolp never paid Frederickson's fee for the stunt, nor did he pay for the medical bills that resulted from the fall.

In June 1991 Zolp pleaded guilty to racketeering charges for attempting to swindle $100 million from the California Public Employee Retirement System while still in prison for the beer can caper. A classic repeat offender, Zolp apparently lives for the rush he receives when outsmarting other people.

Dishonest Stockbrokers and Investment Advisers

Pick any month and the nation's major stock markets report dozens of scams by stockbrokers and investment advisers. In September 1991 the National Association of Securities Dealers (NASD), a group that oversees the over-the-counter market and stockbrokers/dealers in the United States, expelled, suspended, or fined nineteen brokerage firms. Seventy-one brokers were barred from the industry, suspended, or fined. At the New York Stock Exchange, one firm and twenty brokers were disciplined in the same month. The American Stock Exchange cited six professionals, one of whom suggested to two customers that they should trade through his wife's account. The violations included stealing stocks and bonds from customer accounts, charging customers for services not rendered, and accepting kickbacks from companies seeking stock sales in down markets.

The NASD recently reported that Richard Schwartz, a principal in the firm of Richardson, Lyle & Adler Inc. of New York, admitted using an account in the name of Mary J. Kleve to buy and resell stock to generate commissions and keep his brokerage firm going. The account was opened four months after Ms. Kleve had died. Saying that he had spoken to someone claiming to be Ms. Kleve, Schwartz used her account to sell large amounts of a small company stock at unfavorable prices.

Unscrupulous stockbrokers will urge a client to purchase stock in a privately held company. He will sell the investor shares for one price, pay the issuing company half that amount, and pocket the difference.

The Keating Con

A chapter on investment scams would be incomplete without the story of Charles Keating, Jr. Keating and his son, Charles Keating III, who were found guilty on securities fraud charges in early 1992. From 1986 to 1989 Lincoln Savings & Loan's investments in real estate development loans and junk bonds were fueled almost entirely by sales of risky bonds issued by Lincoln's parent-company, American Continental Corporation. More than seventeen thousand people lost close to $250 million when Keating's empire crumbled in 1989. Lincoln's collapse cost taxpayers $2.6 billion.

Thousands of retirees living on fixed incomes and desperately needing their interest income on savings lost everything on the junk bonds bought at Keating's Lincoln Savings & Loan. Bogus land deals and other phony transactions created false profits that deluded bond buyers into thinking they were making safe investments in buying Lincoln bonds. In effect, Keating simply talked investors into taking their savings out of insured certificate of deposit accounts and placing the money into risky noninsured financial instruments while he lined his pockets. (For additional information about real estate fraud, refer to Chapter 13, "Real Estate Scams.")

Probation officer Thomas Aiken, who cited Keating's "callous disregard and betrayal of trust" as a bank owner, recommended a long sentence for Keating, noting that all of his victims who were contacted stressed that they would rather go hungry than see him go free.

Steven Whittle of La Palma, CA, testified at Keating's federal racketeering trial that he and his wife went to Lincoln Savings in 1988 when a certificate of deposit matured. Although Whittle was planning to cash it in because the new interest rate was lower than at other thrifts, the teller suggested the Whittles buy securities sold by American Continental Corporation. After reviewing American Continental's annual report, which showed five straight years of profits, Whittle agreed to purchase one hundred thousand dollars in bonds. The interest checks stopped in April 1989 and Whittle's one hundred thousand dollars became part of the country's costliest thrift failure when American Continental Corporation sought bankruptcy protection, rendering the bonds worthless.

At the heart of the hoax were the salespeople of Lincoln Savings & Loan, who duped customers into buying uninsured American Continental junk bonds by peddling the securities as government-backed, risk-free investments. American Continental did not use underwriters or brokers; instead, it relied on its own employees to sell the high-risk bonds.

The customers were not sophisticated investors who talked regularly with brokers or who had financial planners to manage their investments. Many were elderly Lincoln depositors with no investing experience. Some simply wanted to put their money into insured Lincoln Savings accounts but were persuaded instead to buy the junk

bonds. Many customers were never given prospectuses on their investments, while others received them in the mail after they had purchased bonds. Instead, the victims were sold after being shown glossy
pictures of Lincoln projects such as the Phoenician Resort hotel complex in Phoenix. Many of the elderly who invested their entire life savings were forced out of retirement by the collapse. Several bondhold-
ers committed suicide as a result of their financial losses. (See Chapter
10, "Confidence Games Against the Elderly.")

The worse conditions became at American Continental Corporation, the more aggressive the salespeople at Lincoln Savings & Loan
became. They hid the truth about American Continental's increasingly dire situation. Court testimony revealed that federal regulators
had told Keating as early as December 1986 that the savings and loan
did not have adequate capital for its risky ventures. Superior Court
Judge Lance Ito stated that it was apparent by February 1989 that a
catastrophic event was going to befall Keating's companies, but Keating continued to allow ACC's junk bonds to be sold to Lincoln Savings
investors. Keating ran his companies into the ground while taking a
huge salary and European trips on private jets.

Even after selling five hundred thousand dollars to seven hundred
thousand dollars in bonds a day at Lincoln, American Continental
filed for bankruptcy on April 13, 1989; Lincoln Savings & Loan was
seized a day later. After the regulators took over Keating's holdings,
they discovered that many of Keating's transactions were nothing
more than fraudulent schemes designed to increase the value of Lincoln S&L and provide more money for his lavish spending habits.

Judge Ito handed Keating a ten-year prison sentence and a two
hundred fifty thousand dollar fine. At Keating's sentencing, victim
Harriet Lapsey insisted that Keating "stole bread out of the mouths of
thousands" of senior citizens. Others who lost money with American
Continental described Keating as a cold-hearted criminal, a psychopath in a suit, and a cold, calculating thief who regarded hard-working
people as stupid. Their comments would describe most con artists who
steal trust as well as money from their marks.

Most financial planners will tell you not to invest more than 5 percent of your cash assets in noninsured, high-risk investments. If Continental American's investors had followed that one simple rule, the
losses would have been significantly less and fewer lives would have
been ruined or lost.

How Can You Protect Yourself?

The lure of the quick buck often seems irresistible, especially when investment returns are slim. Investors should be wary, however, because promises of high rates of return appeal to greed. You've worked hard to earn your money, so make sure your money will work hard for you. Here are a few tips to help you protect your hard-earned dollars.

First and foremost, be prudent and think before buying.

Always remember: if it sounds too good to be true, it probably is. Investment schemes come in all shapes and sizes, but the better the offer, the more suspicious you should become.

Never risk more than you can afford to lose. A simple rule in the investment business to remember is: The higher the return, the higher the risk.

Beware of deals "guaranteed" to provide easy, quick returns and higher-than-average profits. Be concerned if you're promised a "sure thing." An investor's skepticism should be higher with promises of high returns. Every percentage point above the going Treasury bond rate should throw up a red flag to the potential investor.

Never invest in anything offered in unsolicited telephone calls, and never discuss your finances with a stranger over the phone.

Never invest money in anything that is not insured. If you're told an investment is insured, ask for proof.

Never purchase investments on tips or rumors. Be safe and get all the facts first. Plus, it's illegal to trade securities based upon "inside information" not generally available to other investors.

Deal only with a licensed stockbroker and a major stock brokerage firm. Inquire about your broker's experience and background, and have him or her confirm this in writing.

Beware of any deals in which the salesperson declares that he or she is not going to make any commission or profit on the transaction. Such declarations should alert you to the possibility of fraud.

Investigate the company in question. Call the department of corporations, the department of insurance, the department of state, or your state comptroller's office to learn if the company is registered. Companies trading in futures contracts are regulated by the Commodity Futures Trading Commission (CFTC) and the National Futures Association (NFA), the industry self-regulatory group. The Securities and Exchange Commission (SEC) regulates the securities and securities options business, and the National Association of Securities Dealers (NASD) is a self-regulatory organization. The Federal Trade Commission (FTC) has jurisdiction over franchises and other business opportunities. Find out if either the company or salesperson has ever been cited by federal or state authorities for illegal or questionable activities.

Review the company's track record.   Before investing review the company's last annual report, financial statements for the past three years, and projections. Verify that the financial statements have been audited by a reputable firm.

Ask for and check business, bank, and client references.   Then retain your skepticism: References who respond too readily or glibly may be accomplices of swindlers.

Ask for information about the firm's litigation records.   Have there been any lawsuits, bankruptcy proceedings, or charges of fraud or deceptive practices?

If a firm cannot answer your questions or refuses to answer your questions, avoid making the investment.

Don't ever let a salesperson make you feel stupid for thoroughly investigating his or her proposed investment.

Before investing in any enterprise, check with others in similar businesses to see if the price you've been quoted is reasonable.   Before making any stock purchases, check the quoted price per share with another brokerage firm. Ask what price you would receive if you wanted to sell the stock instead of buy it.

Talk with the firm's long-standing customers.   Ask for the names of other investors and call them.

Do not get involved in an investment program you do not understand.   Before you give money to anyone make sure you have in your possession a prospectus that provides a complete analysis of the proposed investment and its risks. Do your homework and read it.

Before you enter into any business agreement have your attorney and accountant or financial adviser go over all the details and documents. Discuss your investment plans with professionals such as your accountant or financial adviser, and research the field of investments.

Beware of dealing with any firms located outside the United States. It's nearly impossible for the average investor to obtain financial information from an independent and reliable source when dealing with offshore companies, and it's generally even harder to trace and recover your money. Although many legitimate companies may be headquartered offshore, con artists find the distance from the continental U.S. attractive.

Never make rushed decisions no matter how much pressure the salesperson exerts. "Limited time offers" should be avoided. The con artist wants your check or credit card number now so that you won't have time to reconsider your decision. It's better to pass up an opportunity of which you're unsure than unnecessarily risk your precious savings.

Beware an investment when the salespeople emphasize the profitability of recruiting others versus making sales or providing services.

Beware of an investment that must offer a "free gift" in order to attract investors.

Stay away from "private offerings," especially those where substantial discounts are offered.

Don't think that your prior successes in investing are a guarantee of success in the future.

Don't speculate unless you thoroughly understand and can manage all of the risks involved. You'll be gambling with your money—not investing—and the average investor will most likely wind up a loser.

Keep accurate logs of all your conversations and dealings with your salesperson or broker. You should become alarmed if the person you've been dealing with becomes inaccessible or fails to return your phone calls.

Once you've invested, follow those investments. There's no guarantee that what started out as a valid investment won't turn into a swindle later. Verify the statements you receive from your broker.

What Can You Do If You've Been Swindled?

If you're unable to totally resolve your problems with an investment, demand your money back immediately. Be prepared for every excuse in the book why you shouldn't get it. If necessary, threaten to contact the proper authorities.

If you're suspicious that the offer being presented is not legitimate, or you feel that you've been duped, contact your attorney, the nearest Securities and Exchange Commission or Commodity Futures Trading Commission Office, your local police department, your state attorney general's office, the department of corporations, or your local district attorney's office. If the mails are used in a bogus investment opportunity, the U.S. Postal Inspector will want to know, and if interstate commerce is involved, the Federal Bureau of Investigation (FBI) will become involved. You may be able to save someone else from falling prey to an investment scam.

CHAPTER 9

Scams on the Doorstep: Home Business Opportunities

There is a quiet revolution going on across America, as employees pack up their work and take it home with them. They're called tele-commuters, and they spend at least one day each week working at home. Who are these revolutionaries? Most are white-collar profes-sionals ranging in age from thirty-five to forty-five, more than half are college graduates, and their average household income is forty-two thousand dollars per year. They are usually married and have small children, so many are motivated to work at home to offset child care expenses and to take a more active role in raising their children.

There are many reasons for this change, but probably most impor-tant is the development of effective computer networking via modem and increased ease of telecommunication with telephones and fax ma-chines. The office is less a place than a state of mind, and these profes-sionals are making the most of it.

There are currently as many as two hundred thousand official tele-commuters nationwide, and they may account for a third of the na-tion's workforce by the end of the 1990s. A recent Gallup research pro-ject suggests that the work-at-home trend will grow 8 percent by the end of 1995.

And white-collar workers aren't the only ones getting out of traffic.

Forbes magazine reported that six hundred thousand industrial employees work at home. Labor unions consider this trend a serious threat to their existence, since home workers rarely join unions, and they are fighting to limit people's right to work at home.

Working at home is not for everyone. It requires self-discipline and the cooperation of family members to make it work. In addition, many home workers discover there are legal barriers to the operation of a home-based business, such as zoning restrictions and tax laws that can make it tough to meet income targets. It is clear that society will be forced to make adjustments as more and more people turn their homes into workplaces.

Most of us dream of having our own business, and the home-based business can be a great investment. Start-up and operating costs are often lower, since there is no need to lease or furnish office space. But a home business brings all the challenges a traditional business does, and it should be approached with the same careful consideration.

Unfortunately, many people don't look before they leap into a home-based business. They often think it isn't a serious investment because it's something they do at home, or they may view it as just a way to make some extra money. Such naïveté can lead to frustration and expenses they never dreamed of, like local business taxes and a federal self-employment tax of nearly 15 percent. Or worse, they may fall victim to a con artist offering big profits for little work. When it comes to home-based business and work-at-home programs, there is no free lunch, despite what the pitch men will tell you.

Envelope Stuffing

One such scam was Cassiopia, the brain child of veteran work-at-home swindler Arthur Zelson. He had created a great front for his activities. Using phony identification, he secured a bulk-mailing permit, bank accounts, and a post office box. He had even filed a report about his company with the Lancaster, PA, Better Business Bureau. On paper, Cassiopia was a legitimate business.

Zelson rented mailing lists and sent over forty-six thousand solicitation letters in a two-week period to people across the country who had expressed a previous interest in work-at-home programs. The solicitations explained that Cassiopia would supply the envelopes, labels, stamps, and fliers describing "contests of skill involving word games."

Participants working at their own pace at home would prepare the envelopes for mailing and return them to Cassiopia. They would be paid fifty cents for each envelope.

Zelson cashed in when people sent him a security deposit that he promised to refund if they left the program. It started at twenty-five dollars and went up, depending on the number of envelopes the participant wanted to stuff per week. Over five thousand people fell for this unlikely scheme, one of the oldest in the book. After all, why would a direct-mail company spend a significant amount of money mailing material to be stuffed to people around the country only to have it mailed back again?

It should be self-evident that any legitimate mailing house would have machines and staff that could do the job far faster and better than an individual could. And yet con artists like Zelson continue to use this scam to defraud people with disabilities, the unemployed, parents with young children, and the elderly. The common denominator in this equation is the desperation and gullibility of those who seek some way to earn a little extra cash. These scams are increasingly popular as economic times get tougher.

The good news in this case is that Zelson was caught by postal inspectors and prosecuted for mail fraud. He is currently serving a forty-one-month prison term. The U.S. Postal Inspection Service confiscated $174,000 from Zelson's eight bank accounts and tracked down twenty-five hundred people who had responded to Cassiopia's solicitation. They returned every penny these victims had invested, ranging from $25 to $1,725 each. A stop-mail order sent several thousand other responses back to those who had sent them. Zelson's victims fared pretty well, considering that most people who fall for such mail-order scams never receive any restitution.

The envelope-stuffing program is the most common and persistent work-at-home scam. In its classic form, people send money for information on the envelope-stuffing program and receive instructions to buy space in newspapers or magazines to run ads with the same wording they responded to in the first place. If the individual innocently follows the con artist's advice and dupes others into sending money, he could quickly find himself under investigation by law enforcement officials.

At-Home Production

The ad reads something like this:

How would you like to earn $600, $1200, or as much as $3000 per week by spending ten, twenty, or thirty hours each week working in your home for me? All you have to do is send $295 for each milk culturing kit. You simply pour our powder mixed with water through a strainer and allow it to separate in a cool storage space. The more kits you convert for us, the more money you will earn. One handicapped house-wife in Denver prepares twelve kits per week for me and earns $3000 per month. You can do it, too. It's so easy and so profitable—for both of us. The demand for this precious patented milk-cultured powder is unlim-ited. You decide how much money you want and order the appropriate number of kits. Send in your $295 today and see just how easy it is to become financially independent.

This work-at-home scam netted the con man millions of dollars before he was caught. Initially, he paid for the kits that were processed and sent in. Then, as in all Ponzi schemes, a feeding frenzy of sorts followed. Everyone who sent in $295 received a check back for $600 ordered multiple kits. They encouraged their relatives, neighbors, and friends to do the same. But, no matter how it's sold to the public, a Ponzi scheme is still a Ponzi scheme.

"There is no hard and fast way to identify a scam in advance," said Shirley Rooker, president of Call for Action, a nonprofit consumer hotline based in Washington, DC. "But you shouldn't have to pay to work. You should be getting paid."

Another popular scam involves assembly of toys, baby shoes, plastic signs, or electronic circuit boards for resale to the supplier. The victim may have to buy a sewing machine or other equipment, then pay for the components, all of which are purchased from the promoter. When the product is made and returned to the company, the worker receives notice that it didn't meet specifications. They're out their investment and time, and they're stuck with worthless merchandise.

Chain Letters

Some work-at-home promoters dress up chain letters as employ-ment opportunities. They claim they are legal, but chain letters are illegal lotteries. The promoter gets his victim to mail money to people or businesses listed on the original letter. Guess who's waiting at those mail drops? That's right: the con artist picks up the cash and is on his way, a richer man at his mark's expense.

The variations on these schemes are only limited by the fertile imaginations of the perpetrators, and are fueled by the gullibility of those who fall for them. They want to believe they can earn big money proofreading or reading manuscripts for publishers, clipping coupons, raising lab animals, or even watching television. Sad to say, it just isn't so.

Information for Sale

One enterprising group of teenagers pulled in two hundred fifty thousand dollars over the course of two years, selling information about in-home employment opportunities. They had it all: national advertising, a toll-free 800 number for quick response, and brochures offering callers additional information for the paltry sum of twenty-seven dollars.

Operating out of one of Southern California's most wealthy communities, San Marino, the group ran their scam under the rubrics of Prime Opportunities, U.S. Networking, and Networking America. When authorities apprehended the ringleader he was driving a thirty-five thousand dollar sports car purchased with profits from the scam. The six high school students, ranging in ages from fifteen to seventeen, faced charges of felony grand theft, conspiracy to commit grand theft, and theft by false pretenses.

One of their ads said it all. "To be honest, it sounded too good to be true, but I decided to give it a try and I am glad that I did! I took in $1,500 last week and only had to work four hours." Only if you stole it, like these young con artists.

Home-Based Franchise Opportunities

The International Franchise Association reported that franchise businesses, ranging from auto dealerships to retail stores and restaurants, accounted for over $700 billion in 1990, a third of all retail sales in the country.

Some smaller investors find independent turnkey business systems to be their best bet. These operations resemble franchises, but do not carry a company name, continuing support, or national advertising. They do provide business plans, marketing, training, computer systems and software programs, and they are less expensive than franchise businesses.

Home Office Computing published an article in October 1991 that described seventy good turnkey and franchise operations currently on the market. And that's just the tip of the iceberg when it comes to the wide range of legitimate business opportunities available. A little research can guide investors to a wealth of money-making opportunities.

Growing right alongside these legitimate enterprises are phony franchises and independent business opportunities promoted by con artists. They have become so prevalent that it is growing increasingly difficult to tell the bona fide opportunities from their bogus counterparts. The variety of scams is endless.

Many investors are attracted to mail-order business opportunities because of the lucrative nature of the market—topping $200 billion in 1990—and because many of these opportunities can be run from home. Con artists find this a very attractive option, promoting such business opportunities by mail and disappearing with the investment capital of their victims. They promote them through ads in consumer publications and business journals, promising huge returns with virtually no expense or effort. Sound familiar? Investors soon learn that the products are substandard and promotional materials and instruction manuals are worthless.

One couple in Colorado paid $675 for sixty thousand earthworms, which they were told would produce nearly 4 million worms by the end of one year. The firm guaranteed to buy the worms back, generating a $144,000 annual income for the investors. But the earthworms didn't multiply. They started dying, because the average home did not provide the conditions required for reproduction. The couple lost all the money they had invested.

Franchise scams take advantage of people who seek the security of starting a business backed by the experience and products of a nationally successful company. High-pressure salespeople offer their victims fabulous promises and great supporting material, including sales projections, testimonials, and slick brochures. They urge the person to act immediately so as not to miss out on the opportunity.

Once the deal has been made and the money has changed hands, the con artists may disappear or the franchiser go out of business. In other cases, products, services, store locations, and training programs may fail to meet the standards stated at the outset. Advertising and promotional materials and corporate support prove nonexistent or inadequate.

Vending Machine Fraud

Vending machine frauds involve sale of poor quality equipment to an investor who is led to believe he or she will turn great profits simply by following the program, in which the promoter fills the machines with their products and places them in specific high traffic areas. The unsuspecting buyer soon discovers that the promoter has placed the machines in areas where they are competing against other vending machines that have better products for less money, making it impossible for the investor to make a profit.

One man invested nearly $5500 in vending machines and the small toys they dispensed. True to form, the crooked company placed the machines in terrible locations that were 138 miles apart, making it difficult to service the machines. It was a financial disaster for the unhappy investor.

Shady Multilevel Marketing Distributorships

Multilevel marketing, also known as direct sales, is as well known as the Avon lady. It is a large and lucrative part of the U.S. economy, giving countless people the opportunity to make money in their spare time, selling a wide variety of products to their friends and neighbors. The Direct Selling Association, founded in 1910, is the national trade association of multilevel marketers. They report that direct sales top $10 billion annually, promoted by over 4 million salespeople, 81 percent of whom are women.

The system is fairly simple. Participants are independent business people, called distributors, who market products to consumers and small businesses. The distributors also recruit other distributors to join them in the business, supplying them with products and training to help them succeed.

Legitimate multilevel marketing business opportunities have made participants rich, but only with the application of good old-fashioned hard work and persistence. There is no such thing as easy money in direct sales, but the money can be very good, indeed, once you establish a list of regular customers, recruit others for your distribution network, and train them well.

The shady version of multilevel marketing is the Ponzi or pyramid scheme. In many ways it resembles its legitimate counterpart, but it stresses quick profits made by recruiting others to join in the program rather than profits through sales of products. Some of these scams pay no attention at all to the product line; recruiting becomes their only product as new recruits are paid commissions for signing up other investors.

The promoters of these schemes fail to point out that market saturation will eventually make it impossible to continue this endless round of recruiting, and the investors on the low end of the pyramid will only lose money. The mathematics are simple: If one person recruits ten investors, each of whom recruits ten others, within seven steps there would be over 10 million investors in the program.

Steps	Investors
	1
1	10
2	100
3	1,000
4	10,000
5	100,000
6	1,000,000
7	10,000,000

It doesn't take a nuclear physicist to figure out that this equation doesn't add up. People keep passing money up the line in the pyramid, but if no one is making an effort to sell any products, there's no chance that those on the bottom of the pyramid will make money.

Do people actually fall for these scams? Ask the twenty-two thousand investors who bought into the direct-marketing program being peddled by David Sterns in Southern California. Le Patch was purported to be the new diet miracle, a patch that released appetite suppressants directly into the skin. Federal prosecutors later said it couldn't work the way Sterns claimed. It was just an elaborate scam designed to hide the pyramid scheme from investors until it was too late.

Fortunately, investigators finally caught up with Sterns and put him out of business. He was sentenced to nearly five years in prison and required to pay back the $1.9 million investors gave him. In addition, he received a fine of three hundred thousand dollars and was ordered to serve three years in "supervised release" following his prison term. It's too bad they can't supervise such crooks on a permanent basis, since they usually are up to their old tricks as soon as they leave custody. (For more information on investment fraud, see Chapter 8, "Investment Cons.")

How Can You Protect Yourself?

If you are interested in a home-based business or just want to add a few extra dollars to your coffers with home employment, it pays to be cautious and do your homework. There are a lot of scams masquerading as business opportunities, but you can usually spot them if you know what to look for.

Be on the lookout for these key characteristics of a scam or any variation of them:

- Promises of high returns for little effort
- No skills or experience necessary
- Requirement of an immediate response, or pressure to sign a contract immediately
- Testimonials from nameless people who claim the offer changed their lives
- Advance fee required or a large fee payable before you receive anything in return
- Evasive or incomplete answers to your questions

Investigate before you invest. Legitimate home employment programs should be able to respond to the following questions:

- What tasks will I be required to perform? Ask the potential employer to list every step of the job.
- Will I be paid a salary or on commission?
- Who will pay me?

- When will I get my first paycheck?
- What is the total cost of the work-at-home program, including supplies, equipment, and membership fees?
- What will I get for my money?

Get references and check them out. Don't get involved in any business that won't give you references. But also be wary of references that are too glowing. They may be accomplices of a flimflam man.

Above all, don't believe everything the company representative tells you. Remember, a con artist will promise you anything to get your money but will never deliver the goods.

Before you select a home-based business package such as a franchise, turnkey operation, or a multilevel marketing program, you should first take an unabashed look at yourself. Make a list of your good qualities as well as your weak points. After all, any business is going to be dependent on you to make it work. Compare your list to the job requirements for the business opportunity and see if you meet them. Imagine you are hiring yourself to run the business. Do you measure up? If so, you have a good chance of succeeding and should proceed.

Get your information in writing. The Federal Trade Commission requires that the sellers of some types of business opportunities must supply certain information in writing before a contract is signed. This list can also serve as a guideline for anyone thinking of investing in any business. Insist on getting the following in writing:

- The business background of the principals of the company, including any lawsuits and bankruptcies
- An audited financial statement of the company for the past three years that includes operating revenues, source of revenues, and a profit and loss statement
- A complete description of all initial and future charges you must pay, and all other obligations you may incur
- A full description of assistance the company will provide, including training programs, site selection, and financial assistance
- A description of the conditions under which the contract may be terminated or modified by either party
- A list of the names and addresses of others who have purchased business opportunities from the company

- Proof of earnings claims, including the percentage of purchasers who have actually achieved the results claimed
- A description of any restrictions, including restrictions on what and where you must buy and sell.

Research your business opportunity by contacting the Chamber of Commerce, Better Business Bureau, and consumer affairs office. The public library, a business dealing in similar products, and an attorney who specializes in business law could also serve as good resources. You can also check with the attorney general's office or regional Federal Trade Commission office.

Take your time making a decision to invest even a relatively small amount of money in a business opportunity. Ask questions, get written information, and follow up on all references and resources before you spend a dime.

Have a disinterested party, such as your accountant or attorney, review all material and give you an opinion. A legitimate promoter will appreciate your thoroughness and recognize that you are only making sure your investment is well spent.

If you decide to invest, get all conditions and promises in writing in a contract reviewed by your attorney and signed by the authorized agent for the company.

If you are looking into multilevel marketing programs, contact the Direct Sales Association for more information about their members and the business of direct sales. Take a careful look at the products, up-line distribution network, training aids, and overall operating style of the company before you sign up. Would you use the products yourself? Do you feel they are worth the price charged for them? Do the company's claims about their effectiveness seem reasonable?

When investigating multilevel marketing opportunities, do the same kind of homework you would do if you were buying a large business franchise. After all, the amount of time and effort you will put into developing your direct-sales business will be no less than you would spend on any other business. Spend your time as wisely as you spend your money and you won't have any regrets.

If you decide direct sales is for you, beware of pyramid schemes. Look for these warning signs of a pyramid scheme disguised as a direct-sales program:

- Is the initial product investment substantial, apparently far larger than the value of the products in the kit?
- Do the salespeople offer you "free" merchandise to convince you to invest?
- Will the company buy back unsold inventory, or are you stuck with it?
- How aggressively does the company promote sales of its products to consumers, as opposed to recruitment of new distributors?

What Can You Do If You Think You've Been Defrauded?

First, attempt to get a refund from the company. Be persistent, and complain however loudly you must. The average business doesn't ever hear from 96 percent of its unhappy customers, according to the Direct Selling Education Foundation. Tell the company that you plan to contact law enforcement officials.

If the company refuses to refund your investment, contact the Better Business Bureau, the local consumer affairs agency, the attorney general's office, the Federal Trade Commission, and the U. S. Postal Inspector in your area (if the mails were involved).

CHAPTER 10

Confidence Games Against the Elderly

People over sixty-five make up only 12 percent of the population, but approximately 30 percent of the victims of consumer fraud are seniors. And consumer fraud is an underreported crime. Many victims don't come forward because they feel foolish or fear their families will think they are incompetent to manage their own funds. The American Association of Retired Persons (AARP) estimates that senior citizens are conned out of over $10 billion annually. Scams range from home maintenance rip-offs to phony investments and sweepstakes that "guarantee" their victims will be winners.

Health-related scams are among the most common, offering elderly people everything from the fountain of youth to in-home assistance. A stunning example of this type of fraud has even been seen on nationwide television. "I've fallen and I can't get up" is the unforgettable tag line of the famous television commercials promoting Lifecall Emergency Services Systems. Minnesota Attorney General Hubert Humphrey III knows them very well. In fact, his office and the attorney general's office of Arkansas recently filed a joint lawsuit against the company.

"In our suit, we allege that consumers who called the 'no obligation' toll-free number were promptly visited by teams of high-pressure salesmen, trained to frighten and bully their victims—many of them invalids—for up to five hours." Humphrey reported that these pushy salesmen convinced elderly people to sign a $3,600 four-year lease for the devices. The same devices could have been provided by a local hospital for ten to twenty dollars per month, with no long-term lease required. (See Chapter 12, "Medical and Health Fraud.")

What makes seniors so vulnerable to these types of crimes?

"Seniors are isolated and alone. When someone shows them attention, they like that. And that's how they're duped," said Maureen O'Bryan, senior coordinator for the Cook County (Illinois) State Attorney General's Office. She added that seniors grew up in another era, and many tend to be too trusting of strangers. One elderly woman recently lost fourteen thousand dollars to a prison inmate with whom she'd been corresponding. The con sent her altered U.S. postal money orders and asked her to send him money in exchange. Because she's afraid to tell her family that she was duped, she's trying to pay back the bank herself.

Many seniors become desperate to preserve shrinking buying power and fall for investment scams that are simply too good to be true. Others experience loss of memory and health problems that make it difficult for them to fend off unscrupulous people.

It seems there is no safe haven for vulnerable seniors. Despite security patrols and programs intended to alert residents to the dangers of confidence schemes, retirement communities like Southern California's Leisure World are easy pickings for swindlers. Many of its residents have sold their homes and businesses, so they've got plenty of cash and often don't know quite what to do with it. In a five-year period, the county received reports of over sixty-five cases of fraud perpetrated on residents of Leisure World. Considering how many cases go unreported, law enforcement officials consider this just the tip of the iceberg. It's suspected that hundreds of cases have gone unreported.

Leslie Gall, known as the Sweetheart Swindler, made good use of the loneliness and trust of single women he met at seniors' dances in Florida and California. At the time of his arrest he was carrying fifty-four thousand dollars in securities he had stolen from his latest mark, and a map with all the Southern California senior centers circled in ink. He confessed that he targeted elderly women and "made them feel Number 1."

The Fraudulent Equation

Regional Chief Postal Inspector Jack Swagerty, Western Region, presented a report on mail fraud to the Senate's Special Committee on Aging in 1990. He detailed the five steps a con artist takes to develop any type of scam that you might encounter.

The con artist begins by planning the scam and selecting a target group, such as senior citizens. Next, he creates a cover for his operation that will make him seem believable. At this point, he approaches his intended victim and makes his pitch. He takes advantage of the person's trust, ignorance, or greed, manipulating his emotions to influence him to act impulsively.

The fourth step requires the victim's voluntary participation, by investing money, for example. *The victim must assist the con in order for the scam to work.* The con artist then completes the scam by covering his tracks, concealing his crime so he can go out and find another victim.

Fortunately, no plan is foolproof, and there are ways to catch the con artist at his game. First, be aware of the way in which you are being manipulated emotionally. High-pressure sales tactics and promises that are too good to be true, such as big returns on investments or miraculous results from a product, should set off your alarms. In order for his scheme to work, the con artist must get you to make a financial commitment. If you don't take this step, the scheme collapses.

This is the point at which you can take control of the situation. Refuse to turn your money or property over to the con artist. The con artist is well aware that he must make you feel compelled to participate, so he tailors the scam carefully to be irresistible to his victims.

In this case the best defense is a good offense. Don't take what strangers tell you at face value. Do your own homework; find out if the promised product is all it's cracked up to be before you buy. If it is legitimate, the seller can wait until you check out him and his product with your lawyer, accountant, and other advisers.

There are countless variations on the basic formula of the scam, and a successful scheme can be run on people from any age group. But there are certain categories and classic rip-offs of elderly people that appear again and again. Let's look at some of the most common scams perpetrated on elderly people today.

Investment and Estate Planning Scams

The "get rich quick" investment scams are many: real estate, stocks and bonds, IRA and Keogh plans, oil and gas drilling, business franchises, foreign currencies, precious metals and coins. You name it, someone will sell it to you at unbelievable prices.

Wilma Riggeria, eighty-two, learned the lesson of the wolf in entrepreneur's clothing the hard way. It cost her her entire life savings. A charming man cultivated her carefully, took her to lunch frequently, and even gave her a tour of the plant where his partner planned to manufacture an oil filter that would never need replacement. Her good friend even promised to take her dancing.

After she had written him a check for $61,000, it turned out he'd been giving her a song and dance all along. She was left a sadder but wiser woman. "I feel like I've been hypnotized. I'm not that dumb. Really. I never thought that this could happen here."

Even professional people with considerable knowledge and experience can be the targets of investment scams. In the case of a senior vice-president of a major marketing firm, the con artist baffled him with the sheer volume of material he provided. The VP was presented with a book over four inches thick containing extensive information on a mining project: letters of credit, assay reports, geology reports, deeds, photographs of the proposed site and equipment, and a detailed outline of the projected return on his investment over time. It was an impressive presentation, and absolutely phony.

Two years after he invested, the executive filed a complaint with the FBI. When agents asked him if he had verified the documents he had received he said he hadn't had time to follow up, but his instinct had told him it was a good investment. His impulsiveness cost him a staggering one hundred eighty thousand dollars.

Investments are never something to rush into. Con artists will try to make you feel guilty or foolish if you don't jump at the chance to give them your money. They will use every psychological trick to get you to ignore your better judgment, including your own greed. If you feel like you are on an emotional roller coaster when you are talking to the salesperson, stop and think about the way he is manipulating you.

Another popular area of fraud involves estate planning. Con artists find it easy to take advantage of seniors who are trying to protect their assets for their heirs. This type of scam is especially attractive because the crime often goes undetected until the victim is deceased, when bereaved relatives are left to sort out the legal mess.

An excellent example is the worthless, boilerplate living trust sold at exorbitant prices by door-to-door salesmen with no legal training. Fast-talking hucksters convince their victims to part with large amounts of cash in exchange for preparation of documents that may be no more binding than a note written on a cocktail napkin.

A living trust can be a legitimate part of estate planning that allows heirs to avoid the expense and delays of probate. A trust is a legal vehicle that takes title to an individual's assets. Most people set up revocable trusts that allow them to change or abolish the trust should the need arise. These revocable trusts allow the individual (or grantor) to select a co-trustee, who can take over management of the assets if the grantor becomes incapacitated. In addition, assets pass directly to beneficiaries at the death of the grantor without going through the cumbersome probate process.

Trusts can be difficult to set up properly because the laws vary from state to state. The advice of an attorney who is well versed in local estate and trust law is essential. Because of the expense, trusts are only warranted on estates with considerable assets to protect.

When Marcella P. Abercrombie, seventy-two, made a deposit at her bank in Springfield, IL, she was approached by a woman who asked if she had anyone advising her on her financial affairs. When Abercrombie seemed interested the woman took her phone number and said her husband would call.

Surprisingly, the man showed up at her home that night, stayed for three hours, and convinced her she needed a living trust. He drew one up for her and charged her $1195. If her niece had not spotted the document a few days later and asked her about it, Mrs. Abercrombie would never have learned that she had been taken.

Her small estate, totalling only forty-five thousand dollars, would not even be subject to inheritance taxes, so the living trust was completely unnecessary. Mrs. Abercrombie had to take her case to the Illinois Attorney General's office, but she finally received a full refund. She was lucky. Most victims never even know their investment is wasted.

Loan Frauds

Phony loan brokers descend on beleaguered homeowners, offering to help solve their financial problems by refinancing their homes. Typically, the con artists have read in the newspapers that the properties are in jeopardy of foreclosure. They pressure people into signing documents they haven't read or don't understand, all for the purpose of gaining the titles of their victim's homes. Then they borrow money against the homes' equity before they vanish.

These scam operators look for elderly, fixed-income homeowners who own their property outright and may be suffering from the health problems that come with age. They also prefer victims with poor educations, who may not be able to fully comprehend the papers they are signing.

Loan broker Sam R. Samuelson thought he had found the perfect dupe in seventy-two-year-old Eleanor Davidson. Alone in Los Angeles, and nearly incapacitated by two strokes, Mrs. Davidson was easily taken in by Samuelson's claim that she was in danger of losing her home because of a delinquent one thousand dollar loan. He quickly convinced her to sign a stack of papers that he claimed would protect her right to her home.

She had actually agreed to give Samuelson partial title to her home, against which he borrowed sixty-eight thousand dollars. Davidson was supposed to make monthly interest payments of twelve-hundred dollars for one year, at which time the entire sixty-eight thousand dollars would come due for payment.

A concerned neighbor learned of the foreclosure proceedings and contacted authorities. The Legal Aid Foundation moved to block the foreclosure and saved Davidson's home. Eleanor Davidson was fortunate to have such a concerned, attentive neighbor, but many elderly people who are alone have no one to turn to for help. (Turn to Chapter 13, "Real Estate Scams.")

Telemarketing Scams

Fraudulent telemarketing firms sell products that run the gamut from investment schemes to time-share condominiums and discount vacations. They all have one thing in common: a desire to separate you from your money.

Also known as boiler rooms, these operations consist of large numbers of high-pressure salespeople who sit at banks of phones, dialing numbers and reading from sales scripts. They follow the sun, starting early in the morning calling east coast residents and working their way across the country to the west coast.

The FBI reports that illegal telemarketing companies often target seniors because they are more trusting and make ideal customers. Telemarketing companies purchase lead sheets from brokers who categorize the people listed by age, geographic location, buying habits, and credit card usage. The perfect profile for these swindlers is a senior citizen living in the Midwest who has previously purchased something from a telemarketing company using a credit card.

The telemarketing industry in Las Vegas alone generated an estimated $1.2 billion in gross sales in a recent years. Popular products included vitamins, travel packages, water purifiers, and specialty items like pens, key tags, and baseball caps. Over 90 percent of the victims of the fraudulent telemarketers are senior citizens.

There are many legitimate telemarketing firms, so how do you tell them apart? Legitimate firms will not use high-pressure sales tactics and make ridiculous or unbelievable claims for their products or services. Remember, the con artists can promise you the moon because they don't have to deliver.

Mail Theft and Fraud

The U.S. Postal Service delivers in excess of 180 billion pieces of mail annually. The sheer volume of mail makes an excellent cover for con artists and provides thieves with the perfect opportunity to make off with millions in checks and valuables.

Seniors are good targets for roving bands of thieves who simply drive through neighborhoods with large elderly populations on the day Social Security checks are delivered. They open every box and remove the checks before their rightful owners can pick them up.

Over 70 percent of the people who receive direct-mail solicitations receive no other mail, and the vast majority of people who receive so-called junk mail read every word of it. Companies push an astonishing array of products by mail. Most of the companies are comprised of honest businesspeople, but unscrupulous operators make millions ripping off unsuspecting buyers. Any scheme can be considered a mail fraud as long as the mail is used to carry it out.

The variations on this theme can include many of the other categories, such as: investment and insurance scams, bogus health-care products, discount vacations, work-at-home schemes and phony job opportunities, resort property sales, home-improvement promotions, chain letters, and the infamous "guaranteed" sweepstakes. There are three types of fraudulent mailings recognized by the Postal Service:

- The full-blown fraud, in which the entire operation is designed specifically to defraud people of money. These scams often take the form of phony investment opportunities or involve promotion of a product that must be paid for in advance and is never delivered.
- Mailings that misrepresent the product or make extravagant claims about its qualities or effectiveness. These are usually miracle-cure promotions, weight-loss programs, or cosmetics that purport to be a "fountain of youth." Whatever the product, the claims are false and the buyer ends up feeling disappointed and foolish.
- Mailings that give misleading information or attempt to imply some association with government or law enforcement agencies. A common approach is to put an official-looking seal on the outside of the envelope, along with initials like IRS or FBI. They may also use words like "summons" or "warrant" to capture attention. The main purpose of this ploy is to get people to open the envelope and read it, thinking it has come from the government.

Two of the most active areas of mail fraud involve bogus health-care products and sweepstakes that guarantee you will win—as long as you keep sending them money.

Health Care Fraud

The modern snake oil salesmen push bogus health-care products that guarantee to cure everything from arthritis to cancer and Alzheimer's disease. Their products are seldom delivered, and if they do arrive, prove to be useless and overpriced.

Two bogus companies selling adjustable beds took cash in advance from nearly two thousand seniors. Then the companies sent notices that they were going bankrupt and pocketed the money. Needless to say, the buyers never received the beds they had ordered. Postal inspectors successfully prosecuted the cases and sent the perpetrators to jail. Unfortunately, the victims never got back a dime of their money after spending between two and four thousand dollars for a bed. (See Chapter 12, "Medical and Health Fraud.")

Sweepstakes Scams

People on fixed incomes are particularly vulnerable to these get-rich-quick schemes. Mailings that often appear to have some official or government connection arrive promising guaranteed prizes. The only thing "guaranteed" about these contests is that you'll be the loser if you send them any money.

Retired banker Archie Thatcher lost forty-two hundred dollars on the promise of winning ten thousand dollars to $10 million in a bogus contest promotion in Minnesota. "You're in a quandary. You've worked and saved up over a lifetime, and here's a chance to multiply it," Thatcher said, surprised by how easily he fell for the scam. "Hook, line and sinker, I fell for it."

A contest that charges money for participation is considered a lottery and is illegal in most states. Put simply, if you have to pay to play, don't. You'll be happy you didn't. (See Chapter 16, "Sweepstakes Fraud.")

Home Repair Scams

Name any kind of legitimate service a homeowner might require and you will find some light-fingered criminal making a fast buck. These schemes can range from price gouging and shoddy workmanship to outright theft perpetrated by criminals who misrepresent themselves to elderly people.

One courageous eighty-two-year-old in the Chicago area turned the tables on a quartet of con men who burst into her home claiming to be from the gas company. Rafaella Torino was told she had a serious gas leak and her house was about to explode. When she demanded to see their credentials, they told her there was no time for that. Then she called the police.

Torino's grandson drove up at that moment and blocked the driveway with his van. The men lost their nerve and ran, pursued by neighbors and passersby. One stranger even called the police on his cellular phone and followed a cab carrying a suspect until police arrived to apprehend him.

Torino's daughter summed it up after two of the men were sentenced: "They met their match."

Not everyone is as quick-witted as Mrs. Torino. But knowing what to look for can help protect you from these slippery criminals. Here are a few popular versions of the game.

Price Gouging

The salesman promises bargain prices for carpet cleaning, but on inspection says the carpets are too dirty and the price goes up dramatically. Security officials at Southern California's Leisure World retirement community report that residents have paid as much as twenty-five hundred dollars for carpet and drapery cleaning.

Disappearing Deposit

A contractor offers to do some home improvement work for a set fee. He gets a substantial deposit and is never seen again. In one recent case, a Van Nuys, CA, man was collecting down payments for roofing work that he never did. He wasn't even a licensed contractor.

Unnecessary Work

The con artist sells the homeowner a product or does work that is not needed in the first place. Unsuspecting homeowners are duped into buying new furnaces or air conditioners, or authorizing unnecessary repairs to an existing system. Scare tactics are often used with elderly citizens. A Pompano Beach, FL, man used telephone solicitors to set up appointments for air-conditioning unit inspections and cleanings. The inspectors would tell the customers that they needed new air-conditioning units or repair work, even though in some cases the existing units were less than two years old.

Shoddy Workmanship

The contractor does the job, but does it so poorly that it is obviously not worth the money paid for it or must be redone. One distraught homeowner reported that she was promised a newly paved driveway, but ended up with a load of plastic foam peanuts that had been painted black to simulate asphalt. Needless to say, the contractor had been paid in advance and was long gone.

Charity and Religious Rip-offs

Phony door-to-door crusades are favorites of con artists, especially if they involve a recent natural disaster, famine, military conflict (such as the Gulf War), or stories of family tragedies that have made the news, such as a police officer shot in the line of duty.

Sometimes you can't even trust a man of the cloth. By the time authorities caught up with Reverend Roy Greenhill, he had sold nearly a dozen unsuspecting investors the same shares in a Born-Again Bible he planned to publish. He did actually test-market a few of the Bibles, but an investigator testified at his trial that he had obtained so many personal loans that he could "go to the moon or the Bahamas or whatever."

He was only exaggerating slightly. Greenhill had taken over one-hundred-fifty thousand dollars from investors for royalty rights to the new Bible. Taking money from eighty-five-year-old Harvey Rivery proved to be his undoing. Rivery realized he was being flimflammed and went to the authorities. "I'm a Christian. I believe in ministers," Mr. Rivery said. "But I don't believe in con men, and that's what he is."

Evidently the court agreed with Rivery. They sentenced Greenhill to five years in prison for thirteen violations of the Georgia Securities Act. (Also see Chapter 15, "Fraudulent Fund Raising.")

Bank Examiner Scam

This is one of the oldest cons in the book. The con artist contacts the person by phone and says he's a bank examiner or law enforcement official investigating embezzlement by a teller at a local bank. He convinces his mark to go to the bank and withdraw a sizable amount of money to help entrap the teller. The con artist then meets the person outside and takes the cash as "evidence." The con and the cash disappear, never to be seen again.

Contrary to what con artists would have you believe, bank examiners, FBI agents, and police officers do not use civilians (or their money) in investigations of embezzlement, fraud, or theft. If someone calls you asking you to take money out of your bank account, you can bet it's only for his benefit.

An eighty-seven-year-old woman was taken not once but three times by the same swindler who called and identified himself as a bank executive investigating fraud at her bank. Following his instructions, she cashed a check for twenty-six hundred dollars and met a man, identified only as "Code Five," in a parking lot across the street. She turned the money over to him as the "evidence" and went home. The bank executive called twice more, and she cashed two additional checks totalling five thousand dollars and gave the money to the mysterious man.

When the banker didn't call to tell her how to get her money back she told her neighbor, an accountant, about the incident. He called the police, but it was too late. "Code Five" and the woman's money were long gone.

Another version of this scam involved crooks posing as police officers who confiscated eleven thousand dollars in "counterfeit" cash from an eighty-one-year-old woman, who foolishly kept the money in a lockbox in her home. Making matters worse, she allowed them to convince her to cash in over ninety-six thousand dollars in certificates of deposit and turn the money over to them.

Care Givers Who are Care "Takers"

These individuals are among the most insidious operators in the con game. Posing as nurses, home health aides, and others in the caring professions, these swindlers invade the homes of frail, elderly people who are in real need. They take advantage of the vulnerability of people who are sick, confused, and often out of touch with reality in order to gain control of their lives, finances, and property.

Family members who try to ensure the best care for their elderly relatives find out that it isn't always so easy. Take the case of Pasadena, CA, resident Nancy Slocum, who hired a live-in care giver from the local nurses' registry to assist her eighty-five-year-old aunt, Florence Walker.

Slocum took a trip to Mexico, confident that her aunt was well cared for, only to return and learn that the nurse had sold Walker's condominium, had a new will drawn up naming herself as the sole beneficiary, and had purchased two one-way tickets for herself and Walker to fly from her home in California to Tennessee. Impressive accomplishments in only two weeks' time.

Thanks to the quick response of Walker's attorney, who called to inform Slocum that the nurse was trying to get power of attorney, they were able to halt the escrow and recover control of Walker's assets before it was too late.

Regrettably, most cases like Walker's are never prosecuted because victims with failing memories make poor witnesses, leaving their families with little recourse. Nancy Slocum didn't want to press the case because she felt her aunt had suffered enough. The care "taker" walked away, probably to con some other unsuspecting elderly person.

There are many opportunities for financial abuse in such caring situations, so take the time to protect the older person's interests. It's often hard for relatives to find out about financial abuse until it's too late. But the California Department of Justice offers these warning signs:

- Any kind of unusual activity in checking or savings accounts
- Another party obtains power of attorney when the elderly person is clearly unable to comprehend his or her own financial situation
- An elderly person who cannot comprehend the serious nature of the transaction transfers the title of his or her home (or car or boat) to a "friend"
- A new will is drawn up even though the older person is clearly incapable of making a will
- New acquaintances express affection for a wealthy older person
- Valuables, like jewelry, silverware, and art, are suddenly missing

- A care giver isolates an older person from friends and family, telling the person no one wants to visit
- Someone promises life-long care for the elderly person in exchange for the deed to all property and money
- Forged signatures on checks, or checks and documents signed when the older person cannot write.

How Can You Protect Yourself?

One of the best ways to defend yourself against the myriad of con artists and their schemes is to borrow a phrase from the DARE anti-drug program: Just say no. If you don't buy, you can't be ripped off. One cagey ninety-year-old had this to say about hucksters who appear on her doorstep or call her on the phone: "I just tell them I'm not interested, because I'm not interested—and I don't open my door to strangers."

When in doubt, consult an expert you can trust. You know more experts than you might realize. Call your lawyer, accountant, physician, pharmacist, banker, or financial planner if you have questions or suspect fraud.

Beware of high-pressure sales tactics. If a salesperson pressures you to "act now or miss out on a fabulous deal," you can assume he's just trying to part you from your money.

The best protection against unscrupulous telemarketing firms is to refuse to buy. If you feel you are being unduly pressured or the product seems too good to be real, just hang up the phone.

If someone calls you and asks you to take money out of your bank account, get his or her name and phone number. Then hang up and call the police.

Investigate the company and the investment before you invest. If someone is pressuring you to invest money with promises of very high returns, slow down and check all possible resources for information on any investment and the respective company before you commit any funds. Demand that the salesperson provide you with materials proving the legitimacy of the investments and show the papers to your financial advisers. Call your broker, attorney, or accountant for advice and assistance.

Contact the Better Business Bureau, the Securities and Exchange Commission, and the National Association of Securities Dealers for information about the investment firm and its standing in the industry. Find out if the company is registered, and ask if it has ever been cited by federal or state authorities for illegal or questionable activities.

Always get information about a purchase, charity, investment, etc., in writing. Secure complete information on the product or service and follow up on it before you buy. Find out if the claims made by the seller are reasonable. For example, if it's a health care product, ask your doctor or pharmacist.

Never buy real estate except through a licensed broker.   Have your lawyer and/or financial adviser look over the proposed transaction before any monies change hands.

Never buy prepackaged trusts or other legal documents from people who call or write to you.   Talk to an attorney, who can advise you whether or not a living trust is warranted for your estate. He can prepare legally binding documents for you that will provide full protection for you and your heirs.

Beware anyone calling himself a "foreclosure expert."   There's no such thing. The only expertise this person has probably involves stealing money from innocent people. If you need financial help and advice, talk to your lawyer, banker, accountant, and/or certified financial planner.

Never give your credit card number, bank account number, or Social Security number over the phone to a firm you know nothing about or to someone who shows up on your doorstep unannounced and uninvited.   These numbers are worth their weight in gold to swindlers, selling for fifty to a hundred dollars and up. A good rule of thumb is to give your credit card number only when you have made the call yourself (to hold a room at a hotel, for example). Find out why the firm needs the information and look into the legitimacy of the firm and its request.

Make arrangements to have Social Security checks and other kinds of pension and annuity payments deposited directly to your bank account.   It saves a trip to the bank, guarantees the funds will be available when needed, and gives peace of mind, as well.

Don't purchase products by mail unless you know the company and its reputation. Remember, anyone can buy advertising space or mail solicitations.

There are many worthwhile charities that deserve support. Some even solicit door-to-door. However, there are so many phony solicitors around, your best bet is to make donations through organizations you know, such as your church or local community agencies.

Demand to see the credentials of anyone claiming to be a law enforcement official or investigator. Be wary of anyone who quickly flashes a badge and claims to be a police officer. When in doubt, make him or her wait while you call the police station or other authorities to confirm the person's identity. And don't worry about insulting the person by being careful.

Be cautious when anyone shows up at your door trying to sell you something when you have not asked them to visit. Ask for references and check them very carefully before agreeing to let the party into your home and/or purchasing anything from them.

If you have to pay to enter a sweepstakes, don't play. Mail-order sweepstakes are frequently rip-offs.

If you think you need home repair work or require lawn maintenance, consult a trusted friend or family member for a referral, and check references before hiring anyone. An honest businessperson will be able to provide you with the names of clients. Be wary of anyone who wants a large deposit before any work is done. Demand that all estimates be given in writing with complete details of the work to be performed. Get several quotes before you have work done. Who knows? You may find out that you didn't need repairs done after all.

Plan ahead. Consult your attorney to make arrangements to protect your assets and to assure that your wishes are carried out if you become incapacitated. Select a responsible person to have power of attorney to prevent a swindler from taking advantage of you or your relatives.

When hiring a care giver for an elderly relative, get several references and check them out carefully.

What Can You Do if You Think You've Been Defrauded?

If you suspect that an older relative or friend (or yourself) has been a victim of a scam, report it. No one should worry about feeling embarrassed or foolish. Contact the fraud unit of your local police department, the Better Business Bureau, the state attorney general's office, the Federal Bureau of Investigation, the department of consumer affairs, the U. S. Postal Service, or the Federal Trade Commission.

CHAPTER 11

Business Bunco

Perhaps the easiest mark, the richest mark, and the mark least likely to prosecute a con artist are rolled into one: a company. A con artist might write checks against a company's accounts, send firms phony invoices, purchase products for a business that it does not need, produce counterfeit products that look like theirs, take advance fees for loans that are never made, place phony price tags on their merchandise, illegally redeem millions of dollars worth of coupons, sue them for sexual harassment that never happened, sue them for injuries on the job that never happened, illegally gain access to their computers, or set up phony mergers, and the list goes on.

Companies are infiltrated and attacked by their employees, suppliers, customers, competitors, stockholders, accountants, lawyers, partners, and lenders. When a company does uncover a con artist in its midst, management may hesitate to prosecute because they fear adverse publicity, and they don't want to encourage others to do the same thing. A company may institute new procedures and/or security measures. Although policies, procedures, and check-and-balances systems may help to protect companies and minimize losses, the con artist usually finds a way to take advantage of the very systems meant to keep them out.

For example, an insurance company's policy to pay claims quickly—a surefire winner in the customer service arena—can result in increased payments of fraudulent claims. A company's new purchasing policy requiring multiple bids on purchases in excess of five thousand dollars can give management a false sense of security. The purchasing agent can set up phony businesses or simply create three companies.

According to policy, he selects the lowest qualified bidder even though the lowest bidder (which he'll make sure is him) is five times higher than a legitimate supplier would have been. The company orders the merchandise, the purchasing agent ships the goods or provides the service requested, and then bills the company using a new, corporate name. The company pays the bill and the purchasing agent has earned not only his regular salary but made a big "bonus," too.

The most invaluable tool in the battle against business fraud is knowledge. If a company knows its weak spots—where it may be infiltrated, how it may be attacked—it can protect itself. To that end, I will present a comprehensive review of some of the most common methods used by con artists to fleece companies.

Nothing can help companies protect themselves if they fail to check employee and vendor references, and do their homework before entering into any business relationship with someone new. Many a con artist was arrested while working in a position of trust involving substantial amounts of money. Many of them had extensive criminal careers that would have been detected with a simple background check. Impostors are hired every day to purchase products and services for companies, to manage corporate funds and assets, and even to guard precious commodities. One of the best safeguards is a stringent hiring practice that includes background checks and reference verifications.

Of course, with the onslaught of wrongful termination lawsuits came corporate gag orders on employee performance. If a company tells a human resources manager who is attempting to verify employment that the employee in question was fired for theft or embezzlement, the company stands a good chance of being sued for impeding the employee's ability to get a job.

Because of the modern-day obstacles imposed by what some may label an overly protective legal system that makes it nearly impossible to verify employment and reasons for termination, the human resources staff may need assistance. If the human resources staff is small or nonexistent, I suggest hiring employees through an employment agency so that it can assume the legal responsibility for conducting in-depth background checks as necessary. Contact a good private detective agency when hiring for sensitive key positions so that a thorough background check will be made.

A good human resources manager can compare credit and employment data against information supplied by colleges, professional organizations, personal references, and an applicant's past co-workers. In recent years it's become popular for applicants to "fudge" or downright lie about their educational background, but that's one area that can be verified. Contact heads of any professional organizations to which an applicant belongs to verify membership, and question level of involvement. A thorough screening will usually uncover any inconsistencies between fact and fiction, if they exist. When inconsistencies are discovered an experienced human resources manager or recruiter may simply need to address them with the applicant. Or he or she may need to obtain municipal and superior court documents (if the applicant was convicted of a crime) that are public record. While workers compensation claims may not be considered or held against a potential employee, a history of similar work-related accidents may give cause for more extensive inquiries.

How much a company learns about a potential employee (or other individual or business) depends upon how much time and money it can or wants to spend. If management finds out later how disruptive and costly an employee who's a con artist can be, I am confident that most companies would have decided to err on the side of caution. And having to train a replacement is expensive. When hiring an employee, no matter what level in the company, always remember the saying, "Penny wise and pound foolish."

Toner Phoners

There are as many variations of this telemarketing scam as there are companies invoicing one another. The most successful goes something like this: The caller pretends to be conducting a survey and asks for the office manager when he calls. He then states that he is conducting a corporation-wide survey for the president of the office manager's company on ways the firm can save money. What kind of fax machines do they have? How much fax paper do they buy and when do they buy?

What kind of copiers do they have and how much copy paper do they use per month? Which kind of computer paper do they prefer? The office manager is thanked for his time and told that he will receive a copy of the completed survey.

Frequently the call will come in during the lunch hour, when the purchasing agent is out. The telemarketers have been known to say that their computer is down and they need the name of the purchasing agent, the type of copiers in the office and their serial numbers, and the make and model of the fax equipment. Or the caller may say that he has office supplies at a tremendous cut-rate price because his delivery truck has broken down nearby. He may have found out the name of the regular supplier and say that "Fred" asked him to call. The caller may say that there's a going-out-of-business sale, so the party on the other line needs to make a commitment to a certain number of containers of toner, or rolls of fax paper, or whatever he's pitching, because supplies are going fast.

Always they put on the pressure to order on the spot, to make a commitment before the bargain prices are no longer available. Unfortunately, many employees have taken the bait.

Of course, when the products arrive, they're inferior in quality and usually overpriced. The invoices also state, "All sales are final." These office supply schemes, perpetrated by telemarketers known as toner phoners and paper pirates, cost American businesses at least $50 million every year, according to the National Office Products Association and upwards to $350 million annually, according to retired U. S. Postal Inspector Larry Johnson, who spent many years investigating telemarketing crimes.

Often, the victims aren't aware they've been scammed. Yet even when the victims discover they've been caught up in a con game, the unscrupulous telemarketer is often beyond legal reproach because of his or her carefully scripted sales pitches.

Phony Invoices

Often, a "survey" such as the one just described precedes another kind of scam. Instead of questions about office supplies, the caller queries the unsuspecting staff member about the kind of yellow page listings the company has, its cellular phone bills, the facsimile equipment usage, or perhaps the company's 800 numbers.

One to two weeks later, the accounting office receives a piece of paper resembling an invoice for yellow page advertising and one for 800-number directories or maybe fax number directory listings. The "invoices" (which are actually solicitations for business) arrive at just about the same time of month accounting usually receives the real invoices. The supplier names are almost indistinguishable from the names of the vendors the company uses. National Yellow Pages becomes National Yellow Pages, Inc.; GTE Cellular becomes GTEC. Most of the phony invoices include the name of the office manager as the answering agent for the company, which lends an air of authenticity.

The invoices are paid. Not until the legitimate invoices arrive does anyone become suspicious. By that time, the checks have been cashed and the swindler is long gone. Although it's virtually impossible to determine actual losses incurred by businesses from phony invoice schemes since so many go undetected, estimates go as high as $100 million annually.

According to U. S. Postal Service regulations, any bill, invoice, or statement of account due that is really a solicitation must have one of the following disclaimers in 30-point type or larger if it is mailed:

> This is a solicitation for the order of goods or services, or both, and not a bill, invoice, or statement of account due. You are under no obligation to make any payments on account of this offer unless you accept this offer.

or

> This is not a bill. This is a solicitation. You are under no obligation to pay unless you accept this offer.

Bankruptcy Fraud

Companies need to sell their products in order to survive. In a highly competitive world there is a lot of pressure to sell more products. Sometimes the pressure is so great that companies let down their defenses against con artists.

Operating alone, Mylo Hughes formed and bankrupted over 100 corporations. The fifty-five-year-old con man would form a corporation under a name similar to a well-recognized name. For instance, instead of RCA, he would call his company RCA Electronics; instead of GE, he would use General Electronics, a subsidiary of GE New York. He called business credit reporting companies and volunteered credit information so that when companies called to verify the credit history of a Hughes company, they basically were told what Hughes had told the credit reporting firm.

The stage was set. Hughes would order small quantities of supplies on thirty-day credit terms. He paid the minute he received the invoice. Each month, the orders increased. By the third month, the corporate mark was positioned for the fall. Hughes would call up, excited about a major order, and demand a huge delivery. "Send me all that you have," is always music to a sales manager's ears.

The sales manager would push the credit department to release the goods. After all, Mr. Hughes had paid on time and his credit report was solid. When the goods arrive Hughes sells them at wholesale to an unsuspecting distributor out of state on a cash basis. Many times this soft-spoken, unassuming businessman in his gray pin-striped suit talked suppliers into shipping large quantities of goods as often as six times before he would file Chapter 7 in the federal bankruptcy court. Indeed, his corporations were bankrupt: With suppliers' invoices piling up, all of the goods sold and the money going into his pocket, the corporations had all debt and no assets.

When Mylo was finally apprehended by federal agents for bankruptcy fraud, he was able to produce a cashier's check for $1 million to bail himself out; then he jumped bail. A con man can get pretty rich pretty fast when he runs a business with no overhead and all of the revenue goes into his pockets. Variations of this scam fill our bankruptcy courts every day. Many times con artists will take advance fees to produce a product or perform a service and then bankrupt their company.

Purchasing Agent Con

It is not uncommon for the Mafia and other organized criminals to use their influence to arrange for an associate to get hired as a purchasing agent, or blackmail a purchasing agent to cooperate with them. And many purchasing agents have willingly conspired with con artists of every imaginable affiliation to systematically steal from their companies. Many of these cons go undiscovered because most companies have no system of checks and balances to detect them when they happen.

Some of the cons are very simple. For example, all a purchasing agent has to do is disqualify all vendors except the one with which he really wants to do business. He can disqualify the competition because they are too new or underfinanced, produce inferior quality products or cannot meet specifications or required delivery dates. The purchasing agent can wait to place the order so that other vendors are disqualified because no company other than the one he has already selected can make the delivery dates. Of course, the selected vendor knew immediately that he was going to get the order, so he started to produce the goods long ago.

The purchasing agent places an order with his partner to ship products he does not need or more parts that he does need, and always at very high prices. The invoice is paid and the co-conspirators split the profits. Many purchasing agents will set up a distributorship with ten, twenty, or perhaps as many as a hundred suppliers. Each distributor marks up the cost 100–200 percent, and the purchasing agent purchases everything the distributorships sell at highly inflated prices. As a cover, the agent tells the employer that the purchasing department prefers to buy from one single source in order to get maximum volume dollar purchase discounts or because it saves a great deal of time.

More complex purchasing schemes involve purchasing agents who set up phony supplier companies, order supplies and services that the company does not really need, or authorize payment yet never receive the products or services at all. Sometimes purchasing agents have been known to receive goods through the back door, take the receipt notation out of the computer and resell inventory to their company by simply sending a second, maybe even a third invoice for the same material. If a purchasing agent teams up with an accounts payable manager or others in management, there is no limit to the possible financial losses that may ensue.

A major grocery store chain located in Eden Prairie, IL, hired Herbert M. Michaelson to purchase merchandise for them. He immediately set up a bogus company named Preferred Promotions to resemble one of the store's divisions. This scam was set up in 1982 and wasn't uncovered until 1991. Michaelson convinced suppliers to overcharge the chain by 3–8 percent. Most of the overcharged items were nonfood products like antacids, soap, polish, detergent, and over-the-counter medications. Upon payment, the suppliers paid Preferred Promotions a commission equal to the overpayment. The checks from the suppliers were deposited in a Preferred Promotions account at National City Bank in Minneapolis, MN. The FBI found $415,000 in the account when they finally caught up with Michaelson.

According to his indictment, a major Cincinnati-based company and a large Chicago-based firm were two of the suppliers that had agreed to Michaelson's proposition. Companies in five other states were reportedly involved in the scam. Michaelson was charged with mail fraud, interstate transportation of stolen property, and money laundering in a twenty-five-count indictment.

Con artists like Michaelson can operate in one place for years and earn millions of dollars while reporting an income of thirty-two thousand dollars to fifty-five thousand dollars per year. One daring con artist in New Jersey told his co-workers he had won the lottery, which explained how he was able to drive a new Porsche and live in a million-dollar house. Of course, the only lottery he ever won was landing his job as a purchasing agent.

Fraud Against Cashiers

Improperly trained cashiers in department stores and restaurants are favorite marks for streetwise con artists. Probably the simplest of all cons against cashiers involves change. "I gave you a twenty-dollar bill, not a five-dollar bill. Please give me the correct change." Many times the con man will have an accomplice standing behind her who pretends to be just another customer. The accomplice immediately agrees that a twenty was given to the cashier. Usually, change for the larger bill is made. A con artist who is successful ten out of fifteen times can earn a pretty good living.

If the cashier places the bill to be changed on top of the drawer, making the denomination of the bill impossible to argue, the con artist may use a double-switch technique. Asking for change for fifty dollars, he'll receive two twenties and a ten; he'll then give the cashier the ten to pay his bill. After palming one of the twenty-dollar bills he received from the cashier and placing another ten in his hand, he'll then insist that he just gave the cashier a twenty-dollar bill. Sleight-of-hand tricks are commonly used by magicians as well as con artists. While the process sounds complicated, it's not difficult to learn to palm money.

One con artist in Denver, CO, went from store cashier to cashier, and with each cashier's help, counted the money in each of the cash drawers. Telling the cashiers that accounting was taking a midday audit, he took the cash from each drawer and produced receipts for the amounts he took. It was not until the end of the day, when accounting asked about the meaning of $24,176.04 in receipts, that the con was discovered.

When a cashier and an accomplice work in concert, the losses can be astronomical. In one scenario, the accomplice brings two-thousand-dollars' worth of merchandise to the cashier, who rings up a ninety-dollar sale. Sometimes, cashiers will ring up five dollars in sales and give change for a one-hundred-dollar bill. Carried on over weeks, months, or years, these conspiracies can result in substantial losses. Bartenders are notorious for pouring drinks, collecting money, and not ringing the sale up in the register.

A favorite retail store scheme is to switch price tags on merchandise. If a con artist is working in concert with a cashier, he can buy dozens of items at one time without fear of detection. Moving a ten dollar price tag on a shirt that is on sale onto a one-hundred-fifty-dollar jacket can net a con man an easy $50 on the black market. If he can move this merchandise ten times a day, he can earn an easy fifteen thousand dollars per month, tax free.

A Florida couple suspected of using sophisticated equipment to put false price codes on merchandise in stores around the country were charged with attempted swindling. Lester J. Marshallton and Janet L. Marshallton were charged with conspiracy to commit theft by swindle from K mart and with possession of a theft tool. According to prosecutors, the two were part of an organization that traveled around the country applying falsified bar code labels to items, buying them at reduced prices and later returning them for full credit.

According to Richard Hodsdon of the Washington County, MN, attorney's office, "This is a big business, not just a cute little crime." The Marshalltons were probably clearing six thousand dollars to seven thousand dollars per day. For example, the Marshalltons might apply an altered bar code to a trolling motor worth $189. The altered sticker would carry a sale price of $18.90.

Following their arrest, the couple indicated that they would look for the least-experienced cashiers and buy the item for the lower price. After leaving the store they would create a falsified receipt from their base of operations in Florida. The merchandise would then be returned for the original price.

The scheme fell apart when Janet Marshallton tried to return security lights to a K mart outlet and a sharp clerk spotted what appeared to be an odd zip code and asked Marshallton to repeat her address. Store manager Tom Trevers said, "She couldn't even remember the phony address."

Marshallton fled, but police arrested her and her husband a few blocks away. The Lincoln Town Car they were driving contained merchandise from various discount stores, along with maps identifying Target and K mart stores in the area, a notebook listing discount stores throughout Minnesota, a device used to print price code stickers, and a book with code numbers for various items.

Embezzlement

To embezzle, according to *The American Heritage Dictionary,* is "to take (money, for example) for one's own use in violation of a trust." In most cases embezzlers have been given too much authority. If one person has transaction authority, bookkeeping responsibility, and cash collection ability, the stage is set to allow the embezzler to function undetected for months, even years.

A trusted payroll accountant can add five or ten names to the payroll without detection in a company with several hundred employees. The people would be as fictitious as the phony bank accounts set up by the accountant; with ten phony I.D.s in hand, the accountant goes from one bank to the next, opening up bank accounts. The checks are then deposited into these accounts. The accountant withdraws money from each account and deposits it in his personal bank account under his own name. Companies without a checks-and-balances system in payroll and firms with a high turnover of personnel are most susceptible to payroll fraud schemes. This type of scheme could go undetected indefinitely if the payroll employee works in collusion with someone in the human resources department.

Accountants or others in trusted positions who have check writing authority can issue checks to phony suppliers, pocket cash transactions, divert incoming checks to personal bank accounts, submit phony expenses for reimbursement, and, with enough scheming, take money from just about any account while making the transaction appear normal by simply altering the books.

Priscilla Marvin, an attractive forty-year-old bookkeeper, lived in a modest home in Streamwood, IL, and drove a midsize car that was ten years old. A well-liked individual and a trusted employee, Priscilla possessed a positive attitude in the office and good work habits; she was always on time and never missed a day at a well-known bottled water company. But the company's routine external audit uncovered a pattern of deception and a lapping con game (skimming funds from payments temporarily in order to cover previous skimming) that surprised those who knew Marvin. Between December 1988 and May 1989, Marvin took cash from the daily deposits and replaced it with checks from other collections. In less than six months she pocketed $52,865, according to a Cook County, IL, indictment.

The New Western Bank lost $1.2 million, according to another indictment involving a trusted employee, Nicholas Planken of Setauket, NJ, and an alleged accomplice, Harry Samuels of New Rochelle, NY.

According to the indictment, fifty-one-year-old Planken was employed as a vice president of marketing for the bank. According to Assistant District Attorney Barbara Kornblau of Nassau County, Planken used his trusted position to authorize the placement of advertisements in Harry Samuel's newspaper, *The Trade Union News*. According to an internal audit, the advertisements were never actually run, and *The Trade Union News* did not exist. Both Samuels and Planken were charged with grand larceny based on the false advertising invoices that were submitted by Samuels and paid by the bank after being approved by Planken.

In addition, the district attorney's office suspects the bank may have been defrauded further by the partners, who allegedly padded bills and split the proceeds afterwards. This embezzlement scheme allegedly went on between 1983 and 1992.

A con man on the inside of a company can requisition a piece of equipment, such as a personal computer, and list his accomplice as the designated supplier. The accomplice overbills the company for the computer and then splits his profits with his man on the inside.

Diane A. Mickelson, a forty-six-year-old marketing expert, was hired by a large medical equipment company to conduct market surveys. Diane authorized two hundred fifty thousand dollars to be paid to three market survey firms over an eleven-month period. All three companies were owned by her. Ramsey County, MN, District Judge James Campbell gave Mickelson a three-year prison term for her deception and ordered her to pay restitution. The sentence was later reduced to six months in a county workhouse. That equates to almost fourteen hundred dollars a day.

Joseph Monreal, a marketing director for a large midwestern brewing company, admitted that between 1983 and 1987 he made two hundred ninety-five thousand dollars by authorizing payments to Hispanic community groups that did not exist and for events that never took place. He received kickbacks and wrote checks for events such as the "Citywide International Softball Competition," which never took place.

Many embezzlers are turned in to authorities by friends, relatives, and estranged lovers, yet many are not found out until they quit their jobs, are hospitalized, or die. One Connecticut comptroller for a large advertising agency embezzled over $3 million during his fifteen years with the company. Only after his death did his scheme become known. Interestingly, it took just two weeks for the new comptroller to uncover it.

Product Counterfeiting

You can buy a "Rolex" watch on the streets of Manhattan for less than fifty dollars today. You can buy a "Picasso" print for ten dollars and a pair of "Nike" shoes for twenty dollars. The only problem is that none of these products are authentic. Merchandise counterfeiters make clothing, perfume, auto parts, videotapes, and even fishing reels under well-known names, thus depriving the real manufacturers of their rightful profits. Furthermore, if the buyer really believes that she bought a genuine article and it does not work properly, it reflects poorly on the real manufacturer. These knockoffs are largely manufactured, formulated, and sewn in Taiwan, Hong Kong, and Russia in sweatshops that do not produce quality goods.

According to the International Trade Commission, foreign counterfeiting costs American companies around $50 billion per year. That's an estimated 1000 percent increase since 1982. The International Anti-Counterfeiting Coalition places losses at an even higher $61 billion. Approximately a quarter of a million jobs are lost in Detroit's auto industry alone due to auto part knockoffs. When jobs are lost taxes are lost, and everyone suffers.

The income losses to counterfeiting and the huge expenses of enforcing intellectual property rights make it hard for many firms to recover. This is especially true where research and development costs are high but the resulting product can be easily and inexpensively reproduced. For example, the pharmaceutical industry reports that to get a new product launched could take up to ten years and up to $160 million, but the resulting product may be readily duplicated by a good chemist.

False Advertising

Like people, companies can fall victim to false advertising. With some pretty sophisticated advertisements, con men target companies for advance fee loan scams, or they may advertise the ability to raise large sums of money with limited and general partnerships. For upfront fees of anywhere from ten thousand dollars to one hundred thousand dollars, they may promise to raise between one hundred thousand dollars and $5 million. After receiving payment they always find numerous reasons not to raise the money, such as "the company is too new," "the products are not exciting enough," or "the owner of the company has a poor credit history."

You may have seen the following advertisement (or one similar to it) for reverse mergers with an existing public corporation. The ad reads: "For $25,000 and ten percent of the stock, a company that wants to go public can do so in less than 30 days." The alternative for most companies is one year of preparation time, stringent securities requirements, and one hundred thousand dollars in legal and accounting expenses.

While many companies want the use of public money, few understand the problems of being a public company, including the reporting laws, the filing costs, and the possibility of inheriting preexisting problems from the public company into which they reverse merge.

Typically, a company that has gone public but essentially has outlived its usefulness will consider allowing a company with good sales revenues and interesting products (like exciting, newly patented devices) to fold its assets into the public shell and then turn management over to the new company, as the Board of Directors simultaneously resigns from the public shell.

Many times the public shell has a horrible history. It may have marketed drugs that killed people, phony gold mine interests, school buses that had brakes that failed, or other such products. The promise of being a public company with public investment may be very inviting to the owner of an undercapitalized company, who may be willing to pay a large fee in order to accomplish the merger. Many con artists make a significant income by taking advance fees to set up a reverse merger and never actually set it up.

Miscellaneous Business Con Games

Not as popular, but certainly just as devastating as other corporate cons, are cargo thefts arranged by employees strategically placed in a company's shipping department. Often employees are found stealing customer lists, supplier lists, equipment, inventory, and supplies to set up competitive businesses while working at their regular jobs. Foreign agents have been known to sell joint-venture participation in foreign companies that do not exist. This joint-venture con is a very popular con game in Russia.

Coupon Fraud

Millions of dollars are paid out for coupon redemptions when the product was never bought. Not all coupon scams are perpetrated by your typical con artist but by retail store managers, senior citizens, and even church groups. On April 15, 1992, the Rock Valley Christian Church's congregation and friends of the Rock Valley Christian School in Rock Valley, IA, were confronted with rebate fraud charges.

A visitor entering Rock Valley, population around twenty-five hundred, would immediately notice a huge billboard east of town that proclaimed, "Get High on Jesus." Liquor is frowned upon and church attendance is inordinately high. This town was, in fact, a hotbed of fraud. The Christian school was running a highly organized racket that had swindled some of America's best-known manufacturers out of more than five hundred thousand dollars. For years the church congregation pooled their rebate coupons, proofs of purchase, and cash register receipts, sorted them accordingly, and then submitted them for cash. The proceeds went to the Rock Valley Christian School and the Reformed Christian School.

Families would bring in their empty cereal boxes, empty bottles, and proof of purchase coupons, which were then matched with cash register receipts reflecting those items. Even the local grocery store merchants encouraged the deception by donating cash register receipts. At frequent get-togethers, church and school volunteers sorted out the box tops and universal product code symbols that manufacturers required, then saved them for use with rebate offers. Once matched with cash register receipts, participants agreed to let the group use their name and addresses to submit the rebate claims. When checks arrived the recipients turned them over to the church.

Not all of the townspeople turned over the "loot" to the church. Some senior citizens supplemented their Social Security income with their rebate checks, while other townspeople quit their jobs entirely.

Known as the "cash for trash" program, the fund-raising drive was enormously successful, raising at least two hundred dollars for every man, woman, and child in the northwest Iowa town. There was just one problem: It was downright illegal. Using the U.S. Mail to defraud is a felony. If these individuals—many of them grandparents—had read the small print on the redemption coupons, they would have known that the transfer of rebate rights is prohibited.

The coupon caper might have gone unnoticed forever if the inordinately high rebate response rate hadn't come to the attention of the rebaters. The average response rate nationwide was less than 5 percent; the Rock Valley zip code boasted a response rate of 62 percent! Accustomed to dealing with fraud perpetrated by unsavory characters, investigators from the Postal Service, Proctor & Gamble, and General Foods were a little surprised to find almost an entire town's populace participating in a major conspiracy to defraud.

One Rock Valley citizen, Bradley Kleinwolterink, was receiving nearly one hundred dollars per day. He had shared in the "cash for trash" drive for more than ten years, using dozens of name variations. Kleinwolterink turned his checks over to his mother-in-law, Alta Groeneweg. Alta and her sister, Betty Hoogendoorn, along with thirty of their relatives, used the names of ninety-six children, grandchildren, and great-grandchildren. Coupons were even redeemed in the names of unborn children. Alta and Betty actually purchased their own cash registers so they could match up coupons with cash register receipts on a daily basis.

In exchange for no criminal prosecutions, all participants of the coupon fraud caper agreed to cease and desist. They agreed to adhere to all rebate rules and would no longer manufacture false names and addresses or make their own cash register receipts.

Foreign Investment Scams

Swindling foreigners has become an art form in some countries. In Nigeria, it's become a billion-dollar enterprise. Hundreds of U.S. businesses received a letter from Lagos, Nigeria, offering crude oil at two dollars and fifty cents a barrel below the market price. The letter went on to say that 4 million barrels were available. One businessman from Houston was asked to wire-transfer $15 million in advance after meeting with the state-owned oil company management, high-ranking military officers, and the central bank of Nigeria, which provided the businessman with documentation. He even saw the tanker supposedly carrying the oil. The businessman lost his entire investment when he later discovered that the oil had been sold to someone else. The bank, of course, denied any wrongdoing and blamed the swindle on greedy and gullible foreigners.

Carl J. Smith, a CEO with an export company in Hesston, KS, was offered a $4.6-million oil contract with the Nigerian defense ministry. Even the U.S. Department of Commerce thought the agreement was real, according to Smith. When he arrived in Nigeria to sign the deal he was told by his Nigerian contact to pay a bribe of five thousand dollars. He asked the American embassy representative what to do. According to Smith, "They told me to throw my belongings into a suitcase, walk out of the door, and take a taxi to the embassy, where I would be safe."

Be especially cautious with foreign business opportunities, as con artists work in every nation of the world. Sometimes businesspeople trust foreigners more than they trust people from their own countries. I suspect that is because we let our guard down and attribute many of our suspicions to cultural differences. But, a con is a con in any language of the world.

Putting Up A Good Front

According to Assistant New York State Attorney General Rebecca Mullane, "The women who get into big-league con games in business are sociopaths—extraordinarily manipulative and predatory."

Sharon L. Jelovchan of Casper, WY, had just about managed to buy and loot two state banks before she was caught. She was able to set up a company that netted hundreds of thousands of dollars in fees for insuring the completion of $31 million in contracts awarded by the U.S. Departments of the Army and the Interior. Her company created phony certificates of deposit (CDs) to prove its financial responsibility as a bonding company.

Jelovchan purchased several one-thousand-dollar certificates of deposit from a San Francisco bank. Using sophisticated photo-scanning equipment, she was able to rearrange the numbers so that it appeared as if she had $10 million certificates. Even the paper was the same.

Rather than risking discovery by cashing in the phony certificates, Jelovchan and her associates created a "front" company; with the CDs, Jelovchan established her creditworthiness and her ability to pay any claims against contractors who could not satisfactorily complete their work. She accepted bond orders and charged commissions for issuing the bonds to contractors.

Jelovchan planned to take over two state banks that were in bankruptcy so that she would really be able to juggle around finances. Her scheme unraveled when one of her associates was apprehended while fraudulently trying to solicit money in the name of a United Nations agency.

Postal Inspector Kent Powell commented on Jelovchan's reaction at being arrested: "She was mad she got caught—just furious—and that was her only reaction."

Selling Your Business

If you're thinking about selling a business, be especially careful. John Durocher received three years in prison for bilking business owners out of their businesses, but there are a lot of con artists like him who graduated from the same school of scoundrels.

Calling himself a consultant and an investor with unlimited funds, Durocher advertised in newspapers and on radio for business owners who wanted to sell their companies. He was particularly interested in distressed businesses. As fast as people responded, he presented them with a ninety-day buy-out agreement. Then he would take over the business, put any payments that came in directly into his pocket, and not pay the suppliers. By the end of the ninety days the business was completely bankrupt, and John Durocher merely walked away. He bought dozens of Video Pizza businesses and ran them into bankruptcy. Durocher had two prior convictions in Minnesota and one prior conviction in Texas on similar charges.

How Can You Protect Your Business?

Given the scope of the potential for business fraud, it would be impossible to create an all-inclusive list of how any business can protect itself in each and every possible situation. Explicit protection tips regarding computer cracking and scams related to telemarketing, credit, banking, loans, investments, insurance, and work-at-home opportunities are offered in the chapters covering those topics. Here I've set forth certain general guidelines that can be adapted to the specifics of virtually any business:

Establish specific policies and procedures and incorporate them into a formal manual available for all employees. Make sure it includes ongoing checks-and-balances systems, particularly in accounting, purchasing, finance, payroll, and tax departments, to insure that your company does not turn over its profits to a con artist. Make sure all employees know the company's policies regarding purchasing, receiving, returning goods, and payment. Orient all new employees to the policies and institute mandatory refresher courses for existing employees. Periodically review the procedures and update as necessary.

Check employee references carefully and thoroughly. Credit and background checks should be instituted for especially sensitive positions, such as key financial jobs. A private investigator may provide invaluable assistance; consult your attorney for referrals.

If it appears that a complete check of a candidate will take longer than expected (i.e., you have to wait for a college transcript) and you're really pressed to fill a position, consider filling the job with temporary help. Or hire the candidate on the contingency that continued employment will be based upon a favorable outcome of his or her reference checks.

Develop programs to prevent and deter fraud, not just correct problems after they've occurred. Train all employees—not just managers—to identify areas where the potential for fraud is great.

Consider hiring a security consultant who is an expert in your field to assist you in developing a solid program. Spell out exactly what you want done by what time and get an estimate of the costs of his services in writing.

Teach your employees to be alert, cautious, and suspicious.

Split responsibilities between employees wherever necessary as a checks-and-balances measure. Never give one employee the authority to routinely order goods, accept shipment, and authorize payment. Never give one employee payment authorization, document control, and check writing authority.

Cross-train employees in trusted positions and regularly rotate assignments.

Routinely reassign purchasing agents to different suppliers and product categories.

Establish a company policy that prohibits employees from answering any surveys or questions regarding office supplies, payment cycles, personnel, or other proprietary information over the phone unless they personally know the individual or firm or unless prior authorization has been given by a manager. Train your employees to ask the caller to submit his or her questions in writing. If they are not certain how to handle such a call, they should refer the caller to the appropriate department head.

Make loss prevention a priority in your business by thoroughly training your employees in crime recognition and loss prevention. New employees should be formally oriented to all corporate policies and procedures. Procedures should be reviewed at least annually and a refresher course should be taught to existing personnel every six months.

Only order merchandise with written purchase orders. Never place an order on the phone unless you're absolutely sure the person and firm with whom you're dealing are reputable, and follow up with a written purchase order.

Don't accept delivery of any shipments without being positive that proper authorization was obtained to order them.

Don't accept C.O.D. shipments.

Inspect all shipments in a timely manner in case you decide to reject the merchandise and give reasonable notice to the vendor.

Keep the cargo shipment schedules, routes, and trafficking confidential. Whether the information is stored on a computer or in a file, limit access to this information to those employees who really need to know. Install telephone equipment in all vehicles, so the driver can call for help when needed. Paint your company name, address, and phone number on all vehicles, so if one is stolen, the police can quickly spot it.

Be wary of customers who systematically increase their purchases, then ask for a large credit approval.

Only accept exchanges or returned merchandise for refund with a sales slip.

Never accept a check from an individual without proper identification and a check guarantee card or authorization. Use a check verification service.

Routinely check the geographical origin of returned coupons. If an inordinate number of coupons show up from one zip code or town, investigate for possible coupon fraud.

Clearly identify all company property.

Seriously evaluate the physical security of your business as it relates to employee traffic. If possible, all employees should be required to enter and exit through one doorway. This will reduce pilferage and illegal removal of company documentation. If cost-effective, install a security system that requires each individual to use a card-key for access. Such a system allows for programming access on an individual basis as needed, so that only certain employees have access to the payroll area, human resources file rooms, computer room, etc.

Conduct periodic accounting audits using internal and external auditors.

Watch for telltale signs of embezzlement. These include frequent customer complaints that accounting information is inaccurate; customer invoices that are frequently mailed late; check registers that are not reconciled; frequent inventory shortages; and a large percentage of bad debt written off by the accounting department.

Discourage paying advance fees for anything. If you feel you have to pay an advance fee, place it in an escrow account.

Don't jump at any business opportunity that requires an immediate response, promises extraordinarily high returns, and uses high pressure to get a response.

Educate your sales force, distributors, manufacturers, and even consumers about product counterfeiting. Be on the lookout for counterfeit merchandise in retail businesses, trade shows, flea markets, or being sold by street merchants. Carefully check all returned merchandise for counterfeits. U.S. Customs assists businesses in protecting their intellectual property rights if they are registered with the proper agency. Consult a patent attorney with any questions.

Do business with new suppliers only after their existence and reliability have been verified. Be especially cautious when dealing with foreign entities; if problems arise, it's usually harder to track down and prosecute a company when it's offshore.

When you're considering selling your company, do your homework. Have your attorney and your accountant review all materials and give you an opinion. Get all conditions and promises in writing. Thoroughly check out any individual or business wishing to purchase your firm. Take your time and follow up on all references and resources.

What Should You Do If You Think You've Been Defrauded?

Contact the National Office Machine Dealers Association (NOMDA) for help in combating fraud by paper pirates and toner phoners. It offers guidelines for handling unordered goods and ordered goods that are inferior or overpriced. They also provide a sample letter for revoking acceptance of delivered goods.

If it appears that one of your firm's patents has been violated, call your patent attorney and the U. S. Customs Service.

Report any suspicious behavior to the proper authorities. This may include your attorney, the police, the Better Business Bureau, the district attorney, the state attorney general, the F.B.I., or the Federal Trade Commission. Contact the U.S. Postal Inspector if the mail was involved in the transaction.

CHAPTER 12

Medical and Health Fraud

Medicine. Fraud. What do those two words conjure up for you? Do you have visions of Dr. Kickapoo's magic elixir? Laetrile treatments? Phony prescriptions scribbled out by corrupt doctors? Drugstores holding hands with drug dealers? All of these are a part of what we'll call medical and health fraud. The stakes are high in this arena, not just in terms of the millions of dollars conned, but in human terms as well.

The Face Behind the Con

Nancy is forty-two years old. She has a loving husband, two rambunctious teenage sons, a large extended family, and metastatic breast cancer. For four years Nancy has fought her disease on a daily basis. Almost always, it seems, there is a chemotherapy regime. Some of these treatments last for weeks, others for months. Nancy has forgotten what it was like to have hair or to enjoy the taste of a good dinner. Her name has made its way onto some unfortunate lists and she has started receiving unsolicited brochures from cemeteries, funeral homes, and certain life insurance companies urging her to plan "for that inevitable 'someday.' " Her fear is running high. Her energy is running very low.

Life-threatening disease is a family affair. The cancer touches Nancy's family in a different way, but touches them just as deeply. One could truthfully say that the whole family is suffering with cancer. Now, four years into what seems to be a losing battle, Nancy's doctor offers her another option—an experimental, high-dose chemotherapy treatment that has been tentatively shown to reduce tumor growth in 15-to-20 percent of protocol patients. It also carries a 10-percent mortality rate. Her physician makes it clear to Nancy that this is the last option medical science currently has to offer her.

The frighteningly poor survival/remission percentages, along with the lengthy required hospital stay and hideous list of side effects scares Nancy away from the chemotherapy protocol. For the first time since her illness began Nancy and her husband begin sifting through all of the articles sent to them by well-meaning family and friends about "cancer cures," "alternative therapies," and "experimental treatments." Nancy will do anything to live. With some hard work and luck, she may find her way to peace, hope, and acceptance through these next few months. But to do so, she'll have to maneuver through a maze of scams, quacks, and cons of the most pathetic, unscrupulous sort.

Scamming the Sick

What are the hooks medical scam artists use against the very ill? The most powerful include two of the strongest motivators known to humankind—time and survival.

Time is the monkey on the back of desperately ill or chronically sick people. The terminally ill know they have a limited amount of it. Chronically ill people may spend most of their time in varying states of pain. All of us live on borrowed time, but those of us living in the land of the healthy also live in the land of fantasy that says that death and chronic pain only happen to *other* people. Terminal patients have been told not only that death will be happening to them but, frequently, *when* it will be happening, give or take a few months or weeks, and *how* it will be happening.

Many scams are built on a false sense of urgency: the "only one left—buy now" approach, or "this deal miraculously became available today and will be gone tomorrow" game. The sense of needing to move quickly is a key sales technique used to make potential buyers move *right now*.

Scams perpetrated against the very sick and hurting automatically have powerful motivators working for them. The con artist can sit back and relax. These people know what urgency is. They are living it every minute of every day.

In no situation are people more vulnerable than when their lives— or the lives of loved ones—are at stake. Scams against the sick can be incredibly flimsy. No hard sell is needed here—just the promise, however bizarre, of a cure. People who would never dream of running to Tijuana at the advent of a catastrophic illness may run there and much farther as their medical options run out. Physicians have been known to run that far, even though no one would seem to be more immune to the promise of a miracle cure than a medical doctor.

If someday your life is on the line and you know it, you will instantly and permanently become a different person. That is what gut-level survival instinct is all about. You will do things you never thought you would do, and you will think things you never dreamed you would think. Some of these changes are good; some aren't. For every desperately sick person who delicately hones his or her courage and merit against the sharp edge of survival, there are a hundred others who abandon reason in the face of serious illness. For instance, if your doctor had granted you three weeks to live, and someone in a white lab coat were to tell you that drinking diluted Chlorox three times a day and burying a toad under the oak tree in your backyard at midnight would save you, the new you just might consider it. People say to themselves, "What have I got to lose?" Scam artists know this and count on it.

Americans spend an estimated $30 billion on quack products or treatments annually. A recent list of the FDA's top health frauds included:

* Fraudulent arthritis products
* Cancer clinics promising miracle cures
* Phony AIDS cures
* Weight-loss scams
* Bogus sexual aids and aphrodisiacs
* Cures for baldness
* Anti-wrinkle creams and other "fountain of youth" potions

According to a recent survey, 10 percent of the approximately 38 million Americans who have used a fraudulent product in the past year has been harmed by the side effects.

If Looks Could Kill

Close on the heels of survival and greed, beauty remains a prime motivator, jetting people into the arms of scam artists. Sometimes dissatisfaction with what nature gave you can be deadly. A woman wanted in Los Angeles for injecting women with silicone to alter their facial features is accused of disfiguring and injuring many of her clients.

The accused, a Korean dressmaker, operated out of her shop and left a trail of clients behind her with severe lung problems and necrotic facial parts. Because the silicone injections are so expensive, these clients were willing to put their faces on the line in hopes of coming out of the dressmaker's door looking like movie stars. It was a deadly gamble for many. In medicine, as in most of life, you really do get what you pay for. If you want fuller lips, crinkle-free eyes, and a turned-up nose, it takes a medical doctor to make these changes a success instead of a disaster.

The Doctor Dealership

Many scam artists set themselves up as "doctors" in miracle cure clinics. It's easy to dummy up a fake diploma and set up shop among the four hundred thousand legitimate, board-certified physicians in the United States, and it's astounding just how long a scam of this sort can remain undetected and in full operation. In a small town in Minnesota, Harold Snailem, the owner of a farm-equipment dealership, was investigated for operating a fraudulent doctor's office. For months no one in the small farming town questioned why a farm equipment store would be taking on patients, or why a farm equipment dealer was dabbling in some pretty unusual forms of medicine. An estimated four hundred patients came from several states and spent many thousands of dollars to be cured of high blood pressure, cancer, colds, aches, and pains.

Treatments, which ranged from eighty dollars to one hundred dollars, included the use of a "Target V" machine and a "Light Ray" machine to diagnose and treat cancer. Some patients, who apparently were healthy enough to recognize manure when they smelled it, complained loudly to local authorities. A physician brought in to inspect the curative devices found nothing more than boxes equipped with heat lamps, strobe lights, and fancy dials. Investigators estimate that the clinic made tens of thousands of dollars on these machines and treatments. The patients were lured to the "clinic" with brochures and pamphlets distributed at shopping malls and businesses. Many were terminally ill people who were looking to the clinic as a final hope.

The dealership operators were charged with medical fraud and operating without a medical license. The clinic "doctors" were investigated and authorities found that this wasn't the first time nor the first state in which they had practiced medicine. And I use the term "practice" very loosely here.

Common sense should tell someone not to seek out serious medical care from a pamphlet handed out at a shopping mall, but common sense can take a back seat to the chance for survival.

A Loss Of Ethics

Sometimes doctors lose their objectivity along with their sense of ethics. Dr. Cecil Jacobson, who was instrumental in introducing the prenatal test of amniocentesis to the United States, was convicted of 52 counts of fraud and perjury. The prosecution alleged that he fathered seventy-five of his patients' children by inseminating them with his own sperm while telling them that the donor was anonymous; he was found guilty of only four instances. The other guilty counts were for perjury and mail, wire, and travel fraud used to deceive his patients.

Like a common con man, this revered doctor preyed on the desires of couples who were desperate to have children. Surprised at the guilty verdict, Jacobson commented, "I'm in shock, I really am. I spent my life trying to help women have children."

Higher Authority Scams

Although the hope for medical healing may dwindle, spiritual healing is always an option. Spiritual healing attracts not only the sick but the emotionally troubled as well. There is also a large population of spiritual seekers or New Age enthusiasts in this country who are particularly attracted to spiritualists, "channelers," or healers of many varieties.

A theatrical con artist can wake up in a bed of roses with this type of scam because just about anyone with some creativity and an active imagination can pass as a gifted spiritualist or faith healer. If the practices of these people seem bizarre, dangerous, or lewd, how can you argue with someone who says her instructions comes from a "higher authority"?

A faith healer in Los Angeles County was arraigned on charges of rape, grand theft, and lewd acts on a child. A self-proclaimed folk medicine artist and healer, Oswald C. Ardmore performed candlelight healing rituals during which he asked females to disrobe for spiritual examination and "cleansing." Members of one family gave the man thousands of dollars in cash, jewels, and personal property for these "healings." Authorities are looking for more of his alledged victims.

True practitioners of folk medicine, often called medicine people, shamans, or *curanderos*, are finding more respect and acceptance in genuine healing circles these days. Certain hospitals with heavy populations of Native Americans or Mexicans now have a shaman or *curandero* on staff to offer this specialized healing to their patients. These medicine men and women do not accept outrageously high fees for their services. Sexual acts are not part of their healing repertoire. And, most importantly, they do not promise cures.

Mexico—Land of Sunshine and Medical Miracles

If you are really sick, someone will most likely send you information on quick cures to be found in Mexico. This information frequently comes along with bus schedules for shuttles that will whisk you across the border for a tour of U.S.–supported medical facilities. U.S.–supported medical facilities in this case mean they are supported by U.S. patients with U.S. dollars—lots of them. Because the medical climate is considerably looser in Mexico, many doctors specializing in alternative treatments choose to set up practice there. Many people who aren't doctors set up clinics there, too.

Winding your way through these exotic alternative options can be a very tricky business. Some of the centers focus on nutritional healing and use herbs, vitamin injections, homeopathy, acupuncture, and a wide variety of experimental treatments that are not authorized in the States. Some of these centers are clean, caring, reasonably priced, and cause no harm. There are some voices in the more legitimate alternative medicine community that speak neutrally of some of these Mexican centers.

But there are other centers, too, run by pseudo-doctors, eccentrics, con artists, and flat-out loonies. Sometimes it isn't as easy as it might seem to tell the difference.

James Gordon Keller, a former water-softener salesman, operated the Universal Health Center in Matamoros, Mexico. For many years he treated cancer patients from all over the world with a prescribed three-week intensive regime of vitamin injections, live-cell therapy, a macrobiotic diet, and huge daily intravenous injections of L-Arginine, an amino acid. All of these treatments have been touted to help or even heal some cancer patients some of the time, if you believe in anecdotal evidence, which is, for the most part, the only large body of evidence available to proponents of adjunctive or alternative medicine at this time.

Keller claimed to be able to diagnose and treat cancer with a Digitron D Spectometer—a sort of biofeedback machine—without using CAT scans, blood tests, biopsies, or surgery. His treatment program ran up to three thousand dollars per patient.

Keller was arrested in 1991 after Mexican authorities turned him over to the U.S. authorities, who had charged him with running a profiteering scam through the Matamoros clinic. Keller had been associated with another clinic in Mexico, as well. He could have received more that fifteen years in prison for his crimes, but more than three hundred friends, relatives, and former patients showed up in court to plead for leniency for Keller and to talk of his compassion and caring. He was sentenced to eighteen years in prison, but was given a suspended sentence for all but two years. Keller is prohibited from ever again treating anyone for cancer or any other illness, and was issued a twenty-thousand-dollar fine. The judge, while sternly rebuking Keller's ability to cure cancer, admitted that the treatments brought comfort and consolation to the terminally ill. The judge believed that Keller was truly committed to what he was doing. Keller had spent years working with cancer patients. Money was not his motivation. Still, he was not a licensed doctor, and he was not regularly curing large groups of patients.

Hospital treatments for terminally ill cancer patients run considerably more than three thousand dollars for three weeks. In fact, a staggering percentage of the total cost of treating a terminally ill patient is exhausted during the patient's last six weeks of life. There are those, including Keller's still-living patients, who would say that Keller did no harm, and certainly was no less successful with his treatments than conventional medicine would have been.

The Texas government, which likened Keller to a snake oil salesman, isn't among them. Texas said, in effect, that if you take your car to a mechanic to get it fixed, it doesn't matter how strongly the mechanic believes in his skill if in the end he can't fix your car. Texas said, simply, "Show us a license, then show us some results."

AIDS Profiteering

Of the illnesses that deeply scare people, none is more likely to incite absolute hysteria right now than AIDS. Con artists are delighted to use fear to their advantage and are cashing in on the current AIDS crisis in a multitude of ways.

Sleaze comes in all forms. Theodore Burandt was fined two thousand seven hundred dollars for selling AIDS "disclosure forms" to the public for $22.95 each. The forms were not, of course, legally enforceable, and misrepresented the public risk of AIDS. Purchasers were encouraged to submit the forms to their doctors or other medical professionals to find out if they were infected with the AIDS virus.

Scams of this sort are a sleazy attempt to cash in on the tremendous amount of public misunderstanding about the AIDS virus. Buyers of this fake form evidently didn't consider why on earth any health professional would sign such a form. Most sensible people, health care workers included, would not be inclined or eager to share their medical histories with you, and are certainly not required to.

To date, the only known cases of doctor-to-patient transmission of AIDS are against a former Florida dentist who is known to have infected a small number of his patients. Experts still contend that the risk of this sort of transmission is extremely small. Public fears about this risk are, however, extremely large. Hence, the success of opportunists like Burandt.

The AIDS crisis has also spawned a new wave of scams promising big returns on life insurance policies for terminal clients, including AIDS patients. Unlike legitimate firms that buy AIDS patients' policies and provide needed cash for medical expenses, these ghoulish, unlicensed investments offer potential investors a "menu" of dying patients, complete with life expectancy data and medical history. Investors are then invited to, in effect, speculate on these terminal patients and their insurance policies. One firm's promotional materials for this program promised a "return better than 20 percent annually" with "big bucks" for little or no risk.

Because these firms aren't registered, and are illegally selling securities, there is no way to verify the information provided to prospective investors, or to know if the patients even exist.

AIDS patients are desperate for funds to carry them through the last costly stages of their illness. Many have had their medical coverage dropped, have lost or been fired from their jobs, and have been left with no means to care for themselves. Legitimate insurance firms have instituted programs in which patients with "living benefit" plans can receive their benefits to defray hospital costs and living expenses while they are still alive.

Some patients with no living benefit options sell their policies to brokerage firms for a discount, and the firm becomes the beneficiary. Funding for these programs comes through the stock market, or from tapping large institutional investors for capital. A firm's profit comes from the difference between the discounted price of the policy and its full value received when the patient dies. Patients are not auctioned off in the public marketplace.

Despite the potential for fraud and misuse, this program is providing some much-needed hope for some very sick people. Leave it to the con artists to find ways to abuse, and profit from, any new opportunity, regardless of its origins or intent.

Scamming the System

Although the most macabre aspects of medical fraud involve heartless scams against the sick and dying, the most lucrative aspects involve scams against the institutions and systems set up to administer to the sick and dying. Hospitals, private insurance companies, Medicare, Medicaid, pharmacies—all are bilked of millions of dollars annually.

Health care is an $800-billion-a-year industry. Authorities say annual health care fraud now totals $80 million. How does this happen? It's frighteningly easy. Let's start with a small, unsophisticated case.

Larry has had a rough job history recently. Layoffs have forced him into four different jobs in six years. Luckily for Larry, each of the firms that hired him had a good health insurance plan. Because the firms were midsized or larger, federal law enabled Larry to carry his health coverage at the going group rate for up to eighteen months after he lost each job. When Larry found new work he dropped his Consolidated Omnibus Budget Reconciliation Act (COBRA) coverage by ceasing to send in monthly checks, and he took on the new company health plan available to him. He went through this process of taking over monthly COBRA payments at the group rates, finding new work, taking on a new health care policy, and dropping COBRA four times.

Larry dutifully changed over his health care information with each of his doctors as he took on new plans. But his dental receptionist forgot to bill his new company for a regular exam. Out of habit, she billed his old insurance company. And the bill was paid in full even though Larry had made no monthly payments to this company for over a year. She told Larry all about it.

That got Larry to thinking. After all, it had been a rough few years. He photocopied copies of his last doctor visit, complete with costs for urine tests and X rays, and sent copies to all three of what he thought were defunct policies. And he was paid back his customary 80 percent by all of them. Larry then made copies of every old medical bill he could get his hands on, mailed them to all his old insurance companies, and is now making money every time he goes to the doctor. It seems that insurance companies can find it as hard to let you out of the system as it often seems to get in.

Let's take this a step or two further.

Pharma-Scams

Major Pharmacal Company, through the eager assistance of its president and a handful of enthusiastic employees, managed to squeeze $7.2 million in phony billings from Medi-Cal. For three years the Southern California company received payment for supplies that were supposedly delivered to elderly and disabled Medi-Cal patients. Major Pharmacal submitted hundreds of claims, without the beneficiary's knowledge, for items that were never ordered and never delivered. Although the president fled to the Philippines to avoid arrest, he returned to the United States to face a maximum of ten years in jail and a ten-thousand-dollar fine.

Cons like this happen because Medi-Cal is facing the same problems as many state and federal insurance programs: few resources available to investigate a tremendous amount and complex diversity of fraud. The potential for abuse in the medical system, which is at best a loosely controlled system juggling many billions of dollars, is enormous.

X-Raid

Con artists perceive where there is a lot of money at stake and the controls are loose and sloppy as an invitation to help themselves to the larder. A lucrative case in point involves a health-care fraud scam that conned nine hospitals and three X-ray film manufacturers out of $10 million dollars in New York and New Jersey. The fraud charges included fleecing medical centers through phony billings, kickbacks, and theft. Those involved included hospital officials, employees of the X-ray filmmakers, and X-ray film distributors. Those indicted face sentences of up to ninety-five years and fines up to $3 million. Yet this scam was peanut-sized compared to the potential for fraud in the medical sector.

Scams-on-Wheels

Fraud and abuse account for an estimated 25 percent of Medicare spending. That translates to a cost of about six hundred fifty dollars for every Medicare recipient. With annual Medicare spending topping $100 billion, the most common abuse is billing for services that never happened.

A fraudulent mobile diagnostic testing service operating in the Los Angeles area billed Medicare and private insurance companies for $1 billion in phony claims to approximately fourteen hundred California insurance companies. Rolling lab scams, as they are called, outfit vans with a variety of medical equipment. The vans are then driven to convalescent homes, gyms, athletic centers, churches, and shopping malls, where people are invited to sign up for a variety of free tests and examinations. Then huge bills were sent to Medicare for tests people didn't need or were never performed. For this kind of scam to be successful, someone on the scam team must be a doctor willing to sign off on the necessity for these tests, or a person willing and able to forge a doctor's name to the test request slips.

The $1-billion ticket on this scam makes its perpetrators, two Russian-immigrant brothers whose case is still pending, part of the largest medical insurance fraud case in U.S. history. But officials say they are aware of at least a half-dozen similar operations they suspect are just as large. So far, they haven't the funds to fully investigate.

The most disturbing aspect to this case is that even after Medicare stopped paying the phony bills, the lab rolled on another five years to fleece private insurance companies while Medicare was readying its lawsuit. A recent study by the Inspector General found that Medicare patients of doctors with financial interests in labs receive 45 percent more clinical services than other Medicare patients.

Lack of funding, a failure to adopt a more aggressive policy toward fraud investigations, and a system full of crook-enticing loopholes leaves state and private medical insurance programs with little defense against an enormous array of big-ticket cons. Con artists prosecuted for defrauding a particular insurance company can turn around and work their con on other unsuspecting companies as soon as they can get out on bail, and it may be years before the system can catch up with them again.

Not So Ultra-Sound Scam

It would seem that anyone who can lay hands on some sort of medical equipment can go into business against medical insurance companies. Javed Khan, owner of three New York City ultrasound companies, paid off friends and relatives to pose for hundreds of unnecessary sonograms. He would then forge a referring physician's name onto the sonograms, pass them along to a real radiologist to be "read," and then mail them on to a radiology billing company, which would bill Medicaid. The government reimburses one hundred twenty dollars for sonograms that have been read by a radiologist or cardiologist. Khan would receive huge kickbacks from the billing company.

Khan and his accomplices received $9.5 million from the government in a two-year period. He split the money among doctors, the medical billing company, and others. In the end, Khan collected more than two hundred thousand dollars for his efforts. He was sentenced to just three months in prison.

The Invisible Patient Con

Fraud opportunities in medicine are so tempting that physicians often succumb to the lure. Dr. Mondrian Salomon, a Florida physician, was indicted on Medicare fraud charges for writing prescriptions for people he never treated. Medical supply companies would then pay him fifty to one hundred dollars for each prescription, which they used to charge Medicare for one hundred twenty-five thousand dollars worth of supplies presumably sold or rented to elderly patients. One firm received five hundred dollars from Medicare for nerve-stimulating devices costing the company fifty dollars, according to the indictment. Salomon allegedly also made claims against Medicare directly as well, charging for phony house visits, examinations, and medical evaluations.

In a more gruesome twist, doctors have been known to write prescriptions and order equipment for patients long dead. Sometimes the bills for these services are inadvertently sent to the patients' families, who are often the whistle-blowers for these types of cons.

Golden Pill Fraud

There may well be more drug dealing in the medical industry than you ever saw on "Miami Vice." Federal authorities are cracking down on a nationwide pharmacy scam involving phony drug billings to Medicaid and private insurers, and on diverter fraud, in which prescribed drugs are sold back to the pharmacy for a fraction of their cost and resold to the public (also known as "playing the doctor"). Most of the pharmacies involved in the scams to date have been small, family-run businesses. U.S. authorities believe this sort of drug scam is extensive.

In another pill twist, federal marshals recently seized an East Coast pharmacy that had supposedly been robbed of all of its drug inventory and awarded a commensurately large insurance settlement. But based on the pharmacist's own records taken by the authorities, hundreds of prescriptions continued to be filled before his drug supply was ever replenished.

A new, high-ticket scam in New York state that requires the participation of pharmacists and physicians is costing taxpayers an estimated $150 million a year in Medicaid fraud. The scam works like this: Drug abusers are given prescriptions for narcotics or even uncontrolled substances by unscrupulous physicians. The physician then bills Medicaid for an unnecessary patient visit. The drug abuser turns around and brings the prescription to an accommodating pharmacist. The drug abuser has two options at this point. He or she may fill the prescription and sell it on the street, or sell the prescription back to the pharmacist for a steep discount off the full cost of the drug. The pharmacist can then sell the drug back to the pharmacy for resale, or sell it to bulk drug buyers.

Drug abusers are even finding a specialty niche in this scam, and are focusing on noncontrolled drugs, which are much more difficult to trace than narcotics. Certain drug dealers, known as non-men, specialize in these drugs, which are sold on the street, to bulk dealers, or to ready markets in underdeveloped countries.

If this sort of operation seems far removed from where you live and appears to be the stuff that TV movies are made of, think again. Are you a taxpayer? Do you have private medical insurance? Then every scam, every investigation, comes out of your wallet. Do you know anyone who doesn't complain about the high cost of medical care? Don't fool yourself. Fraud is a big part of it.

Vampire Scams

Equipment, drugs, and fake prescriptions aren't the only items con artists buy and sell in the medical trade. Human blood is a hot item. Sajid Kanchwalla, a young New York State lab employee, and two salesmen, Sabaj Ali Khimani and Rafiq Hirani, were convicted on charges of selling blood for use in needless lab tests and charging the testing to Medicaid. Kanchwalla was sentenced to six months and $19,209 in restitution. Khimani and Hirani received sentences of six and twelve months, respectively, and were ordered to pay $18,309 in restitution.

The salesmen made a commission on the blood sold, and the lab employee collected kickbacks from the lab. This operation resulted in thousands of phony billings to Medicaid, and the arrest of twenty-five people, including three doctors, who were involved in the scam.

Buy Now—Pay Never

No one enjoys paying medical bills. Some people simply don't. Picture this: A woman walks into a dentist's office for her scheduled appointment. She is eager to have her teeth fixed so that she will look dazzling for her upcoming wedding. She gives the receptionist all the necessary information: where she lives, the name of her insurance company, her phone number, her name. After having her teeth reshaped and recolored, she excuses herself for a moment to get her checkbook from her purse. She is never seen again. Dental workers say this happens all the time.

Some play for larger stakes. A California con artist with a long train of fraud and impersonations behind him found himself in the need of coronary bypass surgery, and brought his larceny to bear on the medical establishment. Hiring a New Hampshire phone answering service to pose as "Boston Mutual Health Insurance Company," he instructed the bogus company to answer any inquiries about his insurance and to authorize up to sixty thousand dollars for the bypass surgery. The man went ahead with the surgery in a Mission Viejo hospital; the "insurance company," of course, didn't pay the bill, and the man was arrested in his hospital bed.

Summary

Medicine, healing, and fraud don't happen in a vacuum. The horrendous state of the health care industry in the United States isn't the focus of this book or even this chapter and won't be addressed here; however, suffice it to say that much of the medical and health insurance fraud that occurs does so because it's easy to get away with. And it's easier to overcharge a government program than an individual. Many of the types of frauds discussed appear to be a reflection of today's runaway health care and insurance costs, state and federal budget cuts that make it difficult to investigate and prosecute fraud, and rampant improper payments for phony or padded bills.

But there is a human element to these sorts of cons that is painfully distinct from any other sort of scam people perpetrate against other people. It is a subtle difference, but put simply, lives are often at stake. People are afraid. There is a trust and a caring that people offer up openly in the presence of physical crisis and pain. In the case of certain types of medical fraud, lives can be destroyed or even lost when this trust is broken.

Ironically, the time in our lives when we may be most unable to make rational, clear-sighted decisions is the time when these decisions are required of us. Watch out for the cons who are counting on you to be confused and desperate. Keep your head, and keep away from bad medicine.

How Can You Protect Yourself Against Bad Medicine and Quackery?

If any of this makes you stop and think, *good*. That's the first step in sound decision-making. It's *your* responsibility to protect your health and well-being. Consumers must become more vigilant in the fight against health fraud. At present, only 7 percent of successful prosecutions are the result of consumer complaints.

Rather than deal with how we should "eliminate" our health care woes (that's another book in itself!), I'll focus on what you as an individual can do to help sort out the cons from the cures and the hype from the healing.

First, evaluate yourself as a patient.   Before you select a doctor or a particular therapy, be honest about what you expect from a doctor or practitioner and treatment program, and what you're comfortable with. Don't select a therapy simply because it's the current rage or because it worked for your cousin.

Select a primary physician (an internist or family practitioner) who's reliable and trustworthy before you become ill.   He or she should be board certified or board eligible and affiliated with a teaching hospital.

Communicate openly with your doctor and inform him or her of your concerns or problems.

Never be afraid to ask for proof of licenses and certifications.   Be sure the credentials match the treatments. For instance, chiropractors can also offer massage in some states, as these treatments are somewhat related. But your chiropractor shouldn't be performing fertility testing. And don't assume that all diplomas or certificates are equally valid. Contact your state education department for assistance.

Ask for references, preferably from former patients. A legitimate healer will give them to you. Ask how many people with your ailment this person has treated. If he or she responds with, "I can't let you talk to any of my former patients—privacy issues, you know," look elsewhere. Has he or she ever published any papers on the subject in which you're specifically interested? If so, obtain copies and have them reviewed by a couple of other professionals. Ask these questions whether you are seeking standard treatment or are about to begin a regime of raw liver juice and coffee enemas (a standard of treatment at one well-known Mexican facility since the 1950s). Be critical and evaluate the responses objectively.

Beware of any product or treatment that you are not able to research.

Avoid any practitioner who asks for payment in advance of treatment or who pressures you to commit to a treatment without allowing you adequate time to investigate and research your options. Be very concerned if you hear lines such as, "If you delay, even this treatment may be too late. You have to act NOW."

Never underestimate the value of second and third opinions. Get several opinions from other professionals, but not those who've been recommended by the first doctor.

Be wary of faith healers. If you are seeking spiritual healing and guidance, go in with your blinders off. Beware of someone who tells you that there is just one way of handling your problem, requests for large amounts of your money or property, secrecy, us-against-them language, or orders to recruit other "disciples." This is the language of cults.

Be wary of methods characterized as "alternative" unless all other methods have been exhausted.

If you decide to work with someone in alternative medicine, choose a healer who's been trained in conventional medicine as well, and one who's associated with an accredited hospital or clinic. The association may help provide accountability.

If any doctor or other professional makes unrealistic, overenthusiastic promises of a cure based on what you already know about your case (and you owe it to yourself to know a lot), run. Miracles do happen, but don't bet your life and every dollar you have on one. Hope has a different tone than desperation. A legitimate healer of any kind will be hopeful but honest.

Check with your doctor before you agree to purchase any medical equipment from anyone. And don't accept or use any equipment simply because someone offers it to you free.

Avoid the use of questionable "gadgets." The best you can hope for is an enhancement of placebo effects; the worst is an adverse reaction.

Always evaluate the potential harm of any product or treatment as well as any benefits. If you are using a product or taking treatment about which you're unsure, make sure you scrutinize its impact on your body; watch for new symptoms, side effects, or any abnormalities. Evaluate your progress realistically, and report any problems to your doctor immediately.

Beware of any product or promotion that implies that you won't have to pay for anything because Medicare or Medicaid will cover it.

Beware of any practitioner who exudes excessive warmth and sensitivity. Quacks are often charming and project a feeling of greater than usual concern. Unfortunately, they often are able to produce testimonials from adoring patients who'll swear by this treatment. These are signs of a good sales technique and not necessarily part of a good "bedside manner." If the main qualities a smooth-talking practitioner exhibits are sincerity and understanding and he or she professes to have *all* the answers, find someone else. Don't trust your health to a salesperson.

Beware of any doctor or practitioner who claims to have a special machine or formula that's not available or used by other professionals. Medical journals are the first to report the results of studies on bona fide treatments. If the only place you can find "evidence" of the effectiveness of a drug or treatment is the back pages of a magazine or in a television infomercial, chances are it didn't pass scientific evaluation (if there ever was one).

Beware of anyone who makes blanket statements that accepted treatments (such as X-rays, surgery, or drugs) always do more harm than good.

Stay clear of any doctor or other medical practitioner who claims that others are persecuting him or are afraid of how much he knows. Run if you hear lines like, "The government and the AMA have been suppressing this cure. That's why we have to keep our work secret."

Be wary of advertisements that sensationalize a product or treatment and its results. In 1989, Cho Low Tea was advertised in over one hundred U.S.

newspapers as a natural cholesterol-reducing product. The tea didn't even exist.

Beware of any claim of easy ways to take off weight and tone you up effortlessly. There is no magic pill, diet or device that will take the place of self-discipline to eat right and exercise sensibly.

Don't assume that the advice of talk-show hosts or other celebrities is expert advice.

Beware of products claiming to be the cure for everything from headaches to hangnails. If a product has been on the market or in use for a while and advertised widely, the chances for fraud are smaller than for newer products with less publicity.

Speak to those who've already had the treatment you're considering. How did it work for them? What were the side effects?

Don't let despair color your ability to make sound judgments about your health care. If you're concerned about the efficacy of the treatment you've tried, discuss it with your doctor. If you wish to get another opinion, consult a noted physician who's an authority in the field. Don't abandon the scientific approach or feel that you must resort to the nearest charlatan, quack, or faith-healer.

Know that there is no such thing as an entirely safe medicine.

Always check and double-check any bills you receive. Often office visits or treatments are billed twice or three times, and sometimes treatments or examinations that were never given appear on a bill. It's up to you to keep the insurance companies and doctors' bills straight. Unscrupulous medical clinics and medical practitioners are doubling their compensation by sending bills to their patients with a notice reading: "Please pay invoice. Your insurance company will reimburse you," when, in fact, the insurance company pays the medical professional directly.

What Can You Do If You've Been Conned?

There needs to be a more effective way of preventing incompetent physicians and medical imposters from hurting patients. Unfortunately, it's usually *after* the damage has been done that patients or their families realize they've been conned. If you are suspicious of a medical practitioner or healer you or a family member have stumbled upon, trust your instincts and report it to your local authorities.

Medicare beneficiaries who suspect claim fraud should ask for a review of the claim by the insurance carrier handling Medicare claims in the vicinity. Look for the name, address, and toll-free phone number on the Explanation of Medical Benefits form; you can also check *The Medicare Handbook,* which each beneficiary receives, for the phone number.

Individuals with private insurance who suspect claim fraud should contact their carrier and ask for a review of the claim.

Contact the department of consumer affairs, the state attorney general's office, the state medical licensing agency, and the National Council Against Health Fraud (NCAHF), which offers a list of unproven and fraudulent treatments, some of them potentially dangerous. The NCAHF also can refer you to an experienced lawyer, if necessary.

If you believe that a doctor, hospital, or other health care provider has performed unnecessary services or has fraudulently billed you, call a toll-free hotline reserved specifically for reporting fraud at the office of the Inspector General of the Department of Health and Human Services: (800) 368-5779. If you're in Maryland, the number is (800) 638-3986.

If a harmful or bogus product was offered or ordered through the mail, contact the U. S. Postal Service.

If a product is mislabled, misrepresented, or otherwise harmful, contact the Consumer Affairs and Information division of the Food and Drug Administration.

Any false or misleading advertising or labeling should be reported to the Federal Trade Commission (FTC). Also contact the newspaper, radio station, magazine, or television station running the ad.

CHAPTER 13

Real Estate Scams

Not too many con artists are selling Florida swampland these days. Modern-day real estate scams make those ten-thousand to fifty-thousand-dollar investments in alligator land seem like small change by comparison. When one puts crooked real estate salespeople together with buyers and appraisers, banks and other lenders can lose millions of dollars in the time it takes to process a few loans.

In a downward real estate market, a homeowner watches his or her equity diminish uncontrollably. Many times the homeowner ends up owing more money than the house is worth. Homeowners who have suffered through real estate slumps are prime targets of "creative" salespeople. They may offer to buy your home for a price close to your asking price, except that they only pay 30 to 50 percent in cash, with the rest in a note payable in a few years. In the meantime, these unscrupulous dealers may sell the house and disappear with the quick profit, or they might borrow 80 or 90 percent of its market value, default on the loan, and leave the bank to take possession. In either case, you end up with only a small percentage of what your home is worth. Desperate people make easy targets.

I hope you have the opportunity to read this chapter before you buy, sell, or trade property, or lend money on a real estate deal. Few things are more devastating than to lose your home to a fast-talking real estate con artist. Not many insurance carriers will protect you from that kind of loss.

Tricks of the Timber Trade

The Georgia Bureau of Investigations (GBI) reports scams at every level of the lumber business. Groups of con artists rent homes in rural areas that have heavily wooded acreage. They strip the land of its trees, sell the land to the timber dealers, and vacate the homes. When the landlord stops by to collect late rent payments, barren land and an empty house are all that remains. Ten-acre parcels of heavily wooded land can yield ten thousand dollars to twenty-five thousand dollars in timber sales.

To add insult to injury, these same con artists will allow other criminals to dump tons of worthless used tires on the barren land. Now the owner has to locate and pay someone to remove the tires. Because of their very nature, tires are almost impossible to get rid of, and people pay high prices to have them hauled away.

Sometimes con artists will offer to thin out dense forest areas in exchange for the timber, only to cut down every tree in the owner's absence. Tree cutting has been seriously curtailed in the United States as a result of conservation efforts, and a shortage of timber has given rise to illegal timber cutting and distribution. For generations, the timber industry has relied on trust, but wherever a fast buck is available, the con artists can be found.

The timber business basically works like this:

- A timber dealer buys rights to harvest a specified stand of trees from a land owner.
- He in turn sells the rights to a lumber producer or another timber dealer. This is often a paper transaction and the second buyer may not have even seen the property.
- The timber dealer borrows money from a bank to buy trees, in many cases.
- The timber dealer hires loggers to cut and deliver the logs to a mill.
- Trucks with logs arrive at the mill and are weighed. The truck

driver tells the mill where the logs came from and to whom to make the check out.

Here's how con artists take advantage of the timber business system:

- Timber dealers buy timber rights from uninformed land owners at prices below market value and immediately sell the rights at inflated prices.
- Trees that do not exist are sold.
- Loggers and truck firms deliver timber to Company A that Company B has already purchased.
- In order to borrow money, timber dealers represent to lenders that they have acres of trees on their land when in fact they may have less than one acre.
- Loggers sell logs to a lumber producer that supposedly belonged to a timber dealer but were actually cut from trees that the lumber producer already owns.
- After stripping the land of valuable timber, land dealers default on mortgage payments, leaving banks and mortgage companies holding property that's virtually worthless.

The scam artist is having a heyday buying timber rights by conning land owners out of their timber at no or low cost. He then moves in and out of the logging and distribution system, taking advantage of an industry that heretofore operated on trust. Establishing trust and confidence is the name of his game.

The Real Estate Ponzi Scam

The $3.3 million Linda Swarthout conned out of a few hundred marks cost her five years in state prison and a fifty-thousand-dollar fine. In 1983 Swarthout set up a real estate investment business in Newport Beach, CA, called Lido Homes. She urged dentists, physicians, and other professional people to buy second trust deeds on California property. She insisted that the trust deeds offered high interest and they were safe because they were backed by significant real estate in prestigious Los Angeles suburbs.

Almost none of the trust deeds were real. Swarthout typed phony second trust deeds and pocketed the money. She actually paid interest

to the original investors with new investors' money. The original investors gave her letters of reference which she used to bring in other
investors, according to Guy Ormes, the Orange County deputy district
attorney who prosecuted the case. As with all Ponzi schemes, the con
artist eventually runs out of new investors and is unable to pay the old
ones.

The fifty-one-year-old Swarthout had offered the key elements to
many a successful scam: Establish trust, offer a low-risk opportunity
with high-return possibilities, and establish a sense of urgency. She
would tell each prospect that there was not an inexhaustible supply of
good second trust deeds, so he or she needed to get in immediately
and take advantage of the opportunity, or someone else would. Sounds
logical, and for some people it's all they need to write a check and
become another con artist's mark.

A Con Artist with a Law Degree

Daniel M. Schuyler, Jr., a fifty-two-year-old Chicago, IL, attorney,
pleaded guilty to bilking investors out of their real estate investments.
Du Page County Circuit Court Judge Edward W. Kowal sentenced
Schuyler to six months in the county jail, placed him on thirty months
of probation, and ordered him to pay one hundred thousand dollars
in restitution.

Schuyler was a general partner in four real estate purchases in Nap-
erville, IL. Without the limited partners' knowledge, he obtained loans
on the properties and pocketed hundreds of thousands of dollars.

Jerry G. Feffen, one of Schuyler's investors, was told by Schuyler
that he was putting up money as a general partner. During the trial,
that was determined to be untrue. Although the Illinois Attorney Registration and Disciplinary Commission may initiate proceedings to suspend or revoke Schuyler's license to practice law, Schuyler may very
well be able to go back into the limited partnership business in less
than four months if he behaves himself in jail and gets released for
good behavior. Assuming he stole as much as five hundred thousand
dollars and serves only one hundred twenty days, he actually made
$4,166 per day for each day incarcerated. It is difficult to see why he
would feel any need to find another line of work.

Office buildings, apartment complexes, shopping malls, and other
large real estate projects are often purchased by groups of investors. A

legal entity called a limited partnership is frequently used to finance the purchase. A limited partnership typically is comprised of thirty-five or fewer sophisticated investors (which basically means they are experienced in such matters), who have a net worth of $1 million or more, an income of two hundred thousand dollars per year, and a clear understanding of high-risk investments. In other words, if an investor were to lose her entire investment, it should not materially change her lifestyle. Some limited partnerships have more than thirty-five investors, but those usually require registration with a corporate commissioner at the state level or the Securities and Exchange Commission at the federal level.

Whether an exempt limited partnership or registered limited partnership, the general partner is responsible for acquiring, managing, renting, and maintaining the property.

Some unscrupulous general partners take advantage of limited partners by front-end loading, which means exactly what the name implies. Investors put up $1 million to purchase a small strip shopping center, for example. The general partner invests one hundred thousand dollars and puts nine hundred thousand dollars in his pocket. That means the mortgage is going to be higher than what the investors thought it would be. Instead of creating positive cash flow, the property produces negative cash flow. Thus, the investors have to put up more money in order to keep the property from being foreclosed.

The higher the front-end commissions and fees, the longer it takes to earn a return on your investment. To put it in perspective, would you pay $1 million for a hundred-thousand-dollar house? Imagine paying a real estate agent a 900 percent commission on the sale of your house. Are you are willing to pay five thousand dollars per month for thirty years for a house you know isn't worth $1 million? Unsuspecting limited partners get caught up in such transactions every day.

Don't be fooled. Read the prospectus and pay particular attention to the financial projections. Most limited partnerships have a section entitled "Use of Proceeds," where the general partner describes how your money and your fellow investors' money is going to be used. If it appears to be front-end loaded, invest your money elsewhere.

Of course, good con artists won't reveal how much is really going into their pockets. They will disguise the true use of the proceeds by showing consulting service fees, subcontractor expenses, manufacturing costs, travel, and other general overhead expense. You shouldn't be surprised to find out that the general partner owns the consulting company, the subcontracting companies, and the manufacturing companies, never travels, and uses the general and administrative expenses to pay his personal phone, auto expense, mortgage, vacation travel, etc.

Many fine real estate purchases have been made by legitimate general partners who use the funds as stated and earn their fees as the investors earn reasonable returns on their investments. Unfortunately, legitimate general partners may find it difficult to compete for investors' money when con artists are offering twice the interest, more equity, lower risks, and an exciting opportunity. As always, in the end, the real estate deal that was just too good to be true is too good to be true, and the investors lose all of their interest and their principal, as well.

The $40 Million Real Estate Scam

While Daniel M. Schuyler, Jr. was serving his six-month jail sentence for conning his investors out of a few hundred thousand dollars, John B. Warburton, Jr. and three accomplices were being arrested for conning people out of $40 million in more than three hundred fifty property transactions. Warburton compiled real estate listing information from three counties in southern Florida for homes that had no mortgages. In other words, the owners had paid off their mortgages and wanted to sell their properties. That information is available to any real estate agent who has access to a computerized multiple listing database. Real estate was not moving and sellers were desperate to find buyers.

Warburton enlisted the help of Merle C. Bodine, Cynthia Warburton Smyth, his daughter, and his son-in-law, Timothy James Smyth. All were later charged with grand theft, fraud, racketeering, and conspiracy to commit racketeering.

As con games go, this one was pretty ingenious. With the promise of high returns, the Warburton clan raised money from investors; the security for their investment was the first mortgage on a house. Playing off the desperations of those trying to sell their real estate in a down market, they then offered the sellers half of their asking price in cash. The remaining half would be paid out of a real estate contract sale. The sellers would take the 50 percent payment (which came from the private investors), sign over title to their properties to Warburton, and expect monthly payments after the house sold.

This was a perfect scheme for older couples whose families had grown up and left home, leaving them in a home that was too large for just two people. They could take the fifty percent up-front payment and buy a mobile home or smaller home for cash and then live off the payments on their original house. That is how the deal was sold to the sellers. So far, so good.

The Warburtons then reduced the selling price of a house and "sold" it on a contract-for-deed basis: the person seeking to own the home would make monthly payments for five years and then pay a large balloon payment in order to own the property. In truth, Warburton pocketed the buyer's monthly payments and the first mortgage holder (the investor) foreclosed the property.

According to Michael LaFay, the assistant state prosecutor handling the case, "Mr. Warburton has mentioned privately that he never, ever planned on paying the second mortgage holders." The original homeowners were left with only half the selling price and a worthless second mortgage.

In tough times, "creative" and often fraudulent real estate financing becomes commonplace as sellers' desperation rises.

Su Casa, Mi Casa Scam

Detectives investigating this scam called it sophisticated. Five people were arrested in Miami on October 3, 1992, by the FBI for conning banks out of real estate loans.

The five men and women targeted a home, then researched whose name was on the title. One member of the ring would apply for a driver's license under the owner's name using a forged birth certificate for identification. When the driver's license came in, he would apply for loans at banks, mortgage companies, and private lenders under the title holder's name.

According to Metro-Dade detective Richard Davis, the group netted $1.4 million. Since most of the title holders were insured by Attorney's Title Insurance Fund, it suffered the majority of the losses. However, in some cases, the title holders did not have insurance, suffered from Alzheimer's Disease, or were old and feeble-minded. When they received inquiries from the lender regarding the new, fraudulently obtained loan, they ignored them only to find themselves in the street without a home and with nowhere to go.

Make no mistake about it: Con artists are ruthless, heartless, callous
people who can cost their marks everything they own—including their
dignity and their lives.

Sometimes Cons Con Cons

Marla Donato told her readers in a *Chicago Tribune* article on June
23, 1991, that she had been scammed. After she placed a mail order for
a gift, Marla was notified that she was a lucky winner in the National
Pen Sweepstakes. Her prize was five thousand square feet of unimproved land in the District of San Felipe, Baja California, Mexico.

Since she was not a Mexican national, her property rights would
terminate in the year 2019. She was informed that her property might
overlook the Sea of Cortez and was near the beach. Her only expense
was $28.50 per year for real estate taxes.

Subsequent mailings said that a swimming pool, whirlpool, and
tennis courts were going to be constructed, and scenic photographs
were enclosed.

With a few friends, Marla drove to California and then headed
south to San Felipe, where they did indeed find a swimming pool, a
whirlpool, and a tennis court. They also found a yellow seminar tent
where, Marla writes, "a tanned dude with slicked-back hair" was telling the crowd that their deeds were indeed worthless.

However, he offered to buy them for two hundred dollars each,
and told the small crowd that instead they could trade their worthless
deeds for a truly valuable lot a few miles inland with RV hookups, electricity, and septic tanks for a one-time purchase price of around $4900
plus an annual maintenance fee of $375. Or they could go to the Sierra
Highlands, ten miles from the beach, for no trading fee and the same
amount in taxes. Marla drove out of town to see the lots firsthand.

She found lots with identifying markers such as, "Earl and Jane
North of Yakima, Washington, Population 2." She walked for miles
trying to find a lot with a view of the ocean, which could only be accom-
plished by standing on the tips of her toes. Finally, she decided upon a
lot.

Marla headed back to town to stake her claim. Fortunately, before
she did she discovered that no building was allowed on the Highlands.
In fact, no building was allowed on a majority of the land the develop-

ment company had purchased because it was a federally protected Mexican bighorn sheep preserve.

The scam artist had taken a lot of $4900 payments from the Earl and Jane Norths of the world. And what about the original con artists who first leased the land? How many payments of $28.50 had they gotten, not to mention the money they received for unloading the land to the *second* group of con artists? (For additional information on sweepstakes, turn to Chapter 16, "Sweepstakes Fraud.")

The Apartment Rental Scam

After winning the confidence of Herman and Harry Frickee, two brothers running an upstanding, ethical buying service, by saying he had a connection with the state Banking Department and could get them a special license, Grafton McCandless began plying his trade.

First, he told his new acquaintances and their friends and employees about no-collateral, guaranteed-approval loans. No one seemed to question the three hundred dollar nonrefundable fee or the fact that there was always one delay or another. Until the day he just disappeared.

Grafton McCandless had also been advertising in a Brooklyn newspaper that he had apartments to rent. As calls came in from people who wanted to rent apartments, Grafton would simply scan the classified listings for apartments that met the caller's requirements. He'd agree to meet the caller at the apartment site. The impeccably groomed man would arrive a little early and tell the owner or manager that he was a real estate agent who needed an apartment for a client who was building a house or refurbishing an apartment. In his warm Caribbean accent, the friendly Grafton would reassure the owner or manager that there would be no fee for his services. He was happy to help them out and take care of his customer at the same time.

When the mark arrived McCandless showed him the apartment. If the mark liked what he saw, McCandless had the mark make out a check to him for the first and last months' rent plus a security deposit. McCandless drove directly to the mark's bank, cashed the check, and conveniently disappeared. To avoid detection by any irate marks, he'd simply revise his ad copy and rotate the ad placement into different newspapers. He even "sold" a few houses.

Unfortunately for McCandless, he made a classic mistake that the really professional con man seldom makes: He stayed around the area too long. Harry Frickee and a buying service employee spotted Grafton in the Borough Hall subway station in Brooklyn. Harry called the transit cops and Grafton McCandless ended up in jail, facing grand larceny, criminal impersonation, and criminal possession of stolen property charges.

Low-Cost Loan Deal

Thomas Ulysees Andrew bought a small tract of land with a small down payment. He placed stakes to indicate lot sizes, had an artist draw three pictures of modern, well-appointed homes, and placed an advertisement for the properties in the local newspaper. What the ad failed to mention was that Andrew had been convicted in Illinois for theft by fraud.

His ad touted a small down payment, prices half of any other builder's in the area, and extras such as lawns, driveways, cable TV installation, and remote-control garage door openers at no additional cost.

Prospective buyers flocked to see the lots. Andrew accepted down payments to hold the property, agreeing to place the money in escrow.

As you've probably guessed by now, the escrow account was never opened. Although Andrew disappeared with the money, he was arrested later and will soon be brought to trial.

Gospelgate

A chapter on real estate scams would be incomplete if I failed to cover "Gospelgate," the story of Jim and Tammy Faye Bakker and their infamous Heritage U.S.A. sales program.

Found guilty on twenty-four counts of fraud and conspiracy, Jim Bakker was sentenced to forty-five years in a federal penitentiary and fined five hundred thousand dollars for bilking his many followers out of $158 million and keeping $3.7 million from the PTL ("Praise the Lord") ministry for himself.

Telepreachers now raise over $1.5 billion annually. So it wasn't unusual for his followers to respond when Bakker offered "lifetime" partnerships for donations of one thousand dollars or more. Their donation entitled the donor to three free nights a year at the Heritage U.S.A. park for the rest of their lives. Unlike legitimate time-share programs that sell limited and restricted use to multiple owners, Bakker oversold. In fact, he sold tens of thousands more partnerships than promised, and he still hadn't built all those that he'd advertised. Much of the money Bakker raised went to pay operating expenses. In short, Bakker could not deliver on his promise, and that constitutes fraud. Jim Bakker became just another con artist. (See Chapter 15, "Fraudulent Fund Raising.")

People trusted the Bakkers, but trust is the con artist's best friend. Bakker's supporters were made up of many denominations who'd seen Jim and Tammy Faye on television pray for the sick, the disabled, and spiritually lost souls. Miracles were attributed to their close personal relationship with God.

Thousands of people mortgaged their homes, borrowed from their credit unions, banks, and relatives so they could visit the Bakkers' retreat and enjoy an inexpensive vacation and maybe, just maybe, see Jimmy and Tammy Bakker in person.

To show that greed was Bakker's primary motivation, the prosecutors presented a damaging list of some of Jim and Tammy's outrageous expenditures. The PTL ministry had once spent over one hundred thousand dollars for a private jet to fly the Bakkers' clothing from the East Coast to the West. Because the Bakkers enjoyed the smell of cinnamon rolls in their room, a hundred-dollars' worth of the pastries were purchased, only to be removed from the room without being eaten. There were endless shopping sprees, an air-conditioned dog house, and a secret suite at the Heritage Grand Hotel that had gold-plated bathroom fixtures.

Bakker's attorneys said he intended to fulfill his promises and that everything he did—including keeping two sets of books—was part of his faith ministry. His critics were chastised for their unholy attacks on the ministry. The Bakkers often acted like persecuted martyrs.

Denying his guilt did little to help Jimmy Bakker. He went the way many con artists do—directly to jail. Judge Robert Potter, known to many in Charlotte, NC, as "Maximum Bob," sent a clear message that he objected to letting white-collar criminals off with light sentences when he pronounced Bakker's heavy sentence.

The forty-five-year sentence was reduced to eight years in 1992. And Bakker continues to receive letters from stalwart fans who think he was railroaded. Ponzi, the con artist whose name has become synonymous with pyramid schemes, received letters and money when he was in jail, too. Some marks simply refuse to believe they have been taken, even after the con artist is sitting behind bars. It hurts to know you let someone take such advantage of your good intentions. For the religious zealot, it may even destroy his faith.

What Can You Do To Protect Yourself?

Only deal with licensed real estate brokers and reputable developers. Ask for references from friends and relatives. Contact your local consumer protection group, Better Business Bureau, and Office of Housing and Urban Development for any information they may have on the people and business you're thinking about buying from. The clerk's office at the local courthouse can tell you if there have been any civil actions brought against the seller or developer (unless the names have changed).

Always visit any land or property before you buy, and inspect it completely. Speak with people who are already living in the area or development. If there is an owners' association, meet with the directors and ask plenty of questions.

Beware of anyone selling land and/or property primarily as a tremendous investment opportunity.

Be skeptical of any high-pressure sales techniques that try to force you into an immediate commitment to buy.

Beware of any unsolicited phone calls about investments in land or property. Although there are many legitimate telemarketing firms and valid investment opportunities being offered by phone, there are probably just as many fraudulent telemarketers with phony real estate investments. Always ask for any information in writing. Read about the opportunity and thoroughly investigate it and the firm behind it before making any kind of commitment.

Investigate the land and property values of the area in which you're interested. Speak with a variety of real estate agents and other people familiar with the specific neighborhood or location. Make sure you ask about resale values. Check the newspaper and real estate brochures to compare prices.

Don't buy any property without first getting an independent appraisal.

Visit the tax assessment and county recorder offices to find out about property appraisals, and the planning department to find out about future plans for developing the area.

If you're interested in buying land that's not been developed, ask about who is required to put in the roads and utilities for water, electricity, and sewage.

Ask the developer and the planning commission about the existence of any zoning regulations, environmental conditions, or any restrictions that might make developing the land and/or property difficult, protracted, or costly.

Don't buy from a developer who assures you that in order to get a decent mortgage you must buy from him.

If you're skeptical about the price and payment terms, check with a local bank before making a commitment.

Examine all contracts carefully before you sign. If you're not very experienced in buying real estate, have an attorney or financial adviser look over any agreements before you sign them. Always find out about any cancellation rights you might have.

Before you buy, find out what your rights are under the Interstate Land Sales Full Disclosure Act, which is administered by the Department of Housing and Urban Development (HUD). The Act generally applies to developers selling or leasing through interstate commerce. Write to HUD to find out if a seller is subject to the Full Disclosure Act.

If you've accepted a free trip to see a piece of property, always go back home and think about the proposal before you sign anything.

Retain copies of all promotional materials you received, along with any newspaper write-ups or sales letters you received. If you find that the property you bought has been misrepresented, the materials may be important documentation.

What If You've Been Defrauded?

Complain immediately to the seller in writing.

If you're not satisfied with the response and subsequent actions of the seller to rectify the problem, you may want to speak with an attorney to find out what your rights are.

Write to your local consumer protection office, Better Business Bureau, the district attorney, or state attorney general if you think you've been defrauded.

File a complaint with the Federal Trade Commission (FTC). Even though the FTC doesn't normally address individual cases, the information about your complaint may be part of a pattern requiring action.

CHAPTER 14

Insurance Cons

Security isn't just an emotional issue these days. Security is big business in America. Most of us are well aware that life is a risky proposition, and insurance companies have worked long and hard to cement that idea in our minds. A drive in the family car is an accident waiting to happen. Sickness can easily force your entire family out onto the streets if it involves a hospital stay. And if nothing else gets you, there are always ladders, tornados, floods—almost anything at the wrong time and wrong place can injure or kill you, and if you die, what happens to your spouse, your kids, your grandkids? Where will they get the financial security they need?

From insurance companies, of course. For a fee, your insurance company can help cushion the pain of falls, breaks, crashes, fires, earthquakes, you name it. It's a jungle out there, and Americans are willing to pay many billions of dollars a year to thin out the trees a little bit. In fact, each and every year insurance companies sell almost $400 billion in new policies to Americans.

For many families, insurance bills make up the biggest bulk of their monthly expenses, outside of rent or mortgage. We can insure our homes, our cars, our belongings, our health, and our lives. Some of us even insure particular body parts, like hands, noses, and legs if we entrust our income to them. Ironically, in the case of insurance we pay out large sums of money hoping that we will never have to collect, because if we do, it means we are hurt, sick, dead, or victims of some horrible natural disaster. Many of us can't afford the insurance we need. Others of us, terrified by the unknowns in life, are sold far more insurance than we could ever use. The purchase of insurance is an emotional event, and insurance agents know that they can sell some of their biggest policies to simple, frightened people who may have just lost a not-too-distant relative, or been just a few towns away from the last killer tornado. Insurance sales literature is full of what-if innuendos. What if a tree falls on your home? No trees nearby? What if your neighbor plants a tree and it falls on your home? A lot of money trades hands on the gamble of life and the accidents it may or may not have in store for you.

Some people don't wait for accidents to happen or for that big insurance payoff to suddenly come their way: When you have businesses that are established for the sole purpose of paying off when life accidentally dumps on you, you have an entire subculture of people happy to concoct some pretty creative "bad luck." The American Insurance Association believes that 10 to 25 percent of all claims filed may be phony. That would be a *minimum* of $20 billion dollars each year. This estimate, huge as it seems, is a very conservative one that is based only on direct, accountable losses. The auto insurance industry alone believes that an estimated $17 billion in insurance payoffs is lost to auto fraud artists each year.

Who pays for this rampant scamming? You, the insurance consumer, in the form of higher premiums.

Insurance authorities claim they can't put an exact figure on the cost of fraud because there seems to be some confusion on the part of the public about what really constitutes insurance fraud. A phony accident, sure; lying about theft of certain valuables, yes. But a lot of people look the other way when it comes to "slightly" inflating the cost of a car repair, or telling their employer that their car, accidentally fender-bendered over the weekend, was hit during the course of doing business. These seemingly small infractions add up to millions nationally, and, yes, they constitute fraud. Just check your dictionary.

The *indirect* costs of insurance fraud, which are incalculable, are possibly as large or larger than the direct expenses—or benefits paid out. Attorney fees, time lost to "recuperating" employees who were never injured in the first place, court expenses surrounding lawsuits, and the costs of fraud investigation all raise the roof off the real costs of conning the insurance industry.

Everyone Gets To Be a Victim

Insurance scams are truly equal-opportunity cons. Virtually everyone gets the opportunity to be a victim. Insurers may even find that some of the funds they borrowed to run their companies just don't exist—the lender was a con looking for some lucrative investment money. Needless to say, this doesn't bode well for the strength of the insurer or the security of the insured. The extent of this problem, which is a big one, is finally receiving national attention.

Some companies that claim to be insurance providers just plain aren't. The organization is a shell, collecting hundreds of thousands of dollars in premium payments and pocketing the money.

Then, of course, there are the thousands of amateur actors and actresses who fake wrecks, falls, burglaries, even death to cash in on insurance policies that can run into the millions. Who are these people? Just about everyone from common consumers who inflate damage estimates and stage injuries to attorneys, doctors, and insurance people who manipulate an easy system. Then there are the big players: organized crime and even terrorist groups looking for large sums of money to fund their illegal activities.

Some of the scams worked on insurance companies are incredibly complex, requiring a large host of cooperating businesses and individuals all playing particular roles to ensure the success of the scheme. Others are as easy to execute as falling off a log.

When Your Premiums Support Lifestyles of the Rich and Famous

A portion of the premiums paid by policyholders must be earmarked to pay claims. Premium diversion can result when premium income is applied improperly (perhaps to phony operating costs) or when insurers simply take the money and run.

Insurance people know how the business works and know how to make it work for them, if they want it to. Frequently, insurance scams involve people in the insurance business, from sales to underwriting. Phony companies that supposedly move money from one place to another are easier to set up than you would care to imagine. And insurance companies have a lot of money to move around. Though over five thousand insurance companies control approximately $2 trillion in assets, the industry isn't policed by a federal agency but by state regulators.

A group of law and accounting firms thought it was purchasing millions of dollars worth of professional liability coverage from American International Group (AIG), one of the largest insurance conglomerates in the world. In actuality, those millions helped buy three insurance executives an estate in Philadelphia, stacks of rare books, walls of fine art, antiques, a $2-million certificate of deposit, and a bed that once belonged to Mexican Emperor Maximilian. The beneficiaries, Richard Scholl, Scholl's roommate, and Salvatore DiTripani, enjoyed the opulent lifestyle the accountants and lawyers were unwittingly contributing to until their scam was exposed and they were found guilty of fraud and insurance swindling—to the tune of $18.5 million.

It seems it all began in 1986 when Scholl was a senior underwriter for an AIG subsidiary. AIG had insured a large group of accountants and attorneys, and Scholl had sought out a reinsurance company to help to cover the policy. With policies of great magnitude, insurance companies often seek out reinsurance companies to help share the financial burden and the risk. Scholl contacted Transatlantic Reinsurance Company and senior underwriter Salvatore DiTripani. Together, the two hatched a scheme and a shell corporation, International Reinsurance Brokerage Corporation (IRBC), which they said was an intermediary of Transatlantic. The accounting and law firms were instructed to pay their premiums to this bogus corporation. DiTripani issued a reinsurance policy exposing his company to claims, but conveniently never recorded the policy with Transatlantic. The premiums started rolling in to IRBC.

This scam could have gone on indefinitely if not for the savings-and-loan crisis. AIG began an investigation to determine its level of risk during that time, and inadvertently stumbled upon the hole where the missing money should have been. This time, the bad guys were caught. The mansion, its bed, and all its goods have been sold off for $17 million, and the money has all been given back to AIG, which accepted it in a plea bargain.

The Case of the Phony Assets

In what has come to be known in the industry as the "one-second solvency test," state regulators conduct their annual audits of insurance companies. But insurance companies usually know when to expect the regulators and have ways of making sure they're issued a clean bill of health, even when they don't deserve one.

Insurers who claim phony assets frequently scam their policyholders by refusing to pay claims, often because there's simply no money. Insurance companies have been known to borrow or rent assets—or to simply lie about their assets—in order to pass these inspections. The now-defunct World Life and Health Insurance Co. of Pennsylvania claimed among its assets so-called treasury bills from an Indian nation that was actually a sandbar in the Rio Grande River.

It's estimated that over 40 percent of American insurers buy reinsurance overseas. Although insurers of large properties often use reinsurance companies for protection, more and more insurers are learning the hard way that their reinsurance companies are grossly undercapitalized because of inflated or even phony assets. This can force the insurer out of business.

Reinsurance companies are not regulated, and they assume little or no risks. As a result of the supposed assets of the reinsurer, an insurance company may decrease its reserves accordingly. Yet the insurer's risks remain the same. Before it was forced to close its doors, Executive Life Insurance Co. of California paid $3.5 million for reinsurance credits of $147 million; the reinsurers had no legal liability to pay the company's claims.

The FBI is currently investigating over one hundred twenty fraudulent insurance-company insolvencies.

MEWA Scams

Small businesses often find it difficult to acquire health insurance for employees. Many small companies have turned to multiple employer welfare arrangements (MEWA), in which several companies band together by pooling their monies to get the desperately needed insurance. Although created by Congress to help the small businessman, there is even less regulation of MEWAs than with ordinary insurers, so many small businesses have been defrauded.

A recent General Accounting Office (GAO) report revealed that from early 1988 to mid-1991, almost four hundred thousand people had failed to receive payments for MEWA claims in excess of $123 million.

When All Else Fails, Just Fall Down

"Slip and fall" schemes fall at the bottom of the pile when it comes to creative scamming, but it's surprising how lucrative they can be. Virtually anyone who needs a quick five thousand dollars to ten thousand dollars need only fall in front of some business with enough insurance to cover these sorts of "accidents." These scammers are frequently caught by the greed bug: One fall is never enough, and it's often only a matter of time before they "trip up" and file one too many claims.

One of these trip-and-fall scam artists was even bold enough to claim state disability several times while waiting for settlements on a number of her phony accidents. Another called up and offered his insurance agent some cash to be sure his admittedly phony claim got processed. These schemes and those who perform them aren't usually particularly clever.

"I Forgot to Bury the Treasure" Scam

If you have something that's worth a lot, and you want the insurance money but you don't want to part with your treasure, you can always claim it's been stolen or destroyed. However, if you try this scam, be sure that you remove the item from your home before the insurance adjuster comes calling. You would think this would be obvious, but the owner of a supposedly stolen Andy Warhol print didn't, and when the adjusters and the police showed up at his door, they found the print—insured for six thousand dollars—hanging on the wall. The owner of the Warhol print was released on six thousand dollars bail, but the print remained in custody.

The Invisible Employees

With insurance premiums going through the roof these days, some employers are looking for less expensive ways to insure their workers. One of those ways is to claim a much smaller work force than really exists, or to claim a less risky business venture than is actually being run. Workers' compensation insurers are estimating that these types of falsifications could easily be costing the industry hundreds of millions of dollars a year.

Employers are charged for the number of workers they employ, plus a fee associated with the riskiness of the work performed. For instance, in the state of Connecticut, the rate for roofers is $46.30 for every $100 of payroll; secretaries cost only about 46 cents.

In one case, a firm changed names three times: They essentially became three brand-new companies so that when they applied for insurance their record showed no previous claims and they could qualify for a low insurance rate.

Often, this kind of scam isn't detected until the claims start rolling in. The claim reviewers, at that point, need to be savvy enough to recognize when accidents are happening that are totally unrelated to the type of business being performed. When mail clerks are falling off roofs, there's a problem. When the claims outnumber the employees and their dependents, the invisible employees are at work, and the insurer has a headache on his hands.

Of course, the cost of such premium scams is passed on to customers in the form of higher rates.

Broken Alliance

"This was more than a money-making scheme," said U.S. District Judge Judith Keep. "It was a violation of the public's trust in lawyers—which is not good anyway." Judge Keep was referring to the Alliance insurance scam, which resulted in one of the largest prosecutions of lawyers in U.S. history. In all, twelve lawyers and six law firm employees and clients were convicted of bilking an assortment of insurance firms of more than $50 million in just four years.

Lynn Boyd Stites—formerly of Kumble, Wagner, Heine, Underberg, Myerson & Casey, the nation's fourth largest law firm until it was dissolved in 1988—the alleged mastermind behind the Alliance, wasn't around for sentencing. He skipped town shortly before his arraignment.

Lawyers are frequently stereotyped as a sharklike group of professionals who get their teeth into a case, any case, and chew every last cent out of it. That's exactly how the Alliance, a group of lawyers, became so successful. Targeting clients of insurance companies whose policies covered legal fees in the event the client was sued, the Alliance masterminded ways to inflate and extend cases and skyrocket the legal costs. For the most part the Alliance didn't need to stage accidents or libel suits. They just took simple cases and complicated them, and took complicated cases and managed to never get them settled.

How did they do it? Working together, it was easy. Attorneys created work and income for each other by conducting needless depositions, cross-claiming for damages against each other's clients, and even going so far as to pay kickbacks to clients so they would be content to remain defendants instead of settle the claims against them. The Alliance attorneys made sure their clients never settled out of court, and they worked diligently to add controversies and additional grievances to the cases as they went along. In certain cases, the Alliance attorneys apparently recruited plaintiff attorneys to sue their own clients.

Fugitive Stites allegedly acted as a franchiser, enlisting more unscrupulous attorneys, paying their start-up fees, and providing them with clients. For this, the prosecution alleges that he collected huge kickbacks on the insurance billings.

Some people would say this is "business as usual" for attorneys. The insurance companies that were defrauded wouldn't say that at all. The Alliance scam was unusual in its complexity and in the number of people involved who worked so effectively together. But just as many scams requiring careful coordination and mutual trust are put together by only one or two desperate or greedy people.

Bombs Away Scam

Authorities had visions of terrorist activities associated with the Persian Gulf War and Saddam Hussein when they uncovered six crude pipe bombs at a storage tank facility located just ten miles from a prominent Navy base. There was terror involved, all right, but not the kind the authorities originally feared. The owner of the highly flammable methane gas inside the tank was terrified about the sixty-six thousand dollars he owed the tank leasing company in late lease payments. The methane owner had bought the gas as an investment, but could never find a buyer. After running out of possible disposal options for the 2 million gallons of gas, including a consideration to dump it in the ocean, he decided to try and make money on his methane the only way he could—through his insurance company.

First, he doubled his insurance on the gas by telling his agent that he had a firm buyer in China, which raised the value of the gas considerably. His gas was now worth $2.7 million to him, if he could cash in on the insurance. Then he hired a couple of fellows to wire his tank and one nearby to make it look like terrorist activity. Methane is highly flammable and it all would have created quite a commotion if his plan had worked out, but some tank farm employees found the bombs and called in the authorities. His plan went up in smoke, but because of a faulty fuse the gas never did.

You Bet Your Life

A Washington baker whose life was in personal and financial shambles decided that the only solution was suicide. But the baker was not interested in dying, so he decided to stage his suicide so that his wife and family could collect on his two hundred thousand dollar life insurance policy. On the appointed day, James R. Church kissed his wife goodbye, headed for the bakery, ran his car into a nearby river, and peddled away on a bike to start a new life one hundred fifty miles up the road.

The baker found out that starting a new life is every bit as tough as fixing an old one, and what made things even tougher was when he read in the newspapers that his insurance company wasn't going to pay his wife. At this point he did what perhaps any other inexperienced but naively hopeful con artist would do. He developed—and quickly recovered from—a sudden case of amnesia and went home to his wife and kids. Amnesia is just as hard to fake as suicide, and it wasn't long before the whole truth came out. At that point, the courts decided that his life was indeed in shambles and that prosecution wasn't in order, but counseling certainly was.

Fraud on Wheels

There is something about automobiles that whets the appetite of many serious con artists. Maybe it's because the choices for payoff are so limitless. You can crash cars, steal them, use them to cause other accidents; the possibilities are endless.

One small town in Massachusetts recorded 3556 cars stolen in a recent year. That translates to a per capita rate of one car for every nine people. Many cars end up in the Merrimac River. Authorities know that many are stolen by the eight to twelve gangs specializing in car theft so that insurance money can be collected. Also, more than twice as many people in this little town are hurt in auto accidents than the national average. The town is a nightmare for insurance firms.

A Santa Ana, CA, attorney, his partner, and his wife conspired to collect millions of dollars in insurance payments by staging phony accidents and collecting on the claims to heal the supposedly injured through extensive physical therapy. Jose Jesus Toribio, his wife Adriana, and personal injury attorney Thomas Mullen were part of a fraud ring that staged more than one hundred fake auto accidents that cost insurance companies up to $1 million during a two-year period. Mullen and Toribio would pay "crash victims" to stage the accidents, then send the victims to Adriana, a physical therapist, for treatments that ranged up to three thousand five hundred dollars. Most of the clients never had any therapy. Not coincidentally, Toribio owned the physical therapy clinic, and later bought another to handle his increasing workload. Bills were sent to auto and medical insurance companies, and the attorneys split the take.

When the scheme was uncovered at the end of a two-year investigation by the California State Highway Patrol and State Department of Insurance, Toribio and Mullen requested the right to make restitution to the insurance companies. The providers denied the request and said they felt time in jail would serve everyone better. So did the judge, and the two are now serving sentences of almost seven years. Adriana, who pleaded guilty to fraud charges, received a prison sentence of two years in exchange for her testimony.

High Stakes Big Rig Games

There's a dangerous game being played on the Los Angeles freeways called *el toro y la vaca* (bull and cow). It's a high-stakes game played by the very gutsy and very poor. It goes something like this:

A large rig is rumbling down the road when a cheap car, loaded to the fenders with impoverished Hispanic immigrants, swerves up close in front of it and slows down. The rig driver looks to his right and left for an escape route if he needs it and finds none. He is flanked closely on both sides. Suddenly, another car slices in front of the car ahead of him, aiming too late for a freeway exit. Under his nose and right beneath his cab, the Hispanic passengers lay down quickly in the back seat of their car as the driver slams on his brakes. With nowhere else to go, the big-rig driver slams on his brakes, too, but his momentum is too great and he smashes into the car ahead of him. The accident victims, complaining loudly of back and neck pain, wait for a highway patrol officer to take an accident report, then head off to an attorney to begin an expensive settlement process.

Authorities in Los Angeles believe that there are at least five organized rings of this type of fraud currently in operation on their highways. Each arrest seems to lead to more arrests and more evidence. No one has found the way to the top of these particular rings yet, but investigators strongly suspect they will find attorneys and doctors coordinating the process. At the bottom of this food chain are the accident participants, and there are a lot of them. The game requires cars to run alongside the trucks to trap the rig into a specific lane. Another car must cut off the lead car to give it a legitimate excuse to slam on its brakes on the freeway. The lead car must be packed with passengers so that the maximum number of claims can be filed.

One of the sleaziest elements these scams have in common is that organizers rely on poor ethnic groups to play out this horrible game. Although the organizers of these rings collect tens of thousands of dollars on these staged accidents, the participants who actually risk their necks in the accidents receive as little as one hundred dollars for putting themselves under the wheels of big-rig trucks.

An informant from one of the rings claims that four to six accidents of this kind are arranged each week.

The trucking industry is stunned that they have been targeted for these scams, and can't understand why anyone would willingly put themselves in front of an oncoming eighteen-wheeler. It's simple:

Commercial trucks are guaranteed to carry insurance, and lots of it. Why stage an accident of this complexity and risk if there's an uncertain or unlikely payoff, such as would result from hitting an uninsured driver? Also, insurers for the trucking industry are often willing to settle out of court, which the organizers of these rings are hoping for. There's less of a chance of a ring being uncovered if its phony accidents don't come under the scrutiny of a full court.

Organizers of these rings, whoever they are, are making out like bandits. Those who play "bull and cow" often aren't as blessed. In the livestock world, bulls don't frequently smash cows to the ground. On the highways, immigrants are losing their lives for a hundred-dollar gamble that the truck's wheels will stop before they hit the passenger compartment. It isn't a good bet. And when passengers are killed the drivers are finding themselves up on murder charges. Those at the bottom of the game take the risk, and the fall. They also end up doing the jail time while authorities continue to search for the masterminds behind this deadly game.

Horses Falling for High-Stakes Premiums

Barn manager Harlow Arlie coaxed Streetwise, a seven-year-old gelding, into a loading van for what would be the horse's last ride. It wasn't that Streetwise was sick. It was simply that his insurance policy made him worth much more dead than alive. Investigators from Florida's state Agricultural Department, tipped off to something foul at the stable, watched from hiding as Arlie reached behind him, pulled up a crowbar, and smashed it into Streetwise's back leg. There was a sickening sound, like the shattering of a dry tree limb, and Streetwise screamed out in pain and terror. He thrashed wildly for a few moments and then collapsed in a stricken heap to the bottom of the van, moaning. Arlie called the vet and within an hour—a long and agonizing hour for a horse with a shattered leg—Streetwise was humanely destroyed.

At his hearing, where he pleaded guilty to insurance fraud and felony cruelty to animals, Arlie talked about a scheme to cash in on the horse's twenty-five-thousand-dollar insurance policy. Streetwise's owner was willing to pay Arlie and his partner five thousand dollars to maim the horse. Arlie also talked about "big people and heavy bread," implying mob involvement in the new wave of mysterious horse deaths in the high-stakes thoroughbred industry.

Horses, like children, are completely vulnerable to attack. They are easy, trusting targets, and lucrative ones to boot. Equine insurance specialists believe that up to 1 percent of all horse deaths may be insurance-motivated killings. But the numbers could easily be a lot higher. Why this attack on the lifeblood behind the sport of kings? Officials are pointing fingers at the recession. Also, changes in tax laws back in 1986 suddenly made horse ownership syndicates much less profitable. In 1984, the average price for a yearling colt at the prestigious Keeneland July Yearling Sales was up to about six hundred thousand dollars. Today, it's dropped to almost half of that.

Instead of that old adage of buy low, sell high, there are people in the horse industry who have bought high and are killing to stay there. These "horse lovers" include racing professionals, businesspeople who buy and sell horses for profit, and organized crime members. When the bottom drops out for the horse for whatever reason the contracts go out along with it. Horses are commonly poisoned, electrocuted, burned or beaten to death, shoved out of moving trailers, and run off yachts to drown.

Take the tragic case of McBlush, a three-year-old colt. McBlush was insured as a foal for one hundred thousand dollars. After permanently injuring his leg in a paddock accident, McBlush was suddenly worth no more than 50 cents a pound—the going price for horse meat. McBlush's owner, a Connecticut businessman named Gerald Minsky, made a deal with his dentist, Dr. Joseph Brown, to kill McBlush in a manner that couldn't be detected by the insurance company. Brown, who was fifty thousand dollars in debt to Minsky, was happy to accept the job to clear his bill.

So McBlush was led to water, but he didn't drink. Instead, he was injected with it—filthy water from a slop bucket plus a lethal dose of insulin. McBlush died an agonizing death the next day and Lloyds of London paid Minsky his one hundred thousand dollars. McBlush's premature death would never have been discovered if Dr. Brown hadn't shown up at Florida's Calder Cup races with a pocket full of hypodermic needles and a slew of suspicious drugs. Enjoying his new-found financial freedom from the death of McBlush, Brown was on his way to fulfill another death contract at the races. But this time authorities had been tipped off to Brown's intentions. Unfortunately for Brown—but luckily for his unsuspecting equine target—there's little room to negotiate when you're picked up with needles and drugs at a racetrack.

Minsky, Brown, and another accomplice are, like their thorough-bred targets, behind bars for a while: The horses are in paddocks; the con men are in cells. But only the horses will be doing any running in the near future.

The Claims Stop Here—When the Insurance Business Declares War

Tired of being a major financial support to con artists everywhere, insurance companies are choosing to invest some of their dollars for their own protection. Some states have created special insurance fraud investigation units. The computer has entered the insurance wars, with programs that have been very successful in flagging suspicious claims and cracking a wide variety of fraud cases. Where state insurance departments and bureaus haven't organized, the local insurance companies have. Many have established their own investigative units. Insurance fraud won't go away, but fraud artists stand a greater chance than ever before of being caught with their hands in the insurance companies' pockets.

Keep Yourself and Your Company Insurance Fraud-Free

There are plenty of ways to play the insurance fraud game. There's room for individuals, companies, and organizations. Yet a recent study by the General Accounting Office (GAO) found that state insurance regulators delayed action in over 70 percent of the cases where they had positive evidence of serious problems. States are underfunded and simply not equipped to combat the international insurance con artist. However, apparently they aren't ready for federal intervention, either. Congress, recently trying to establish a new federal body to regulate the insurance industry, met with great opposition from state insurance commissioners and much of the insurance industry itself.

So what's the American consumer to do? Regrettably, there is no foolproof way to avoid falling prey to insurance con artists. But here are some tips that should help.

Maintain an awareness of the extent of the insurance "games" and many players and parts. Protecting yourself from insurance swindlers is your responsibility. If you have ever spent time in a hospital or on disability, if your home has ever been robbed or damaged, you know the value of insurance and the peace of mind it can bring. The cost of that peace of mind is more than money. It is vigilance.

Investigate thoroughly all firms that you are considering before you buy rather than finding out later that you've bought a "paper policy" from a fictitious firm. Ask for a copy of the firm's financial statement or company report, and don't be squeamish about asking for bank and business references. Besides proving to you that the firm really exists, credible, long-term client references can also shed insight on how quickly the firm has processed claims. They can give you some idea about the level of service you can expect, such as the company's willingness to keep your policy up-to-date and to let you know about changes in the industry that may affect you or your business.

Be careful, even with well-known insurance companies. Allstate Insurance Company, part of Sears, Roebuck & Company, agreed to pay an unprecedented $1-million fine to settle charges brought by the California Department of Insurance for mishandling claims from the destructive 1991 fire in the Oakland and Berkeley Hills. The company was charged with delaying coming to terms on replacement costs, putting customers through a laborious process to get estimates, and confusing their customers about policy terms. The fire, the country's most costly urban brush fire, resulted in insured losses of $1.7 billion. In 1992 Allstate Insurance Company was ordered to accept sixty-two thousand drivers from New Jersey's state-run insurance pool for high-risk drivers because it had failed to comply with a state law requiring all car insurance companies to accept a quota of drivers in the pool. When selecting an insurance company it's best to deal with reliable insurance companies, not ones with a history of fraud and unfair practices.

Specifically find out about:

Registration. Call your state insurance department to make sure the insurer is licensed in your state, which at least guarantees that solvency and financial-reporting standards have been met. Robert Hunter, president of the National Insurance Consumer Organization, suggests that you make sure a company is licensed in the state of New York, which has some of the country's strictest regulations.

Guaranty Funds. Although every state maintains what is known as "guaranty funds" to pay claims in case of default, coverage varies considerably. For instance, self-insured companies and certain group health plans don't qualify.

Creditworthiness. Since understanding the complexities of an insurance company's financial statement is difficult at best, several rating agencies evaluate the creditworthiness of insurance companies. Experts recommend that you don't settle with the evaluation of just one agency; read several. Check with the library for *Best's Insurance Reports,* or contact Weiss Research Inc. (2200 N. Florida Mango Rd. West Palm Beach, FL 33409; (407) 684–8100) for the only ranking of the Blue Cross and Blue Shield plans.

Who actually covers you? Is it a self-insured plan where the employer pays all claims directly? Are reinsurers involved? Ask your agent or check with the employee benefits staff at work.

If the firm is outside of the United States, it may be hard to gather financial information about the stability of the company. In a case like this, ask your banker or a good financial counselor to help you gather information. If you can't get what you need to make a sound decision, look for another company.

Read your policy. Legislation and changes within the insurance industry itself have made it so that policies drafted these days can be understood by regular people. Read your policy closely. Make sure you know what you're covered for and what you're not covered for. I found out the hard way that my belongings were not covered by the Allstate homeowner's policy on my home, even though my Allstate insurance agent had told me that they were. Of course, in a court of law, the written policy is more persuasive evidence than the spoken promise. Make sure you are dealing with an agent you can trust, and know what's in your policy.

If you encounter any problems with your agent, go to the head of your insurance company and request a change of agents. Even in the best of insurance companies you may encounter a rogue salesperson. To keep your business, these salespeople can use tactics that are less than ethical. For instance, they may refuse—even upon request—to release information about your claims to competitive companies, knowing that companies need this information to formulate a bid. Your agent can also stall until the last minute in notifying you of a raise in your insurance premium rates so that you must renew your existing policy or risk being left without coverage while you search for a new one. If you feel the problem is company-wide, seek out a new carrier.

Stay current on industry pricing. As in any business, the cost of the service is whatever the market will bear. If you are not keeping yourself informed about the general costs of the insurance you require, you may be paying too much for it. Being overinsured is a common problem. An insurance salesperson is likely to try to sell you the most expensive and comprehensive package he or she has. Frankly, you probably won't need it. Even if you have a longstanding and trusted relationship with a particular carrier, get an outside bid from time to time to be sure that your policy is competitive and lean. Another way to keep a close eye on your insurance coverage is to ask business colleagues or members of any trade associations you belong to what they are paying for similar coverage.

Beware of anyone who offers you a chance to make a quick dollar by falsifying or inflating information about an accident claim. This can be the tip of the iceberg that can easily sink your *Titanic.* Those at the bottom of the insurance-con food chain are the first caught, the first prosecuted, and the first thrown in jail.

Make sure you understand the complete contents of anything you are asked to sign regarding an accident claim or other insurance matter.

Notify your local authorities and your state insurance commissioner if you sense anything suspicious about an accident that you have either been involved in or witnessed. Fraud may be indicated when one or more of the parties:

- Appears too eager for a speedy settlement.
- Is eager to take the blame for the accident.
- Converses fluently in insurance, medical, or vehicle repair terms.
- Has a history of lots of insurance claims.
- Is driving a rental car when the accident occurs.
- Develops subjectively diagnosed injuries, such as headaches, whiplash, and muscle spasm, only after he or she has consulted with a lawyer.

Other indications of possible fraud:

- The accident is minor but medical costs, repair costs, and lost wages claims are major.
- All the occupants in an accident vehicle are unrelated, but they all contact the same lawyer or doctor.
- The doctor's reports do not vary substantially from one accident victim to another.
- Physicians refuse to itemize medical bills although repeatedly requested to do so.

If you own a business, be on the lookout for phony claims from your employees. Be suspicious of chronically ill employees who have no particular illness of note but file claims regularly against your company's disability and medical policies. Request a second medical opinion from a doctor of the company's choice if you have this option. Read through all claims with your antennae up.

Be on the lookout for "slip and fall" artists who claim an injury on your property and threaten a lawsuit. Call the police and your company attorney in any case where a customer or employee claims damage to personal property while on company grounds.

If You Think You've Been Defrauded

Complain loudly to the consumer advocate group in the state insurance department and the state insurance commissioner if you have a complaint or feel that you have been victimized, and be persistent. According to the U. S. Postal Inspection Service, insurance industry mailings account for almost 3 billion pieces of mail annually, so you need to contact the Postal Inspector if the mail was involved. Finally, since fighting insurance fraud often means going to court, you may need to contact an attorney and the local police.

Chapter 15

Fraudulent Fund Raising

Most bunco artists will do literally anything to make a buck, except work an honest day. Those who prey upon people's generous impulses are among the most heartless, since the money they take from their victims is denied to legitimate charities, as well. These criminals pose as representatives of cancer research foundations, war and disaster relief groups, police and fire organizations, or just people down on their luck. They collect money in increments that range from pocket change to hundreds of thousands of dollars, all in the name of charity. But the only beneficiaries of these activities are the bunco artists themselves.

The American Association of Fund Raising Counsel reported that Americans donated a total of over $122 billion to charitable causes in 1990. Of this total, individuals contributed the bulk of the money, $101.8 billion, while businesses contributed $5.9 billion in money and merchandise. The balance was provided by foundations and bequests.

The donations covered a broad spectrum of issues and interests, with religion leading by a large margin at 54 percent of total donations. Health and human services, which includes medical research, received 18 percent of the total, followed by education at 10 percent.

The remaining 18 percent covered causes ranging from the arts and culture to environmental and public benefit programs.

The Salvation Army is ranked number-one among nonchurch charities, according to the Chronicle of Philanthropy, which compiles an annual listing of the top 400 non-profits in the nation. This well-known charity amassed more donations than any other single charitable institution, a total of over $658 million. Pretty impressive results from all those bell-ringers at Christmas. Since a mere 3 percent of the Salvation Army's expenses are devoted to fund raising, donors do well in giving to the group. This means that more of the dollars given are devoted to the programs and activities for which the group is famous.

There are more than four hundred fifty thousand charities nationwide, many of them small, local organizations that struggle to meet the needs of their communities. And the number of new charities is staggering: nearly two hundred thousand since 1982. As these groups have proliferated, competition among them for funding has become intense, almost cut-throat. At times, even legitimate charities have stepped over the legal line in raising funds.

Borderline Fund-Raising Entities

The real champions of charity fraud, however, are the con artists who have made this a large, lucrative business. The borderline legal fund-raising entities spend more of the money they raise on overhead than they do on the causes they are supposed to benefit. One infamous example of this type of operation is perpetrated by direct mail fund raisers like Watson and Hughey.

"Millions of dollars are diverted from charities like ours by Watson and Hughey and their ilk," said Sharon Swanson, Executive Director of the Cancer Research Foundation.

She wrote a letter to Ann Landers after she received a mailing from Watson and Hughey requesting her support for the Walker Cancer Research Institute in Edgewood, MD. When she took a closer look at the letter she learned that only 0.96% of the funds raised would actually go for research. That's less than one penny on every dollar raised. The balance of the money, 99.04 percent, would be used to cover "administrative costs, fund raising and education associated with the fundraising appeals."

Watson and Hughey is a Virginia-based direct-mail fund-raising firm that raises money for a number of "good causes," but even if the charity is apparently legitimate, the amount of money it receives may be insignificant. The charities on Watson and Hughey's list of clients have included:

- Cancer Fund of America, Knoxville, TN
- Center for Alternative Cancer Research (also known as Project Cure), Dothan, AL
- Walker Cancer Research Institute Inc., Edgewood, MD
- Pacific West Cancer Fund, Seattle, WA
- National Animal Protection Fund, Tulsa, OK
- Social Security Protection Bureau (also known as Foxhall Corp.), Washington, DC
- American Heart Disease Prevention Foundation, Montclair, NJ

Watson and Hughey first appeared on the scene as the fund-raising entity for the American Institute for Cancer Research, which was coincidentally started by Jerry C. Watson and Byron Hughey in 1981. Watson and Hughey specialize in raising funds for small or newly created nonprofit organizations. And their aggressive direct mail campaigns are successful, reportedly raising over $34 million for six client charities in the health-education field. It's unclear how much of that money actually went to the charities themselves.

The National Charities Information Bureau (NCIB), which rates the performance and ethical standards of national charities, has determined that no less than 60 percent of a charity's income should be devoted to its programs. However, according to the Minnesota Attorney General's office, many of the charities associated with Watson and Hughey have come under fire recently for devoting less than 3 percent of funds raised to research, medical care, or other services. While other charitable institutions struggle to meet the needs of their clients, Watson and Hughey clients seem to focus on fund-raising with little investment in the causes they represent.

Another of their clients, Pacific West Cancer Fund, has an interesting operating structure. Incorporated in Delaware, the organization uses a telephone answering service in Seattle and is under contract with a Louisiana company, Academic Services Associates, to perform certain administrative functions. The owner of Academic Services Associates, Donald Tarver, also founded Pacific West Cancer Fund. He's also the president of the United Cancer Council, which has a contract with Watson and Hughey. Keeping it all in the family, Tarver has named his son as Pacific West Cancer Fund's secretary and his daughter is chairman of the board.

One of Watson and Hughey's most controversial ploys was a sweepstakes appeal run on behalf of several participating charities, which misled recipients into thinking they had won one-thousand-dollar or five-thousand-dollar prizes. The mailing also suggested that even larger prizes could be had by sending a donation along with a preprinted form.

Some of the sweepstakes letters were signed by lawyers who claimed they had been retained by the charities to "notify winning contestants of the results of the organization's sweepstakes campaign" . . . "you have won a cash prize in the PWCF $5,000 Sweepstakes." It went on to say that the winner should return the "Winner's Release Form so your prize check can be sent to you by return mail."

One of the lawyers, Thomas R. Fleet, was under suspension from the bar for unethical and unprofessional conduct in both the District of Columbia and the State of Virginia at the time the letters went out. And the charities he claimed to represent had little or no contact with him.

Most people who responded to notices that they were winners received a check in the amount of ten cents. If they had read the fine print on the sheet sent along with the fund-raising letter, recipients would have discovered that the five thousand dollar figure referred to the sum of *all* the cash prizes to be awarded in the sweepstakes. The prize money would be divided among all contestants who returned the release form. In other words, the whole thing was a scam designed to get people to donate money in anticipation of receiving large prizes.

The entire pot of prizes for another one of Watson and Hughey's contests consisted of a check for one thousand dollars, two Nikon cameras, and two hundred thousand tiny Brazilian emeralds worth no more than a few pennies each. Once again, the promotion was highly deceptive, promising big winnings to donors. (For more information about sweepstakes, see Chapter 16, "Sweepstakes Fraud.")

Using mailers that resemble government agency documents, the two men do business as the Social Security Protection Bureau, offering services to elderly people that the government provides for free, such as obtaining an individual's lifetime wage records. They promote memberships in the bureau to older people and invite prospective members to enter sweepstakes. (Refer to Chapter 17, "Scams Against the Government: Biting the Hand of Uncle Sam.")

Legal action has been taken against the charities Watson and Hughey represent in a number of states, including Missouri, Pennsylvania, Illinois, New York, Maryland, and Michigan. The firm itself has been under scrutiny from the U.S. Postal Service for several years, but thus far they have carefully trod the fine line of legal operation, shifting the responsibility for their misleading direct-mail campaigns to their clients. In the case of Watson and Hughey, the wise donor may wish to simply put such solicitations where they belong—in the trash.

Conning the Charity

In these days of decreasing government and corporate support, charitable organizations are constantly seeking innovative ways to raise the money they need. And this can sometimes leave an opening for enterprising con men, who use the charity's desperation to turn a quick dollar for themselves.

I found myself on the receiving end of one con man's successful plan to defraud a worthy organization and people who donated money to support it. A California charity raising funds for multiple sclerosis research sponsored an auction at a ski resort. The promoter put some very attractive items on the block, including skis, ski clothing, ski vacations, and guest appearances on television shows.

I couldn't resist the opportunity to give my kids the chance to be on television. My bid of six thousand five hundred dollars for three roles topped everyone else's, and I happily presented my children with the news of my gift. A few weeks later I contacted the charity to find out more specific information about the television appearances. They told me that we had both been had by a smooth-talking con man who promised to line up items for an auction that would raise a large sum of money for the charity. He had raised quite a bit of money, but the items promised didn't exist and the con artist disappeared with the funds right after the auction was over.

Everybody lost. I had to accept a sixty-five-hundred-dollar loss and tell my disappointed children that they would not be on television. And the charity lost the income from the auction as well as the faith of those who had donated to the cause.

Gulf War and Other Veteran Scams

Before the Persian Gulf War had actually begun, con artists were hard at work, tugging at people's heartstrings to gain support for non-existent charities purported to benefit American troops in Saudi Arabia. These scams proliferated during the course of the conflict as con artists fleeced people all over the nation.

Residents of a senior citizens' home in Atlanta, GA, received a mail solicitation asking them to send money for gift packages that would be sent to troops in Saudi Arabia. In return for their generosity, donors would receive American flag decals. A large number of the residents responded to the request, but neither they nor the troops ever saw any evidence of their gifts.

The con artists targeted a group of senior citizens because they knew it would be easy to stir patriotic feelings and convince the residents, all of whom had lived through World War II and the Korean conflict, that they were doing a good deed for our boys in uniform.

Voices for Liberty, a nonprofit organization based in McLean, VA, had sold over seventeen thousand nickel-plated "Operation Desert Storm commemorative bracelets" by the time the Illinois Attorney General's Office began an investigation. The firm solicited sales using a computerized telephone system that dialed numbers and played a recorded statement for listeners.

Edwin Fitzgerald of Roselle, IL, considers himself a patriotic guy, but he was offended by the company's tactics. "I get solicitation phone calls all the time, but somebody was exploiting the war, and anything like that is not in good taste."

Kathleen Mott, another Illinois resident, was upset and angry after she received a similar call. She felt the message played on her emotions because she was concerned about her son, who was serving in the Persian Gulf. "They have it worded so that you think you're getting a message from your son or someone telling you he arrived safely. Then you get this message saying 'Order your freedom bracelet for $9.95.'"

Voices for Liberty spokesperson Barbara Jelly said the proceeds from sales paid for the bracelets, postage, and a phone message center that troops could use to contact their families. It was unclear why troops would need an intermediary message center to contact their families.

The recorded message was read by Jelly's husband, a retired navy captain. In the message he identified himself as a captain, which led many recipients of the calls to think he was currently connected with the military or that he was calling from the Persian Gulf. Jane Blocks of Melville, NY, definitely recalled the message saying the captain was with Operation Desert Shield. Voices for Liberty discontinued its telephone campaign when investigators from several states began to look into the group's activities.

In Connecticut, telephone solicitors asked people to donate money to purchase water filters for U.S. troops stationed in the Persian Gulf. The callers reported that service people were going thirsty or getting sick from tainted water. In exchange for each ten-dollar contribution, the company promised to send a $49.95 water purifier to the troops. Needless to say, despite donations the company received, there were no such water purifiers on the ships to Saudi Arabia.

In another scam, con artists asked for calling card numbers, claiming that troops in Saudi Arabia would be able to use them to call home. Those calling card numbers were sold to the highest bidders, who ran up thousands of dollars in phone charges on victims' bills.

The Vietnam War ended nearly twenty years ago, but the emotional scars it left behind still cause pain to those who lost friends or relatives in Southeast Asia. The fund-raising activities of organizations working for the release of American POWs and MIAs missing since the Vietnam War came under the scrutiny of the Senate Select Committee on POW-MIA affairs following a direct-mail campaign.

Direct-mail fund raisers for a group called Skyhook II sent a letter signed by its founder, former New York Representative John LeBoutillier. The letter sought funds:

". . . to launch a carefully planned mission—one that's sure to force the release of every American serviceman now in the hands of Asian communists (including, I'm sure, at least several Medal of Honor Candidates)!"

"All I can safely say here about the mission is that it's built around a small, elite force of Southeast Asians loyal to the U.S. Their job is to rescue just one American POW from the brutality of a hidden Laotian prison camp. Unfortunately, I can't tell you how."

It sounds like the stuff of which adventure movies are made. It is also manipulative and heartless because it plays upon the painful feelings of families who still cling to the hope that their loved ones might be alive after all.

Another group, Veterans of the Vietnam War Inc., raised over $11 million in an appeal for support that said, "Vietnamese leaders told our representatives that American POWs are still alive in Southeast Asia. They admitted it—FINALLY!"

Tell that to the Vietnamese, who have never acknowledged the existence of any remaining American POWs. Members of the Senate committee were incensed that these organizations continue to perpetuate the idea that Americans are being held primarily so they can raise money to sponsor more "rescue" missions. To date, none of these groups have liberated a single American, nor have they shown any concrete proof of the existence of American POWs in Southeast Asia.

Imposters

The Wall Street Journal reported that charity fraud is growing as telemarketers are employed more frequently by nonprofit groups seeking new ways to raise money. It is natural that con artists would capitalize on this trend, posing as representatives of legitimate charities and lining their pockets with the goodwill of those they call.

"It's no longer possible to tell if you're talking to a con artist or a real charity," said Patrick Connolly, an investigator in Pinellas County, Florida.

A veterans' group there hired a telemarketing firm to raise funds for their organization and didn't realize that the firm was dishonest. Using the veterans' group's name, the con artists sold overpriced household items, raising in excess of $10 million over the course of several years. The veterans received less than $1 million, while the telemarketers pocketed the rest for "expenses."

A telemarketing company and the Southwestern Pennsylvania State Troopers Association found themselves on the wrong side of the law when the attorney general's office filed charges against them in connection with a telephone fund-raising campaign. Telephone solicitors were hired to sell sauces, seasonings, and preserves to raise money for the police fraternal organization, but they identified themselves as police officers and implied that the money raised would be used primarily to fund the association's "Say No to Drugs and Alcohol" program.

The worst of these telephone fund raisers are the ones working for fire and police organizations that threaten people who don't give. One woman who wouldn't contribute to a Minnesota fireman's group was told, "I hope there isn't a fire at your house."

An elderly woman in Des Plaines, IL, was frightened by a solicitor who told her that she would no longer receive fire protection services if she didn't donate to the local firefighters' group. The man made such a convincing case that the woman sent money to the group, only to learn that she was one of many victims of a rash of phony police and fire solicitations that hit several northwest Chicago suburbs.

Local police and fire chiefs maintained that these criminal activities wouldn't have been so successful if their own union groups didn't use phone solicitors to raise funds. Residents come to expect calls asking for their support, which only makes it easier for the con artists to masquerade as police officers or firefighters, raking in hundreds of thousands of dollars before anyone is aware of their activities.

"They're not representing anybody but themselves," said Sgt. Al Freitag of the Des Plaines Police Department. "Most victims never call the police or fire department to check [on the validity of callers]. They just take it for granted that they are legitimate."

An Orange County, CA, woman who finally called the local sheriff's office to complain about the pushy tactics of their telephone fund raisers was horrified to learn that the money she had been sending the group for several years was going into a con man's pocket. The police union there had not done any fund raising by telephone *in over sixteen years.*

But the potential for high returns on a low investment—a phone line, a car to pick up donations, and a phone list—makes this type of fraud very attractive to con artists, who use every trick in the book to get people to give them money.

Take the con artist who told people the Lombard, IL, fire department pension fund was bankrupt and money was needed so retired firefighters could buy food and basic necessities. "They're always trying to find that one thing to get you, that one soft spot," Fire Chief George Seagraves said. "If the pension fund doesn't grab you, then they might say the money also goes for children who have been burned. They're always circling, and they don't want to give up."

Steve Carlson fell for a pitch from a man masquerading as a Miami police officer who said he was collecting on behalf of the families of slain police officers. Carlson was happy to write a check for ninety-five dollars. "The cops are targets. They're the good guys. They deserve the support."

Unfortunately, the impostor wasn't collecting for widows and orphans. He was soliciting money for advertising on behalf of Miami Enterprises, which publishes a magazine that lists phone numbers of local police departments and hospitals. John Pierse, president of the company, said the magazine contains a dedication honoring families of slain police officers. He claimed that his telemarketers never promised to give any money to the families, but Miami police and state investigators weren't convinced. Unfortunately, Pierse was operating in a legal gray area that prevented investigators from putting him out of business.

The "circus scam" is another popular phone fund raiser. Con artists posing as members of some benevolent organization contact people and offer to sell them circus tickets that will be distributed to needy children. This scam is especially popular with con artists who solicit from small business owners, and it is quite successful since it appears in virtually every city across the nation on a regular basis. Of course, the circus never comes to town and the con artists make 100 percent profit for their efforts.

Hard-Luck Hustlers

Con artists are experts at playing on people's emotions, tugging at the heartstrings in order to loosen pocketbooks. And they don't always reach people by mail and phone. Sometimes they come knocking on the door with a tale of personal tragedy that is hard to resist.

Brooklyn residents were moved by the story of a neighborhood family who had just lost their seven-year-old son, Joey, to leukemia. The family couldn't afford funeral expenses, so neighbors pitched in and gave a total of ten thousand dollars to the family. Or so they thought, until a sharp police officer uncovered a con artist at work.

Officer Greg Bacalles kept hearing the same story from different people on his beat. But Bacalles became suspicious when the dead boy's address kept changing. Police spokesman Sergeant Tadgh McNamee said, "When he spoke to residents on East Seventy-First Street they told him that Joey's family lived on East Sixty-Ninth Street. When he went to East Sixty-Ninth Street to see if he could help the family, residents there told him they were told that Joey was from East Seventy-First Street."

Bacalles spotted forty-one-year-old Rosie Pazzo collecting money for Joey's family and placed her under arrest. When police searched her car they found a list with the names of over seven hundred other people from Brooklyn and Queens who were also victims of the scam.

Disaster Relief Scams

As long as there are natural disasters, there will be hustlers looking to make a buck from someone else's misery. Before the flood waters began retreating in the Midwest in mid-1993, bunco artists from all over the country were pouring into the area to take advantage of those struck hardest by offering bogus home repairs and overpriced relief goods.

A direct-mail solicitor pleaded guilty to mail fraud charges after he sent out thirty-four thousand letters in the wake of the Los Angeles riots, seeking donations to help victims. He was actually only helping himself to money that should have gone to the truly needy.

Another man called people in the Los Angeles area requesting donations on behalf of a firefighter who had been shot in the face on the way to an arson fire during the riots. Although the police knew about the con artist's activities, they simply didn't have enough information to track him down.

On the East Coast, Hurricane Andrew washed up four slick operators who were collecting money for veterans who had lost their homes. They were former employees of a contract fund-raising company that had raised money for the American Veterans organization Am Vets. But they weren't calling to get money for the vets; they were calling to line their own pockets.

Their scam was a cut above the rest, according to Detective Ben Lowe of the Monroe Sheriff's office. "They did have literature. They had receipts. They had all the paraphernalia."

The group was so convincing that they even fooled a local hotel manager in Key West, who gave them free hotel rooms and phone calls. Hotel records indicated the foursome had made about two hundred fifty phone calls before police apprehended them.

Canister Cons

We've all seen the canisters soliciting donations for worthy causes in retail establishments, usually placed near a cash register to make it easy for people to toss in spare change. Most of these canisters are placed by legitimate charities like the March of Dimes, but there are growing numbers of illicit operators who are making a handsome living off the donations meant for the needy. In some cases the distributors give the legitimate charities a fixed sum and keep the rest as their fee. In other cases, the bogus charity keeps all the funds.

There is virtually no policing of this kind of activity, and many merchants don't ask the right questions of people placing the canisters in their stores.

Robbing the Collection Plate

Con artists make good use of Christian charity, duping ministers and congregations with tales of woe. The increase in scams run on churches and church charities has prompted church officials to ask for identification and proof of need before money, food, and clothing are given out. The Christian Council of Metropolitan Atlanta has created a computer system that links its affiliates by computer, screening potential clients to make sure they aren't making the rounds from one church to another.

"One family we know of has been getting assistance from churches and organizations since 1986," Amy Stickers, director of one area ministry, reported. "And they just cannot understand why we won't help them anymore."

Some people drive around and fill their trunks with canned goods at food donation centers, while others try to get several organizations to give them money to pay the same utility bill. Reverend R. Page Woods is philosophical about it. "It's a matter of survival, so they learn to survive."

But not all these "survivors" are in real need. Many are simply trading on the generosity of church organizations to line their own pockets. Take the case of the pregnant woman who needed an emergency Cesarean section but had no money to pay for it. Several ministers in Marietta, GA, banded together to raise over $1250 to cover the cost of the surgery.

They might never have learned they had been victimized, but when one of the pastors took the woman a potted plant at the hospital she wasn't there. It was all a scam, perpetrated by a con artist wearing a pillow and maternity clothes.

In another case, Reverend Bob Legnoski accepted a collect call from a distraught woman one Sunday morning at his Methodist Church in a small town in Georgia. She told him her house had caught fire that morning and all her family's belongings had gone up in smoke. Luckily, the church service was just starting and Reverend Legnoski called upon the members of his congregation to lend a hand. They came through with $104 in cash and a promise to collect clothing for the woman's family after the service.

But Reverend Legnoski discovered that the duplex where the family was supposed to stay was a fictitious address. "The whole thing was a scam. From now on, I'll ask for identification when someone asks for help, and write down their [auto license] number."

Another "needy Christian" took at least a dozen Orlando, FL–area churches for several thousand dollars with a sob story about how he and his pregnant wife, who was confined to her bed, were about to be evicted. Everyone who dealt with him said the con artist was so convincing that they just gave him money. The con artist was happy to take it and go off in search of other victims.

IRS Roulette

The money is so tempting and the need so great that a legitimate charity can be tempted to indulge in a little below-the-table dealing, as the Nassau (NY) chapter of the Association for the Help of Retarded Children (AHRC) was. Three employees of the prestigious Long Island charity and a donor were indicted in connection with a multimillion-dollar tax fraud scheme. Evidently, the theory was that it was all right to defraud the federal government, as long as money was raised for a good cause.

The AHRC sponsored an annual Las Vegas Nite benefit, inviting the cream of society to gamble for charity. But many participants weren't taking risks at the roulette wheel; they were betting that the IRS would never discover that they were turning an eighteen-thousand-dollar profit on a ten-thousand-dollar donation.

Imagine that a donor in the 90 percent income tax bracket writes a check for ten thousand dollars to purchase chips. In return, he receives a receipt for his ten-thousand-dollar donation and nine thousand dollars in cash under the table. At tax time, he claims the ten-thousand-dollar donation as a deduction and receives nine thousand dollars in tax benefits for his gift. His investment was one thousand dollars and his return was eighteen thousand dollars in combined tax benefits and cash; a much higher return than the stock market pays, even in a good year.

Although the plan raised significant funds for the AHRC, it ultimately robbed them of their reputation and public credibility, according to Mark Blandi, the current executive director. "By their conduct, these people have victimized not only the association and its children, but the hundreds of volunteers and staff whose hard work and dedication have made the AHRC the outstanding charitable organization it is today."

The organization has instituted accounting safeguards to ensure against tax fraud and manipulation of its books in the future. And the IRS and federal prosecutors fully intend to get their money back, with substantial interest and penalties. (See Chapter 17, "Scams Against the Government.")

Summary

According to a study by the Illinois Attorney General's office, fewer than 1 percent of the state's ten thousand charitable organizations operate illegally. But that small number in Illinois alone can take in literally millions of dollars in revenue annually. Only by becoming knowledgeable donors can people prevent this kind of fraud and be sure their money is going to support the causes they care about.

There are no hard and fast rules about charitable giving. Kenneth Albrecht, president of the National Charities Information Bureau (NCIB), recommends, "Your motivation comes from the heart, but your decision on whether and how much to give should come from the head."

How Can You Protect Yourself?

There are some common-sense ideas that can make you a more informed donor who invests wisely in worthwhile causes:

Think about what causes matter to you before you give. Long before you get a solicitation by mail or phone, think about what causes really matter to you. Is cancer research high on your list? Do you want to see more help given to the homeless, or children in need? Are you a big fan of the ballet, the symphony, or your local art museum? Perhaps you think environmental issues are critically important to our future.

Plan your giving before the requests are made. Make a short list of your interests and select the causes you will support on that basis, rather than as a knee-jerk response to mail that arrives on your doorstep.

Decide in advance how much you will give to your chosen charities and don't let anyone pressure you into giving more than you can afford. Consider the option of giving larger amounts to fewer charities. This kind of planning can benefit your favorite charity in more ways than one. Statistics show that it costs just as much to handle a five-dollar donation as it does to process one that is significantly larger than that. So, although your five-dollar donation is appreciated, a larger gift will have more impact on the program you are trying to support.

Get as much information as you can from your selected charities before you give. When considering a charity for inclusion on your list of worthy causes ask for written material on the organization and its programs, along with its annual report or financial statement.

Give to causes that can assure you a substantial portion of your gift will go for programs and activities, not for overhead and fund-raising costs. Take a close look at the percentage of money that is spent on programs and activities. The National Charities Information Bureau suggests that no more than 30 percent of a charity's expenses should be devoted to fund raising, and at least 60 percent of its annual expenditures should be devoted to its programs.

The best defense against fraudulent fund raisers is to get all the written information you can on the charity that is requesting a donation and then check them out with two organizations that monitor the activities of charities nationwide: the Philanthropic Advisory Service (Council of Better Business Bureaus) and the National Charities

Information Bureau (see the "Resources" Section for the addresses and phone numbers).

Mail Solicitations

Mail solicitations are particularly suspect because of the activities of impostors and direct-mail firms like Watson and Hughey. When trying to separate the honest charitable solicitations from their phony counterparts, take the following steps:

Read and evaluate the solicitation carefully, especially the fine print, to find out how much of the money actually goes to the programs of the charity. Does the solicitation describe specific programs that you want to support, or are their descriptions vague and deceptive?

Consider giving to recognized, established charities, such as the USO (United Service Organizations) or the American Red Cross, if the cause is particularly timely, such as aid for victims of a current war or some recent natural disaster.

Check out the charity. If you have never heard of the charity, or if its name seems similar to that of another major charity, don't hesitate to check it out with your local postal inspectors, or write to the Council of Better Business Bureaus or the National Charities Information Bureau.

If a charity's mailing includes address labels, pens, key rings, etc., as incentives for donation, consider refusing to give to that charity. They spent a significant amount of money buying and mailing those premiums, money that might have been better spent on services to benefit the cause they represent. And you are not obligated to send them money, no matter what they may suggest in their literature.

Beware of any mailings designed to look like government documents or charitable groups that have names that make them appear to be affiliated with the government. These practices are unethical at best and probably crooked at worst. In fact, Congress has been working on legislation to prevent this type of mailing.

Return the reply cards with a note requesting that they remove your name from their mailing list if the charity doesn't fall within your range of interests. Be sure to include the mailing label because this information will help them locate you in their computer files. This will save them money and cut down on your junk mail.

Telephone Solicitations

Remember, telephone solicitors can call from anywhere and make any kind of statement or promise they please. Be wary of any solicitation by telephone from an unknown party. There are several other things you can do to protect yourself from these hustlers.

Tell the caller that you want information in writing before you will make a donation. Any legitimate charity will be happy to provide you with the names of the organization's officers, the location of its headquarters, and a full accounting of how its money is spent. If they refuse to tell you, refuse to give them any money.

Get the name of the solicitor and his or her relationship to the charity, the name of the organization, and the programs and activities your donation will support.

Before you purchase goods or services to benefit a cause, get the name of the organization, its address and phone number, and how much of the price actually goes to the charity.

Be wary of any solicitation that uses harassment or high-pressure tactics to get your donation.

Don't ever be afraid to say no, especially if you have doubts about the organization.

Never allow the organization to send someone to your home or office to pick up a check.

Never give a credit card number over the phone, even if the charity seems legitimate.

Send all donations in the form of checks or money orders by mail, and verify that the address is legitimate before you send your money. If the caller offers to send a courier to pick up your donation, you can be pretty sure the group is phony (con artists try to avoid mail fraud charges by using couriers). Always make the check out to the charity, not the individual seeking the donation.

If the solicitor claims to be a police officer or firefighter, ask what division or precinct he or she works for and you'll call back after you verify the story.

Ask anyone who calls if he or she is a paid solicitor and what percentage of the donation goes to the charity. Even legitimate telemarketers may keep 60–70 percent of the money they take in.

Ask if the organization is registered in your state.   Most states require charities and fund-raising companies to register even if their headquarters are in another state. Check the name carefully for sound-alike
titles created to deceive potential contributors.

*Ask if the charity meets the standards of the National Charities Information Bureau
or the Philanthropic Advisory Group of the National Council of Better Business
Bureaus.*   If it's an evangelical group, ask if it has received the seal of
the Evangelical Council for Financial Accountability. Beware of
anyone who says their group is "registered" with any of these organizations. They don't register charities, they *rate* them.

Other Types of Solicitations

*Before making a donation at a charity event or auction, find out who is running the
event.*   Is it the staff of the charity, or some outside promoter who
has been hired for the evening?

Never give your check on the spot.   Instead, have it delivered to the office
of the charity and get a signed receipt.

*Never give money to someone who knocks on your door with a hard-luck story about
themselves or someone else.*   Tell them thanks, but no thanks. Suggest
they contact a local charity or church agency. It is unlikely the
money will be used for the purpose described. In addition, you
can't claim donations to individuals on your tax return.

*Think twice before depositing spare change in canisters that tout obscure charities with
poorly described programs.*   If you don't recognize the name of the organization, save your pennies for a better-known group.

*If you are a businessperson, demand specific information from the people who want
to place the canisters in your business.*   Ask for proof of their nonprofit
status and check up on them by calling the local office of the charity they say they represent. Explain that you are trying to make sure
the money goes where it is intended to go. The charity will appreciate your concern. The canister should also have a clear description
of the program the funds will support and an address and phone
number where potential donors can get more information.

*Ask that your church always seek identification from people asking for assistance and
that they carefully check out the people before giving them cash.*   Many churches

no longer give people cash under any circumstances. Instead, they provide assistance in paying bills and locating housing for people in need. This is a sound policy, since it assures that the person receives basic necessities and prevents misuse of funds.

If You Think You've Been Contacted by a Con

If it's not too late, cancel your check.

Blow the whistle.   If you believe an organization may not be a legitimate charity or if the charity appears to be making misleading solicitations, do everyone a favor and report your concerns. Contact your state attorney general's office and write the Federal Trade Commission. If the solicitation came through the mails, contact the U. S. Postal Service.

CHAPTER 16

Sweepstakes Fraud

Sweepstakes scams were spotlighted by the National Consumers League as the number-one scam of 1991. It's no wonder, as consumers are deluged with postcards promising them vacations, luxury automobiles, jewelry, cash, and a host of other desirable items. In addition, smooth operators call potential victims on the phone to tempt them with tales of wealth and products that can be theirs if they will only send in their money. Some of these hucksters even pose as IRS representatives, pitching the prizes in exchange for payment of a "luxury tax."

The Alliance Against Fraud in Telemarketing (AAFT), a coalition of trade and consumer protection organizations, law enforcement, and regulatory agencies, seeks to alert the public to the high incidence of fraud in telemarketing. The AAFT held a national press conference in late 1992 to call public attention to the alarming rise in fraudulent sweepstakes promotions. The press conference was broadcast by CNN and all three major television networks, and covered by daily newspapers and wire services across the country.

Linda F. Golodner, chairperson of the AAFT, reported that "fraudulent postcard offers have become not only one of the major scams of the '90s, but also a big business which is cutting into legitimate companies' profits and creating a mistrust for all types of prize promotions.''

Over 92 percent of American households have received a letter or postcard in the mail informing them that they were guaranteed to win a prize. Almost one-third of those receiving such a mailing have responded at one time or another. Any direct-mail marketing expert will agree that this is a phenomenal response rate, but it isn't surprising since the mailers offer their customers the chance of a lifetime.

But people quickly discover that there is no free lunch, like the woman who wrote Ann Landers to tell her how she had been ripped off. She fell for the pitch that offered her either a Cadillac, a trip to Hawaii, five thousand dollars in cash, a home entertainment center, or two thousand five hundred dollars in cash. All she had to do was order a beautiful sculpture the mail-order firm claimed was worth one thousand dollars. And they sweetened the pot by letting her purchase it for only $395, and even gave her a money-back guarantee. Too good to be true? Yes. The sculpture wasn't art.

"It was junk,'' wrote F. B. of Fontana, California. "I called and wrote letters trying to get my money back, but I got nowhere. No one answers my letters, and I get the runaround when I call on the phone.''

She never did receive a refund, and there was no sign of any big prize. She said she felt like a fool, and she isn't alone. Only a third of those who respond to such offers ever receive a prize, and fewer than one in five get the prize without having to order some product or pay a fee. And the prizes (and merchandise they purchase) rarely resemble those described in the mailers.

The types of prizes people actually receive run the gamut: cheap jewelry, household items like cutlery and dishes, cameras, lottery tickets, coupon booklets, watches, Liberty dimes, photographs, and checks in amounts from a few pennies to fifty dollars. The prizes are hardly worth the hassle involved in getting them.

When people complain and demand refunds, the telemarketing firm just packs up and moves to a new location, where they set up shop under a new name and do it all over again. In addition, a company that promotes guaranteed prize offers will have trouble securing a credit card agreement with a bank, and will usually process credit card charges through another firm. This practice makes it even more difficult to get refunds because the firm processing the billing is not the company that sold the product.

This is a form of money laundering and violates the merchant agreement the intermediary firm has with its own bank. Consumer protection groups and law enforcement agencies are working with Congress to pass legislation that will make such activities a federal offense.

How prevalent are these scams? The Minnesota Attorney General's Office reported that it receives over three hundred calls per week from people concerning sweepstakes offerings. It is difficult to say how many people are victimized by sweepstakes con artists, because so few come forward to complain to law enforcement officials. Most people chalk it up to experience and vow never to enter another contest.

You Have Already Won . . .

Fraudulent sweepstakes operators take advantage of people's greed and desperation, reaping profits from the pockets of those who can least afford it. And once they get someone on the hook, they come back again and again, draining the victim's resources as long as they are gullible enough to play the game.

A seventy-nine-year-old retired elementary-school teacher found herself in the midst of an endless round of contest scams until she had gambled away her entire savings—nearly sixty-five thousand dollars. By the time investigators entered her north Minneapolis home, the woman had filled twenty-five plastic garbage bags with several thousand notices from sweepstakes promoters.

"We've never seen anyone with this many solicitations, but it makes us wonder how many other victims may be in the same situation," said Doug Blanke, director of consumer policy for the state attorney general's office.

The retired teacher's case illustrates the plight of many people who just can't pass up the opportunity to win the extravagant prizes touted by crooked telemarketers. She was lured into cashing in stocks and bonds and emptying her checking account over six years of playing the sweepstakes game.

"It broke me, absolutely broke me," she said. "I lost my whole life savings."

How could anyone be so foolish? It is remarkably easy for trusting people to be manipulated by the salespeople in these boiler-room telemarketing operations. They promise again and again that the mark will receive the prize if he just orders one more product, pays one more fee, or plays one more time (and sends that entry fee). And the more desperate some people become, the more they will invest in the phony contest, hoping to get something in return.

The typical pitch arrives in the mail in the form of a glossy brochure featuring color photographs of fabulous prizes, including cash awards of up to twenty-five thousand dollars. The participant is asked a simple multiple-choice question that nearly anyone can answer and is encouraged to send his entry immediately with a fee of five to twenty dollars. The material suggests that contestants will win larger prizes if they send more money.

The first mailing is followed up with a mailing marked "urgent" that informs the person that he is tied for first place. He must answer another question and send additional money. Finally, the victim receives a tie-breaking challenge, usually a crossword puzzle with a complicated formula for solving it. Even if the victim manages to come up with the solution, chances are good he will never receive any prize.

Repeat Performances

Once an individual's name gets on the telemarketer's mailing list, it's sold to other con artists. These "sucker lists" are spread across the country, and the people whose names are on them are deluged with mailings and calls from "reloaders" who hope to take the victims for additional money.

Some crooks develop a significant attachment to one victim and keep milking the person as long as they can. Raymond Manning thought he'd found the goose that laid the golden egg when he contacted an eighty-three-year-old woman about her big winnings. He convinced her to send him cash to cover taxes and fees, promising to send her prize as soon as the money was processed.

Over the course of two years he placed more than three hundred calls to the woman's California home, netting from forty to five-hundred dollars per call. The barrage of phone calls nearly wiped out her savings, and her health deteriorated from the stress of the experience.

U.S. District Court Judge Charles Kocoras gave Manning the stiffest sentence he could give by law: eighteen months in prison and payment of full financial restitution to the victim, which totalled over fifty thousand dollars. An angry Kocoras told Manning, "In all my years on the court, I have never seen an individual that I would classify as such a lowlife as you. You are a disgrace to the human race."

Time-Share Tricks

The guaranteed prize offer is a favorite promotional device of promoters selling time-share vacation homes and other types of real estate. Typically, an envelope marked "urgent" arrives, bearing some official-looking seal and an acronym such as FBI or IRS to give the impression the mailing is coming from a branch of the government. Inside, the materials proclaim that the recipient is guaranteed to win one of several exciting prizes, such as a Las Vegas vacation, a television, a food processor, or a grandfather clock. All he or she has to do is come to Marvelous Acres to collect the prize.

In reality, it is simply a pitch to get people to come listen to a high-pressure sales presentation, and the prizes are usually not what they appear. The vacation is free lodging at the Low-Budget Motel ten miles from Las Vegas, the television is a black-and-white import from a country no one has ever heard of, the food processor is a hand-crank egg beater, and the grandfather clock is made out of cardboard. And some of these promoters have the nerve to add a handling charge equivalent to the value of the "free" prize.

Of course, if you fall for the mailing and drive a couple hundred miles to pick up your prize, the promoters figure they might also be able to talk you into buying a lot in their wonderful retirement development. And they may be right, because people keep responding to the mailings.

Business Sweeps

Small businesses sometimes fall for phony prize promotions mounted by fraudulent telemarketers who claim to be selling business supplies, such as paper products, toner for copy machines, or business equipment. The salespeople promise to deliver the prize in exchange for an order. The merchandise is usually overpriced and the prize is rarely what was promised.

The 900-Number Game

It seems 900 numbers have come into their own as devices for scam artists. Victims receive a postcard stating that they have won a car, a vacation, or a cash prize, and they must call an 800 or 900 number to claim it. The toll-free 800 number frequently rolls over to a 900 number, so that the call is charged against the caller's home phone number without his or her knowledge. The victim is told he or she must pay a processing fee or provide credit card information in order to receive the prize. The prize doesn't arrive, but the victim is billed for the call and the processing fee. And if the victim has given his or her credit card number, it is frequently sold to the highest bidder for use in scamming merchants and credit card companies.

IRS Impersonators

Sweepstakes scams take many forms, but one of the worst is the IRS rip-off. If somebody offers you a prize but says you must pay shipping costs or a "luxury tax," you may assume a con artist is at work. Too bad nobody told Kathleen Loadle that before she fell for a con artist's pitch.

The thirty-eight-year-old Washington mother of three was recovering from surgery when John Kevin Ervin called. "When he said he was an IRS agent, my heart started pounding," Loadle said. "Great, I thought. What do we owe the IRS?"

But he had good news for her. Ervin told her he was calling to inform her of her winnings, but she would have to act quickly to claim them because runners-up were waiting if she didn't take advantage of the opportunity. She was entitled to receive a brand-new Mercedes Benz 300E or $52,975 in cash. All she had to do was prepay $535 in luxury tax.

"He asked me if I had that much money," Loadle said. "I said no, but that if it meant getting $52,975, I would find a way. He said, 'Good for you, Mrs. Loadle.' "

Her husband was just getting back to work after a one-year layoff, but she managed to put the money together from her children's clothing allowance and a cash advance on her credit card. She and her family even discussed the things they would do with the money. Some would be used to help other friends in financial trouble and the rest would go into a college fund for their children.

But the money never arrived, and Ervin's indictment on charges of wire fraud and impersonation of an IRS official is scant comfort to Loadle and the other people across the country who fell for his scam. By the time the police caught up with him, he had talked at least thirty-seven victims into giving him over ten thousand dollars in cash.

Another IRS scam showed up in the mailboxes of New Yorkers in August 1992. The postcard said it was a "Public Notification" of an official IRS tax refund. It also said it was a sweepstakes prize. Which one was it?

Neither, according to the U.S. Postal Service, which lodged civil charges of mail fraud against a Fort Lauderdale firm called the Center for Refunds. The Internal Revenue Service was impressed by the nationwide scale of the scam, its sophisticated approach, and its timing. Each fall, the IRS mounts a publicity drive concerning unclaimed tax refunds, but the Florida company beat them to the punch.

Their pitch was both deceptive and confusing, promising recipients checks of up to $5178 for reasons that remain unclear. The cards announced a "Refund Sweepstakes" and a "public notice of IRS unclaimed tax refunds." The mailing was so unclear that even an IRS employee who received it assumed that the IRS owed him money.

Gerard Wilson, customer service representative for the firm, claimed that the mailing was simply a sweepstakes with a coincidental offer for a taxpayer information kit for $9.97. The Internal Revenue Service and postal officials disagree, saying that the kit tells taxpayers nothing they won't hear on the free information line provided by the IRS.

"The company appears to be conducting some kind of scam," said Postal Inspector Rafael Rivera. "They make it appear they have money for you and they'll help you collect it."

IRS officials report that schemes invoking their name are rampant, and some include threats of imprisonment and fines for nonpayment of taxes. In one case, con artists demanded immediate payment of back taxes and offered to send an "agent" to the person's home. Others just try to get Social Security and credit card numbers, then order duplicate credit cards and begin running up big charge card bills.

In all cases, the victims don't owe the IRS any money. They are just unlucky enough to be on the swindler's hit lists.

How Can You Protect Yourself?

There are many legitimate sweepstakes that deliver what they promise, but consumers must arm themselves with information to protect them from the fraudulent telemarketers who prey on people's greed and naïveté.

A sweepstakes by any other name is really a premium incentive offer, and knowing what to look for can help consumers separate the legitimate contests from the scams. The National Fraud Information Center (NFIC) published a consumer advisory that detailed the Direct Marketing Association's (DMA) guidelines for sweepstakes. The DMA, the national trade association of direct-marketing firms, stated it plainly:

Sweepstakes are promotional devices by which items of value (prizes) are awarded to participants by chance without the promoter's requiring them to render something of value to be eligible to participate (consideration). The co-existence of all three elements—prize, chance and consideration—in the same promotion constitutes a lottery. **It is illegal for any private enterprise to run a lottery.**

Beware of any sweepstakes mailing that does not meet the guidelines listed here:

It should never cost money to enter a sweepstakes. Legitimate sweepstakes clearly offer recipients the opportunity to enter the contest without buying anything.

If a premium gift is offered as an incentive for entering the sweepstakes, it should be clear that everyone will receive it.

Descriptions and pictures should accurately and honestly portray the prizes being offered. No price comparisons should be made that do not reflect the real cost (value) of the items unvolved. Fraudulent promoters sell items that are very attractive to the consumer, such as vitamins or water purifiers, but they generally charge more than the product is worth. Be wary of the tricks these hucksters use in quoting prices. An elderly woman from Atlanta bought vitamins a salesperson said would cost "Four-ninety-eight." When she received her charge card bill, the cost was actually $498, not $4.98!

Any guarantees made by the firm offering the prizes must be honored faithfully.

All rules of the sweepstakes should be easy to find, read, and understand.

Don't give any personal information such as your Social Security number, credit card number, credit card expiration dates, or bank account numbers to anyone promoting a sweepstakes. Promoters have lists of credit card accounts and can use the expiration dates to verify the victim's account information. They'll later claim that this disclosure authorizes them to charge items to your account.

Watch out for sweepstakes or prize offers asking you to call a 900 number. You will pay for the call, even if you don't order anything.

Don't be fooled by mailings that display official-looking seals or names that are similar to the departments of the government, such as FBI or IRS. And if the envelope proclaims itself to be "urgent," you can bet it's simply a matter of the seller being in a hurry to part you from your hard-earned cash.

Beware the limited-time offer that requires immediate purchase. Even if your state has a law that provides consumers with the right to cancel orders, collecting a refund from telemarketers can be nearly impossible.

Be suspicious if the promoter requires that you send a check by a private delivery or courier service. He may be trying to avoid investigation and prosecution by the U.S. Postal Service.

Always read the fine print. It will often tell you what you have to buy and what the prizes are really worth.

Before you agree to buy, call your state and local consumer protection office to inquire about the legitimacy and reputation of any telemarketing company.

Greet with skepticism all telephone sales pitches offering prizes as inducements to purchase. Your best bet: Place orders only with recognized firms that have solid reputations.

Be suspicious of any calls from IRS officials that come "out of the blue." Here are some key points to remember:

- The IRS will never come to your home unannounced or ask for your Social Security number over the phone.
- If someone calls claiming to be from the IRS, get a name and phone number and tell him you will call him back. Then look up the local IRS office in the phone book and call the number to verify that the person really works there.
- If an official comes to your home, demand to see identification and don't hesitate to call the local office to check up on him or her.

- Never write a check to an individual or "IRS" for payment of taxes. Spell out the full name: Internal Revenue Service.

Read and understand all the terms of any agreement that you're asked to sign.

The best way to protect yourself from becoming the victim of sweepstakes fraud is to toss suspicious offers in the trash. Although it's possible that you may miss out on big winnings, you won't have to put up with fast-talking hucksters and mountains of junk mail from con artists looking for one more sucker in the sweepstakes game.

If You Think You've Been Defrauded

First, contact the company in question and attempt to resolve the dispute.

If the problem is not resolved to your satisfaction and you suspect fraud, report the company to your local consumer protection agency, postal inspector, state attorney general, Better Business Bureau, and the Federal Trade Commission.

CHAPTER 17

Scams Against the Government: Biting the Hand of Uncle Sam

"When I was eight years old, my parents decided to teach my brother and me a lesson in charity that we would never forget. Instead of celebrating Christmas in the usual fashion that year with lots of presents, parties, elaborate decorations, and endless platters of food, my mother called the Department of Health and Rehabilitative Services and got the name of a nearby needy family. That Christmas, we would learn to be givers instead of receivers.

"Charged up with the fever of the season, my brother and I threw away our gift lists and instead shopped for the two young sisters and brother in the single-mother, welfare-listed family. My father was a professional cook and his income wasn't grand, but we went all out. My mom and I baked cookies and candies and packed them away in decorative tins. Mom and Dad shopped for an especially big turkey and all of the trimmings one could ever imagine.

"A week before Christmas, we packed up our small station wagon with boxes and baskets filled with new clothes, toys, food, Christmas decorations, and lots of loving goodwill. In those days, you delivered your gifts yourself and the givers and the receivers had the chance to meet face-to-face. My brother and I were nervous, but terribly excited.

"Our trip took us through the slums of Oakland and then out into the wealthier suburbs. We were wondering if we had followed the wrong directions when my brother called out, 'That's it! That's the address!' Our nervousness gave way to confusion as we pulled up to a home three times the size of our own. We could glimpse the swimming pool in the back. In the driveway were two large luxury sedans. One was a Cadillac. The street was immaculate, the landscaping flawless. Our Volkswagen seemed piteously out of place. So did we. We were sure we were lost, but then three children and a woman came over to our car. The woman, dressed in an angora sweater and lots of jewelry, said to my mom, who squirmed in her jeans and flannel shirt, 'The agency said you'd be coming over. We'll help you unload.' And that's what they did. Not another word passed between us. They took the boxes as if we were delivery people, chatted amiably to the neighbors who had come over to watch, and vanished back into the house. None of us spoke on the way home. We couldn't. What was there to say? I've never forgotten that Christmas, or what it was supposed to teach me, and I've never trusted the welfare system since."

The friend who told me this story isn't alone in his suspicions. Nor are they unwarranted. In this country, we have many government programs designed to take our money—mostly in the form of taxes—and as many programs designed to give it away. Ideally, those who give, give their fair share, and those who take, take only what is needed. The con artists who abuse this Robin Hood–type system do neither. Tax evasion scams, as we will see, are too numerous to count and too widespread for authorities to effectively enforce. Abuses of the welfare system—the entitlement program most frequently and thoroughly bilked—stagger our imagination in both size and volume. Other forms of fraud against the government—meaning fraud against you and me—range from those in power taking bribes and kickbacks to contract fraud, embezzlement, and unemployment benefits rip-offs.

The ever-present flow of money into and out of the government attracts con artists of all sizes and shapes. Put in an extraordinarily simple form, the government collects money and spends it. Taxes come in many shapes and sizes, as do permit charges and licenses of one sort or another. Who must give and how much? On the expenditure side, money is given away. Who qualifies for it and how much is received?

There is a common belief afoot that if you want to create a program that assures bad service and delivers it at the pace of a snail, just let the government run it. Because of the ever-increasing size and complexity of our government, this adage isn't as far off base as we would hope. Quality assurance and control, checks and balances, and enforcement are not strong enough components of many government programs. Government workers blame the incomprehensible workload. Critics of the system blame everything from bad management to whatever administration is in power at the time.

Meanwhile, in the middle of all of this finger-pointing and blaming, thieves and scam artists are making off with billions of government dollars.

Collecting the money is one of the primary jobs of the IRS. Ironically, there seems to be some challenge associated with dealing with the Internal Revenue Service. Even the most honest of us can feel our blood rise at the prospect of finding some hidden twist that can significantly lower our tax burden. Con artists just take this process a step (or ten) further and lie, cheat, and steal to lower theirs. They "create" the hidden twist. They "forget" how much they earned.

Cons also take entitlement programs and conjure up ways to "entitle themselves" to the benefits. They find desperate people, like immigrants who need permits or elderly citizens who need more than their Social Security benefits, and they offer them "solutions" for a price.

The federal government defines welfare as all entitlement programs funded through taxes. These programs made up approximately $730 billion in 1992, or 43 percent of the total spent by the U.S. Government. There are approximately 14 million Americans on welfare and over 22 million receiving food stamps; one child out of every seven receives welfare.

Let's start our look at government conning with a close look at the welfare system—one of our main means of giving money away.

You Can Call Me Mo . . . You Can Call Me Joe . . . And You Can Call Me . . .

One of the tricks to the welfare con trade is remembering your name. Those who are successful at this game juggle lots of them, along with different personalities, many addresses, and loads of pieces of phony identification. Welfare payments are not typically enormous, but if you are receiving several a month, they can add up to a very sizable income.

Just ask Teresa T. Thomasson. This twenty-eight-year-old California scam artist collected one hundred sixty-three thousand dollars in welfare payments under seven different names. She succeeded in milking the system by using different addresses and by never applying for aid at the same welfare office twice. Her scheme unraveled when she slipped up and filed for Aid to Families With Dependent Children using a name she'd used twice before. The case management computer showed that two other women with the exact same name were already receiving welfare benefits. When Thomasson was arrested she told authorities that other welfare recipients had taught her how to cheat the system.

Sometimes it seems that everyone is in on the game. One group of federal employees, phony document manufacturers, and fraudulent welfare recipients all worked together over a fifteen-year period to net more than $45 million in welfare aid. The success of this con resulted from having so many playing the system from both inside and out.

An even more surprising case concerns a Los Angeles woman who, with the help of family members and friends, managed to collect more than four hundred twenty-five thousand dollars in welfare aid over a ten-year period. Because of a clause in the welfare process that allows the agency to pay a representative of the actual recipient, no one put together the fact that a lot of checks were going to one person. Using fake Social Security numbers, driver's licenses, addresses, and personal identities, the woman kept one name throughout the fraud. When authorities informed the welfare agency personnel that one of the people involved in the ring was being investigated for welfare fraud, her checks continued to be sent! Actually, the agency withheld 10 percent as back payment on possible "overpayments," but when she had the chutzpah to call up the welfare office and demand her money, her payments were restored in full.

Thoroughly frustrated, Los Angeles County District Attorney Ira Reiner understated the obvious when he said, "This is not a sophisticated operation. You simply go in and demand money, and it is given to you. And if your check is cut because you have been caught stealing, you go back in and ask for another one and you get it."

One would think that with all the time, skill, energy, and enthusiasm it takes to invent personalities, locate or make fake forms of identification, keep all those names and addresses straight, and coordinate with other cheats, welfare con artists could easily channel that energy into finding a real job that pays as well as robbery.

Fortunately, the current public attention on government waste and spending is pushing the welfare system to police itself more closely. When it's trendy to save money the public eye fixates on programs that throw it away and don't even seem to know to whom they're throwing it.

Getting Fat on Food Stamps

Arnold is a drug-user. He is also chronically broke. Although he never has any money, he does have food stamps. Let's say Arnold isn't in the mood for food. A friend of Arnold's has told him that the manager of the convenience store on his block will give Arnold cash for his food stamps, so Arnold checks it out. Sure enough, the manager is eager to cut a deal with him—half the face value of the food stamps in cash. Arnold is quick to take the offer, because he's been clean for a while.

The manager collects hundreds—perhaps thousands—of food stamps for cash each month from people just like Arnold. He can cash in the stamps in one of two lucrative ways: He can redeem them for full value from the government; or he can shop for truckloads of food items at a super-discount store and sell the merchandise for an inflated price at his small, inner-city market.

Con artists don't need to be grocers to pull off this scheme. In Los Angeles, two men were sentenced to three years in jail for conspiracy charges in a food-stamp scam. Andrew Beyjamini and Ashley Charles Aji set up stores that did little but buy up black-market food stamps at prices lower than the face value. The stamps went into bank accounts, where the pair received full credit for the face value of the stamps. The fraud netted the men between three hundred fifty thousand dollars and $1 million before their scam was discovered. Evidently, special agents keep a close eye on markets that don't carry any products on the shelves. After this scam, which was the largest of its kind uncovered in the L.A. area, they are watching even more closely.

A few years ago the government began using large supermarkets as well as banks to distribute food stamps. Organized crime stepped in, stealing hundreds of thousands of dollars' worth of food stamps and popularizing a black-market trade. In the Long Island area, an entire network of convenience stores was found trafficking thousands of the stolen food stamps. Managers and employees of these stores had traded cars, appliances, and drug paraphernalia in exchange for food stamps. A New Jersey real estate agent decided that the black market was far more lucrative than the supermarket, so he sold a house for thirty thousand dollars in food stamps. Unless these traded items test out as edible, the traders are in for a surprise: The penalty for this kind of trafficking carries prison terms of up to twenty years, along with two-hundred-fifty-thousand-dollar fines.

By targeting stores with low monthly sales volumes and large food stamp redemptions, federal agents closed the doors on a defunct Brooklyn meat company that had laundered millions of dollars of food stamp money too hot for other small stores to handle. The operation was considered the largest food stamp swindle in the U.S. Department of Agriculture's (USDA) history. The company was acting under the USDA's authorization to participate in the food stamp program given in the 1970s, even though that authorization had been revoked since 1982. But the money was USDA prime, and the owners were just not going to let such a good thing die. They laundered $82 million before special agents reduced their operation to hamburger.

A special food stamp program known as the Women, Infants, and Children (WIC) Program has been designated for pregnant women and women with infants and children under five years of age. It's a nutrition program that uses vouchers redeemable for only certain types of foods and food supplements. A Milwaukee grocery store owner we'll call Bill decided to take a $1-million bite out of the program by selling vouchers to nonexistent women and cashing in on the proceeds. Since most Wisconsin grocery stores redeem about thirty-seven-thousand-dollars' worth of vouchers per year, FBI agents got suspicious when Bill redeemed six hundred sixty thousand dollars. So Bill had a good year—too good. Bill is up on ninety-four counts of fraudulent claims against the government and eighty-seven counts of money laundering.

Officials say that food stamp fraud has reached the $1-billion mark annually. And the food stamp program has whetted the appetite of more than one employee of the Human Resources Administration (HRA). HRA employees have been indicted and sentenced on many counts involving food stamp and welfare fraud. It's as easy as inventing a person and a file. In one particular East Coast case, HRA employees were putting out the word that they would accept bribes of up to fifteen hundred dollars to create phony welfare files. Every industry has its con artists, and employees in an industry often figure into the scam equation. In this industry, it's frequently case workers who consider themselves underpaid. Those who know the most about a system are always the ones who can most easily undermine it if they are willing to throw away their integrity.

Beam Me the Money, Scotty

"Nothing is certain except death and taxes" is an adage only the honest live by. For crooks, taxes are definitely not certain. And clever crooks are finding more and more creative avenues for big-stakes tax evasion and fraud.

Jerome Hearne, a former promoter of women's professional wrestling and a convicted armed robber, found that computers could be a riskier proposition than Amazonlike women or guns. Along with payment of three hundred thousand dollars in fines and restitutions, he is spending fifteen years behind bars for coordinating one of the largest electronic tax fraud schemes in California.

Electronic tax fraud has existed for as long as the IRS has enabled taxpayers to file their claims electronically—that is, only a few years. Honest taxpayers enjoy the program because it enables them to collect their tax refund quickly in one of two ways: They can either have their tax preparer give them a refund instantly if the refund amount is under three thousand dollars, or they can take their return to a bank and get a loan on the refund amount within a few days after the IRS has granted a preliminary "acceptance" of the return. Because the IRS is eager to promote this program, a "preliminary acceptance" means little more than just a quick check to make sure that the person and the Social Security number on the claim match up.

Swindlers enjoy the program for the same reason—fast, easy money. The quicker a cheat can get money into his or her hands, the quicker he or she can skip away with it. Electronic tax fraud is fast and lucrative and growing like mushrooms, particularly in California. With the enormous increase in fraudulent electronic claims filed in just the past year, the IRS's Criminal Investigation Division in Los Angeles is devoting 40 percent of its manpower to investigating this type of fraud alone.

IRS agents say the phenomenal growth of electronic scamming, the tax scheme of the '90s, is spread mostly by word of mouth. Some scammers start out small, seeking returns of only a few hundred dollars.

When they are successful greed strikes, and they go for thousands or tens of thousands.

To file a personal income tax claim, you need to be alive. You need a Social Security number and a W-2 Form. Grifters like Hearne seek out homeless and unemployed people who can easily "disappear" when needed, and give them dummied-up W-2 Forms. Then they help them prepare a claim, or give them all the phony information they need to file a claim electronically with an unsuspecting tax preparer, including child-care receipts, pay stubs, rent receipts, whatever. At this point, the claim filer can request a refund from the tax preparer, who is then reimbursed by the IRS, or take a copy of the electronically filed claim to the bank and request a loan on the refund amount. However the money arrives, it is split among the scammers. By the time the IRS figures out that the claim is bogus the claim filer is long gone.

The success of this scam lies in the W-2 Form. This critical piece of paper must be created. To do this, scam artists often invent dummy corporations with false letterhead stationery, business cards, and perhaps an answering service. Then they "hire" employees and set them up with phony pay stubs and, of course, the W-2 Forms.

Hearne assisted in the filing of as many as two hundred false returns, using similar addresses, company names, and child-care services. He would mix and match the details so that someone who appeared as a dependant son on one claim would show up as a head-of-household on another.

When Hearne was sentenced he complained that he hadn't collected nearly what the government claimed—which was $1.2 million. He also said he wasn't the ringleader—just unlucky enough to be the last one tried in the case—the one everyone else pointed the finger at. And then he said that he was very sorry for the way it all turned out. Now *that* part, I believe.

Filing Off the Teeth of the Tax Bite: Deductions

Everyone loves deductions. We deduct our cars, our homes, our computers, our children—anything to soften the bite of our taxes. A clever con artist can invent a multitude of fascinating deductions, mix them all together, and, voila: No taxes!

Charities and religious donations are especially enticing. Because these are tax deductible, you'd be surprised at what people manage to donate to these institutions to cut their tax burdens. William Blackmore, a seventy-two-year-old East Coast real estate agent, was sentenced to a year on probation and community service work after he pleaded guilty to tax fraud. Allegedly conspiring with two Eastern Orthodox groups, Blackmore would advertise for donations of hard-to-sell properties for an unnamed religious corporation. Then he would send the donor an inflated appraisal that was far above the market value for the property. The donor would write off the property as a charitable contribution, and the religious groups would sell the merchandise for a small percentage of what Blackmore had valued it.

Hiding behind brown monks robes and a designation as friars of a religious order, a group of men in New York managed to shield $20 million in earnings from the IRS. Working outside at secular jobs, they paid no income taxes because they took a vow of poverty and donated all of their earnings to the religious order, or so they claimed. In actuality, they got back all but twenty dollars of each paycheck for "living expenses." The leader of the phony friars, John Brennan, was sentenced to two-and-a-half years in jail. He'll serve that after he answers to charges of forgery and welfare fraud in another state.

Stalking the Endangered Deduction

Just about the only people who harbor much sympathy for big-game hunters are other big-game hunters. So when the enormously wealthy shooters of elephants, tigers, jaguars, and snow leopards start whining that they are being harassed by Fish and Wildlife agents, not many people rush out to pick up protest signs. The agents admit that they are stalking the territory of the rich and famous, looking for large-scale hunting violations that often involve the killing and importation of endangered or rare species. They target the wealthy because middle-income and poor people just don't have the means to jet over to Nepal and bag a snow leopard.

So how does tax fraud fit into all of this? John Funderburg, ex-director of the North Carolina Museum of Natural History, could tell you quite a story about that. Funderburg had big plans for his little museum back in the mid-1980s. Funderburg took a long look at his options for growth and decided to make an offer to big-game hunters that was hard to resist. He would grant them "associate curator" status with his museum in return for hides and heads. According to Thomas

L. Bennett, the special agent who investigated the case for the U.S. Fish and Wildlife Service, "This wasn't hunting. This was killing one of the last of a species and taking it off your tax return."

Here's how it worked. Hunters of the most elusive and rare species have several problems much stickier than killing their prey. One has to do with getting a foreign government to let anyone kill its rare animals. Another involves getting your own government to let you back into the country with your trophies. "Associate curator" status could eliminate both problems quickly. Funderburg offered to write letters to appropriate government officials declaring that the letter-carrier was "collecting" animals for the museum. It would all be in the name of science.

The hunter would pocket his letters, bag his trophy, get an appraiser to put a monetary value on the remains, donate some parts to the museum, and write the whole thing off as a charitable deduction. Deals as sweet as this spread rapidly by word of mouth. Hunters who needed some big deductions but didn't want to bother with all the travel and expense of a big-game hunt began donating truckloads of animal body parts to the museum, and soon Funderburg's little museum was accumulating a very large stash of respectable specimens. It went from being known as the repository for the state's largest watermelon to a well-regarded museum.

Funderburg began working with Chicago appraiser R. Bruce Duncan, who could be counted on to appraise photos of dead animals and skins at sky-high rates so that hunters could take a deduction after donating an animal. Duncan, of course, charged a hefty fee for his service. These inflated appraisals made the museum donation program even more popular—so popular, in fact, that Funderburg soon ran out of room to house all his specimens. Employees later reported unloading truckload after truckload of animal skins and heads on a regular basis. These treasures were eventually stored in an abandoned apartment building some blocks away, where they awaited display in the new museum Funderburg said he was building to house his collection.

But Funderburg never built his new museum because his lucrative con began to unravel when U.S. Fish and Wildlife agents started snooping around. What they found, in addition to reams of museum files and paperwork, was the abandoned apartment building. The damp and the cold, along with less than careful handling by homeless people and vagrants who'd broken in over the previous ten years, had reduced the store of heads and hides to a bug-infested pile of skin shreds and dust.

Because the statute of limitations for civil tax cases is three years, many of the donors will be able to walk away with their donations intact on paper. Duncan, the overly generous appraiser, was sentenced to ten months in jail and received a fine of thirty thousand dollars for the half-million-dollars in appraisal fees he made in just three years. Bruno Willy Scherrer was fined one hundred thousand dollars and sentenced to probation; he got no jail time because his attorney hinted that he might have a budding case of Alzheimer's Disease. And Funderburg was fined a mere five thousand dollars and received probation because he cooperated with the government.

Food stamp violations carry penalties that include twenty-year jail terms and hundreds of thousands of dollars in fines. In this scam, the perpetrators came out with sizable profits even after they paid their fines and served their time. One could say that something stinks here, and it isn't the animal hides. One could say that the U.S. Government, through the IRS and a laughable penalty system, essentially subsidized the killing of some of the rarest animals in the world.

If there is an upside to this story, it has been in the reaction of some of the world's largest big-game hunting clubs. After decades of sponsoring events such as the North American Grand Slam, where hunters get a distinguished designation for shooting twenty-nine of the nation's hardest-to-find big-game animals, these clubs are bowing to public outrage and starting to talk about conservation.

That Ol' Devil Bribe

Swindlers who are too lazy or too unimaginative to come up with schemes to rob Uncle Sam directly try that old standby, the bribe. And in some cases, Uncle Sam is ready and waiting for them. A group of twenty-three individuals, most of them New York Chinatown restaurant and garment shop owners, offered an IRS special agent posing as a corrupt tax agent over one hundred twenty-one thousand dollars to wipe away more than hundreds of thousand of dollars of withholding, corporate, and unemployment taxes owed by their businesses. The investigation lasted three years.

According to federal authorities, David Chang initiated the bribery scheme and brought others to the IRS investigator, who even paid Chang a three thousand dollar finder's fee.

Well, suffice it to say that Chang's bribery scheme didn't work. The Internal Revenue Service expects that sort of thing. You would think that people smart enough to create and run a business would know it.

The Friendly, Fraudulent Tax Preparer

The men and women who prepare your taxes have a wonderful window into the state of your finances. Most of them work hard to get you an honest refund. Some of them would rather keep your hard-earned dollars for themselves. A New York tax preparer, Frederick Schneider, offered to place his clients' monies into various tax shelters. He then deducted these shelters from his clients' tax statements, paving the way for huge refunds. Unfortunately, these tax shelters really existed only in Schneider's mind. But the millions of dollars' worth of payments deposited to them were very real and went into his bank account. While Schneider awaited sentencing, his clients were awaiting their bills from the IRS for fines and back taxes. The bills will be big ones.

In the world of the IRS, no one but you is responsible for your taxes. If your taxes are prepared by a shyster, you will be the one who pays for your mistake, and you'll pay with interest.

Feeding Off Vulnerability and Misfortune

For many older Americans and the disabled, Social Security is the lifeline that puts meals on the table and a roof over the head. Swindlers thrive on vulnerability. This situation makes many of our seniors, with their fixed incomes, sitting ducks for a multitude of Social Security scams.

Rumors that the Social Security Administration is broke have caused trembling in more than one pair of hands, and have also lined the pockets of some pretty sleazy con artists. According to a recent *Forbes* magazine article, by the end of the 1990s, Social Security reserves will reach over $1 trillion. This is three times the rate of annual payments (an estimated $315 billion).

Backed up with fraudulent but official-looking letterhead stationery, swindlers who target the elderly have sent out mass mailings from supposed senior-citizen watchdog groups. The letters say that the Social Security well is bone dry and that it has been drained by corrupt politicians. It begs for donations from its elderly readers for money to legally fight this corruption so that the waters can be restored. If enough money is not raised, monthly Social Security payments will slow down to a trickle—such is the veiled threat of these cruel letters.

Of course, the money rolls in. And, of course, another cheat makes a dollar off someone who is least able to afford it.

Some con artists decide to impersonate the Social Security Administration and other government agencies. They dummy up impressive letters with eagle emblems and offer to sell seniors special brochures that will help them learn about "secret" or little-known benefits that the government has waiting for them. Some of these letters offer forms—for a price—to register name changes or to see if their worker earnings records are accurate. These forms and many others are all available *for free* from the real Social Security Administration. And there are no hidden or secret benefits out there.

Some legitimate businesses plaster the words "Social Security Information" on the outside of their envelopes to encourage elderly readership, when all that's contained inside is sales literature on insurance programs or investments.

Any such "copycat" documents that use a seal, emblem, or other symbol that would lead someone who sees it to believe that there's an affiliation with a government body must carry the following disclaimer, typed and in a conspicuous place:

> This organization (or product or service) has not been approved or endorsed by the Federal Government, and this offer is not being made by an agency of the Federal Government.

An additional disclaimer must be placed on the envelope or mailing container in uppercase letters in a conspicuous place in legible type:

THIS IS NOT A GOVERNMENT DOCUMENT.

One ingenious con used a 900 telephone number to bleed money from the elderly. At first told to call a toll-free 800 number, the caller was then referred to a 900 number. Not until the third time the 900 number was repeated was there any mention of the ten dollar cost for the call. When the 900 line was called there was no mention of any cost for the call, and the phone service rattled off the history of the Social Security program and other bits of worthless information. Seniors calling the number would find out about the charges only when they received their next phone bill. Social Security maintains a 1-800 information number that is remarkably close to the phony number.

As in the case of the big-game tax frauds, the penalties for Social Security scams say a lot about our commitment to ending this kind of criminal activity: five thousand dollars is the fine for falsely implying affinity with the Social Security Administration; the ceiling on the penalty is one hundred thousand dollars in a year. Not a serious fine when a few months' work can net a scammer many times that amount.

Occasionally, a senior will turn the tables and cash in on the system by inventing phony identities and claiming extra Social Security benefits. Leroy Robert Castermetz was arrested for conjuring up over three hundred different identities and claiming benefits for all of them—perhaps up to $1.3 million.

Using the names of contemporary authors, Castermetz allegedly took the biographical information provided in a reference book and obtained birth certificates and duplicate or new Social Security cards. Investigators found hundreds of phony birth certificates at his home, along with photos of him in different outfits with different bank names listed on the back. Apparently, he wanted to make sure he kept his identities straight. The old man was deaf and lived a very spartan life. There was no evidence that he ever spent any of the hundreds of thousands of dollars he supposedly collected from his scam. His attorney speculates that he conjured up this scam because it was an interesting way to pass the time. I guess some folks just won't tolerate any more bingo games.

Just as the fate of many seniors is tied to Social Security benefits, the fate of many immigrants is wrapped in permits. In most cases, immigrants are totally unaware of what it takes to enter and stay in this country, and that's a fact that con artists are delighted to use to their advantage. Day after day, hopeful foreigners pay hundreds of dollars for phony documents they are told will allow them legal entry into the United States. And day after day they are turned back at our borders or shipped home if they manage to gain entry.

When the De Jiminez brothers were sent back to Mexico with their phony work papers, authorities began disarming a scam that would go down in California lawbooks as one of the largest and easily the most profitable of its kind. Robert and Pietro got their permits to work and reside in the U.S. from a firm called the American Law Assn. So did thousands of other hopeful immigrants from Mexico to the Philippines. For a mere three hundred dollars, the organization would grant a work/residence permit to anyone who could pay the fee. It all looked legal. It was supposed to.

The De Jiminez brothers were devastated by the hoax and weren't going home without a fight. They brought a civil suit against the American Law Assn., demanding their money back. They got it—and more. The Assn., also known as La Clinica de Ayuda—The Help Clinic—was ordered to pay each of the brothers twenty-eight thousand dollars in damages. An additional $431,032 was to be remitted to one thousand other swindled clients. Because Susan M. Jeannette, the owner of the Assn. and a one-time paralegal, claimed to have destroyed many of her records, the firm was also required to spend forty thousand dollars in advertising to let unsuspecting former clients know about the case so that as many could be reimbursed as possible. The case is unprecedented in the severity of its verdict. It is meant to serve as a warning that undocumented people are not fair game.

Most often, illegal aliens do not get or demand their day in court. Like the elderly, they are often vulnerable, easy targets. The money they place in the hands of con artists is hard to come by and precious.

While many scams against the government hurt our wallets as taxpayers, those aimed at recent immigrants, the elderly, and the disabled hurt lives in a much more devastating way. Fines and penalties reflect our commitment to curb these kinds of scams. And low penalties send con artists a particularly loud message that our commitment is pretty flimsy.

Protecting Yourself From Government-Related Scams

Scams can't work as easily if you are awake and aware. Con artists succeed in instances where your guard is down and your trust is naively high. Convicted rapists say time and again that they depend on the element of surprise. They go after women who are distracted, lost, or daydreaming. Many of the people who are out to assault your wallet do the same. When you don't ask questions, when you blindly hand your tax preparation over to someone whose references you haven't even checked, when you assume that everything that comes to you in the mail is legitimate, you are setting yourself up to be conned.

We need to take care of ourselves first. Then we must take time to take care of our world. That is what community activism is all about. That's why we need to write letters, to keep our eyes open in our own neighborhoods, and to speak up when something smells rotten.

Look to your business associations and friends for reputable tax preparers and accountants. Remember, the IRS holds you responsible for your taxes. If your tax preparer is less than honest, you will still be held accountable. In your search, focus on finding someone who has been in the business awhile and who has a good reputation for honesty and customer service.

You must be intimately involved where your money is concerned. If your accountant recommends a tax shelter or a deduction that you know nothing about, get a second opinion and even a third. You may be handing your taxes over to a preparer because you don't want to be involved with these kinds of details. But "ignorance is bliss" doesn't hold water with the IRS.

Look closely at all requests for donations—they're not all legitimate. Fraud may be hiding in your mailbox or it may be a phone call away. Embossed stationery and fancy emblems mean only that someone had a good printer, not that the correspondence is official. If you receive mail from the Social Security Administration—or any government agency—that asks for money or disturbs you in any way, call your local Social Security office and your post office and check it out. A few phone calls could save you money and some sleepless nights.

Question the need for unusual permits. Question those who tell you that you need a special dispensation or permit to do something, to go somewhere, to own something. It seems these days that you need a permit to sneeze, but assumptions are dangerous. Con artists feed off assumptions.

Be a good neighbor whenever you see something suspicious or sleazy going on in your neighborhood. Many food stamp scammers are shut down by alert neighbors. Local grocery stores that cater to the food-stamps-for-money drug trade infuriate their honest customers, who are taking the time to make some angry phone calls to the local police and welfare offices. If we don't care for our own communities, no one else will.

Don't underestimate the power of letters to your government representatives. If you want to see stiffer sentences for con artists, if you want to see better enforcement of fraud crimes, tell them. Politicians assume that only one person in ten will write on an issue, so when you write, you are sounding the voice for the nine that didn't.

What Can You Do If You Detect Fraud?

If you suspect fraud, report it to the police and the governmental agency involved.

CHAPTER 18

Credit Repair Scams

Recessionary times are hard on everyone, but the hardest hit are often those who live on the financial edge. Some people live from paycheck to paycheck in the best of times, their incomes so limited that they can barely keep up with their creditors. Others suffer financial reverses because of layoffs, divorce, or illness. Small business owners may find business drops off during an economic downturn and watch helplessly as income dwindles and debts grow. Whatever the equation, the ultimate result for thousands of people is bankruptcy, loss of assets, loss of self-esteem, and credit problems.

It is widely believed that declaring bankruptcy makes it impossible for an individual to get credit for at least ten years. Illegal "credit fixers" cultivate this misconception in order to sell their services to the newly bankrupt. Although it is far more difficult to get credit after declaring bankruptcy, it is by no means impossible. In fact, Purdue University's Credit Research Center reported that 16 percent of consumers who declare bankruptcy establish credit within a year, and almost half re-establish their credit within five years.

Although many credit agencies, including banks that issue credit cards, will not extend credit to those who have declared bankruptcy, there are institutions, such as finance companies, that will make loans simply because the bankrupt party cannot declare bankruptcy again for seven years. The interest rates offered by these institutions will be higher than that charged someone with a good credit history. But it may be worthwhile for someone seeking to re-establish credit, since a consistent record of payments demonstrates credibility and eventually makes it easier to get credit from more traditional sources.

Some people don't want to wait that long, while others are simply duped into believing there is a quick fix for their credit problems. This is where the credit repair "experts" come in. They promise a clean bill of credit health, new and better opportunities for borrowing, and claim it's all legal. Some even have the nerve to say they are affiliated with the federal government.

It's all just another way to part desperate people from their money. There are a number of different systems promoted by these slippery individuals, but they are all shams that only put the participants at risk of prosecution for several different crimes, including tax fraud.

What makes matters worse for law enforcement agencies is that these bogus operations often offer seminars that train others to use their techniques to start their own credit repair agencies.

"It is like trying to handle mercury," said John Lefever, an attorney with the Federal Trade Commission (FTC). "Every time you open an investigation, you grab one of them, it runs through your hands and you discover more clinics pop up somewhere else."

California officials faced a dramatic rise in credit repair scams as the state suffered from a crushing recession in the early '90s. The Internal Revenue Service office in Fresno, which processes the state's tax returns, was the first to spot the problem in early 1992. Officials found that one in every twenty-seven returns was rejected by the computer system because the name and Social Security number did not match. Some of the filers had made honest mistakes, but many were participating in the newest form of credit repair scam, file segregation, which takes advantage of the complexities of the massive computer systems operated by more than nine hundred credit bureaus nationwide.

The Credit Reporting System

The sheer volume of records the credit bureaus maintain and process is staggering. It is a simple matter for dishonest credit fixers to exploit the inherent weaknesses of the system to generate clean credit reports for people who have bad credit histories. In order to understand the way the credit fixers manipulate the system it is important to know how the credit reporting system works.

Banks, insurance companies, department stores, and other businesses that extend credit to consumers subscribe to credit bureaus. These credit bureaus collect financial and employment information on individuals and pass the information to their subscribers.

When an individual borrows money or applies for a credit card the lending institution submits a request for a credit report to its credit bureau. The lender uses this report to evaluate the credit worthiness of the applicant. Ultimately, it is the single most important factor in determining whether or not the applicant will receive the loan or credit card. A good credit report is essential for anyone seeking to borrow money or obtain credit cards.

It's no wonder that people with tarnished credit records often seek illicit ways to improve their appearance on paper. There are legitimate ways to improve a damaged credit record, especially if the credit bureau has inaccurate negative information. Unfortunately, many people seek the easy way to erase their mistakes, which only compounds their problems by adding fraud to the list of their sins.

The Credit Repair Game

People who have developed credit problems are frequently ignorant of their rights and options, making them vulnerable to swindlers who promise to give them clean credit files. People who have declared bankruptcy are deluged with mailings from hustlers offering credit repair seminars at exorbitant prices and credit clinics that will provide new credit records for a large fee.

Some credit counselors or attorneys simply send certified letters to the credit bureau stating that information contained in the person's credit history is injurious to his credit rating and should be reviewed and resubstantiated. The credit bureau has four to six weeks to review the file and request confirmation from its subscribers that the information contained in it is accurate.

Many subscribers simply don't respond, either because they don't have the staff to handle the high volume of such inquiries, or because the record is too old and has been taken off the computer system. The law of averages simply works in the favor of the credit counselor, and many negative reports are dropped from the individual's file, giving him a much better credit report.

The catch is that the individual could have submitted the letter of inquiry himself, with the same result. And he would have saved himself several hundred dollars paid to the credit counselor.

Currently, the most popular approach to credit repair is "file segregation." The basic outline of the scheme involves the creation of a new identity for the client, which he can then use to establish a clean credit record. The problem with this system is that the use of a new identity to obtain credit constitutes fraud and leaves the client open for criminal charges.

First, the credit clinic will advise the client to apply for an Employer Identification Number (EIN) from the IRS. This number has the same number of digits as a Social Security number and is used by businesses for tax reporting. However, it is not intended for individual use and it is a federal crime to obtain an EIN under false pretenses. Then the credit clinic has the client establish a new mailing address, usually a mail drop, and pick a new name to go with his new credit identity.

Kevin Pleasant was just one of many Southern Californians looking for a solution to his credit problems when he attended a seminar offered by Michael Wang. A self-styled credit expert and lawyer, Wang promotes hotel seminars in which he tells people how to clean up their credit files and sells a collection of credit repair tapes and books, including one called "An Investigative Research and Legal Opinion on the File Segregation Method."

Wang claims that his seminars have made him rich, with attendance in excess of ten thousand people, many of whom have started their own credit repair clinics. But he has credit problems of his own, including an unpaid ten-thousand-dollar California state tax bill. Numerous newspapers are also trying to collect thousands of dollars in overdue advertising bills. Hardly a model credit manager, Wang still manages to attract the desperate and dishonest to his programs.

Pleasant was desperate because his part-time income as a carpet cleaner was not enough to keep up with payments on his student loans and credit cards. He didn't think he could afford to pay $495 for the books and tapes Wang was touting, but he left his name when he was promised a free tape. A few days later he received the first of many calls from Consumer Credit Co., a credit clinic run by one of Wang's former students.

They courted him, buying him meals and plying him with promises of the perfect solution to his credit troubles. Finally, Pleasant caved in and signed a contract with the company. He would pay one thousand five hundred dollars in several installments for a new identity. Six weeks later he received a package containing one of Wang's books, an FTC publication on credit repair, his new identity, and three clean credit reports under the name of Pleasant Richard. Pleasant was horrified that the credit clinic had *reversed* the first and last name he had selected.

Their error proved good fortune for Kevin Pleasant because he was reticent to use his new alias, thinking such an odd name would arouse suspicion. He has avoided serious legal repercussions, since file segregation violates a host of criminal and civil fraud statutes.

Use of an alias to gain credit from lenders and credit card companies may lead to wire or mail fraud charges if applications are made by phone or mail. Social Security payments credited to a nonexistent number would greatly reduce a person's retirement benefits. And tax returns filed with the bogus number would never pass through the IRS system, possibly leading to tax fraud charges. All in all, even with his debts and the loss of one thousand five hundred dollars to the credit fixers, Kevin Pleasant came out a winner.

Credit bureaus are beginning to take steps to counter file segregation schemes, which they won't divulge for obvious reasons. However, those still considering this alternative to suffering through bankruptcy should be advised that credit bureaus are highly suspicious of any new files created for middle-aged people. In addition, it just isn't easy to lead a double life.

Associated Credit Bureaus, the industry trade group, reports that anyone who pursues this avenue of credit repair will ultimately get caught. One small mistake, such as mention of an old address on a credit application, can cause the fake credit file to merge with the real one.

Credit card companies are taking steps to address the problem of file segregation, as well. Consumer bankruptcies cost bank card issuers over $2 billion in 1991, and that number could increase dramatically if large numbers of people fail to repay debts incurred under an alias. Vice President Kenneth R. Krone of Visa's bankruptcy recovery program reported that his staff was collecting information on the file segregation scam to pass on to Visa card issuers so they can protect themselves.

Law enforcement officials are working hard to close down these bogus credit repair operations as they spring up. In May 1992 John and Nancy Carruthers were arrested for selling twenty-thousand credit repair kits that extolled the file segregation scheme to unsuspecting customers across the nation. Officials seized the records of their firm, Credit Two, of Ft. Bragg, CA, and discovered that Carruthers had purchased mailing lists of people who had recently declared bankruptcy and proceeded with a massive mail campaign promoting the kits.

Taking advantage of people in dire straits seemed like a good idea to another group of con artists in Minnesota. They started Credit Minnesota, a mail-order credit repair company, similar to the Carruthers' Credit Two, by simply photocopying Credit Two's material and substituting their own name. The Minnesota Attorney General's office filed suit against them and put them out of business before they could do much damage.

Summary

The full extent of file segregation scams will not be revealed until law enforcement officials begin cracking down on individuals who use phony identities to establish credit and get caught. Those who do will discover that a few years of tight credit are nothing when compared to criminal charges leveled at them by lenders, the IRS, and the federal government.

What Can You Do To Protect Yourself From Credit Repair Fraud?

The best advice I can offer is to try and fix your credit yourself. If you can't fix it yourself, it may be best to grit your teeth and leave well enough alone.

Do-It-Yourself Credit Repair

There are several things an individual can do to improve credit without breaking the law or spending a fortune on credit fixers whose activities may or may not be legal. Considering how important a person's credit rating is in our credit-oriented society, it seems strange that most people never even review their credit histories. Instead, they allow lending institutions to control their credit profiles. Consumers who take an active role in maintaining their credit files will be far better off than 90 percent of the population.

First, acquire a copy of your credit report, which you can get for a nominal fee (around ten dollars) from the reporting agency. Credit bureaus operating in your area will be listed in your local telephone directory. The top four bureaus can also be contacted at their home offices.

TRW Credit Information
Services
505 City Parkway West
Orange, CA 92667

Trans Union Credit
Information
444 N. Michigan Avenue
Chicago, IL 60611

CBI/EQUIFAX
P.O. Box 4091
Atlanta, GA 30302

Associated Credit
Services, Inc.
652 E. North Belt, Suite 400
Houston, TX 77060

Compare the information in your credit report to your records. Take note of any discrepancies, particularly if you see negative information that seems inaccurate or if some business you don't recognize has run a credit check on you.

Occasionally, disreputable businesses will run credit checks on prospective customers without their knowledge or permission. This is illegal, and you should request the name and address of the business and contact them to advise them to remove the unauthorized inquiry immediately. Sometimes the credit bureau will assist you in removing such entries, since they cannot afford to have businesses misusing their services.

Making sure the information on your report is both accurate and up-to-date can be very helpful in cleaning up your credit file. These steps can lead to a greatly improved credit report and increased borrowing power:

- Have the credit bureau remove incorrect negative information about your payment history from your file upon verification that it is inaccurate. Bankruptcy information over ten years old and other judgments or late payments should be removed after seven years.
- Ask lenders who consider you a good credit risk if they would be willing to submit positive reports about your payment history if a credit bureau requested them. Then contact the credit bureau and request that they solicit the positive report from the lender and add it to your file. The bureau may charge a modest fee for doing this, but it's a worthwhile expense because the good report will balance your credit history.
- Update your employment information. This is another important part of your credit picture, since your income determines your borrowing power. If you have received a promotion, taken another job, or have increased your income in some verifiable manner, ask the credit bureau to add this new information to your file.

What Should You Do If You've Been Contacted by a Con Artist?

Don't participate in any illegal "credit repair" schemes. It's simply not worth the risk.

If you are contacted by a company making claims that it can provide you with a new credit identity, contact your state Attorney General or consumer protection agency. Notify the Federal Trade Commission. Even though the FTC doesn't handle individual complaints, they may act if they discern a pattern developing.

CHAPTER 19

Computer Scams

One day in 1990, a company that had placed an ad in *Game Pro* magazine somehow made an error. It failed to send two Staten Island teens a poster they'd ordered by mail.

It was a trivial mistake, it seemed. It was no big deal, until that September, when the magazine's publisher, International Data Group, began to suffer the consequences. Nearly all two hundred employees at IDG's Peterborough, NH, office walked into their offices one morning and found that their voice mailboxes had been sabotaged. Normal greetings had been replaced with gibberish spouted in odd voices. Incoming messages had been ruined and replaced with vulgar memos. There were even some recorded bomb threats.

It took IDG almost a full day to restore its phone system, and the sabotaging continued for weeks, mainly because the company didn't know who was causing the problems. It didn't realize that the Staten Island boys were attaining "revenge" remotely, by deftly instructing their personal computer to wreak havoc on IDG's daily operations.

These youths ultimately caused IDG to lose an estimated $2.4 million in business. They typified a breed of con artist that is prevalent these days—known as "phone phreaks," computer hackers, and crackers.

One underground newsletter directed toward "phone phreaks" defined computer hacking as randomly trying (as opposed to sequentially testing) the best phone numbers in order to access telephone systems. Hackers are not necessarily professional white-collar criminals or even vandals; frequently, they are trying to get into a system just to attain some sort of recognition for technical achievement. Some may have strong feelings against big businesses, particularly the telephone companies, but many are simply young men and women with prodigious computer savvy. Most have never been arrested. They're often simply addicted to the feelings they get when they're working on the computer, hot on the trail of breaking into someone else's system.

In his book *Fighting Computer Crime*, Donn B. Parker describes several factors that he thinks assure continued hacking problems. Young people are introduced to computers at very early ages, providing an ever-increasing supply of potential addicts, and experienced hackers and even computer instructors encourage young adults to try hacking. Other important factors are the ease in which computer systems can be compromised, and the failure of many companies to institute internal system controls to combat fraud.

The term "cracker" has recently been applied to professional criminals or other system trespassers who intentionally "crack" or access a system in order to gain information or services from which they will profit. Unlike hackers, who aren't necessarily trying to defraud a business, crackers may work for organized crime, drug dealers, or other big-time criminals who can't risk having their calls tapped or traced. Although some may use the terms interchangeably, for our purposes I'll use the term hackers since it's the term most often used in the industry.

Whether you call them phreaks, hackers, or crackers, the activities of such system intruders cost Americans at least several billion dollars each year. About $100 million is lost to illegal electronic fund transfers alone. Hackers primarily hit big businesses and government institutions because it usually takes longer for the fraud to be discovered, but they can worm their way into home computers, too, and they have a plethora of scams. One New York hacker was charged with federal wire fraud when he allegedly used two computers in his home to generate calls to thousands of pagers. When the unsuspecting individuals owning the pagers returned the call, they were charged fifty-five dollars for the pleasure of hearing a recorded message about two credit cards.

Hackers can steal or scramble confidential computer files, read glowing computer screens from afar, and even instruct a computer to deposit money into an illicit account. A student was able to enter the computer network at the Defense Department and place a disruptive "virus," a program that alters or destroys data, into the system. The first case of desktop publishing counterfeiting was discovered in 1989; with new technology, it's relatively easy to duplicate official government documents, stock certificates, even bank checks. Using computers, embezzlers can manipulate or destroy company records to cover their crimes, or they may add names of fictitious suppliers and authorize payments to come to them.

As well as being able to infiltrate voice mail systems, hackers know how to make millions of dollars' worth of long-distance calls at their victims' expense. AT&T recently recorded over $1 billion in telephone charges it was unable to collect in a year, a large part of that figure resulting from fraud.

Experts agree that no system is 100 percent hacker-proof. The hacking industry, the Better Business Bureau warns, is diversifying these days, and growing. Growing because the computer is becoming more and more commonplace in the American office, and because today's computer systems are more accessible, for honest citizens and hackers alike.

In the past, computer security expert James R. Wade explains in a recent article in *Security Management,* computer systems were typically quite isolated. A system at Company A, in other words, could not communicate with a system at Company B. Barriers to keep hackers out could be simply erected—but they can't be anymore. The new technological era, where information is more accessible and easier to use, has its downside, Wade reminds us, by complicating the security required to protect the telecommunication and computer systems.

Information can now flow freely across nations, into factories and home offices and, in some cases, right into the grasp of a covetous con artist. Indeed, anyone who has a modem—the device that enables computer data to travel over phone lines—is hooked into a vast global information network. Speed dialers, which can readily crack codes and PINs (personal identification numbers), and other sophisticated equipment are also used to penetrate computer networks. Frequently, "insiders" such as technicians, system installers, and others familiar with a company's equipment have been bribed to disclose their customer's most classified information.

Computer users, in such a climate, need to be careful. They need to know how hackers work and how they can be foiled. The following are some of the most pernicious scams that hackers are now pulling off.

Electronic Funds Transfers

For most people, wheat farming takes loads of machinery and hours of arduous work. For Danita J. Suhling, however, it's a different story.

Suhling "changed" a portion of her husband's Springfield, IL, corn crop to wheat by merely pushing a few buttons on her computer keyboard. Suhling used a password to access the crop records of her former employer, the Agricultural Stabilization and Conservation Service, and then altered the files, so that her husband, Randall Suhling, soon gleaned two undeserved farm-support checks totaling $2625. Ms. Suhling pleaded guilty to unauthorized computer use and was placed on probation and ordered to return all of the money.

It was an ingenuous scam, and one that is now perpetrated with frightening frequency. The Better Business Bureau reports that hackers score about $100 million annually in electronic fund transfers. They use modems to break into computer files, and their scams are not easily detectable.

The BBB says that the criminals add names of fictitious suppliers to a company's list of vendors, and then instruct the business' computer to authorize payment to the phony suppliers. The instructions sit nestled in files containing utility bill records and other such minutiae—and often it is months, or even years, before a given company realizes it's paying phony bills.

Data Theft

Much of the computer information sent via modem today is confidential. Banks dispense account information; companies send out new ideas that have not yet been copyrighted. All the little bits of data, as they zip over the phone lines, are exposed; vulnerable like so many pieces of clothing on a line. Increasingly, crooks are stealing transmitted secrets.

The Better Business Bureau reports, for instance, that a ring of hackers recently accessed phone lines transmitting bank transactions to automatic teller machines. The thieves ascertained customers' ATM numbers, and then made their own bogus cards for use at money-dispensing machines.

Computer data isn't just stolen as it's on the wire, either. Electromagnetic sensing devices can spy on computer users as they're inputting and printing data. From a hideout a mile away, they can assess the radiation a computer is generating, decode it, and know precisely what a victim is writing.

Toll Fraud

Robert Gensa couldn't figure it out when odd phone calls starting coming in over the 800 line at his office.

Gensa, a vice-president for Industrial Corp., says the callers were speaking Spanish over the sound of passing busses and cars. They pushed buttons and hung up whenever an IC employee spoke a word—and Gensa guessed that IC was just getting a rash of harassing calls.

By the time his firm got its phone bill, though, Gensa knew precisely what was going on. Hackers had found a way to access IC's switchboard and to subsequently make long-distance overseas calls at the company's expense. They'd found a way, in short, to give IC a serious headache. Gensa said that he finally stopped the calls by disconnecting the 800 number that connected the company to the eastern part of the U.S.

The firm's bills detailed one hundred twenty-five thousand dollars in fraudulently made toll calls. The calls all originated from New York and went to places as distant as the Dominican Republic, Ecuador, and Peru. And though Gensa doesn't know who did all the dialing, it's reasonable to guess that it was immigrants who yearned to connect with their families.

John Haugh, the editor of a national newsletter called *Toll Fraud and Telabuse,* reports that frequently the cons sell access numbers to sidewalk "call-sell" entrepreneurs who, in turn, hawk cheap international calls—from ten to thirty dollars per call—to immigrants too destitute to own phones.

Hackers also peddle access codes to drug dealers and criminals who prefer to use other people's numbers so that their calls cannot be easily traced. And the effects of their scamming is staggering.

Toll fraud, Haugh says, now costs Americans over $4 billion a year, and it has hit hard some of the nation's largest companies and institutions. It's estimated that the average toll fraud bill when a business is hit is ninety thousand dollars. The list of businesses hit by hackers reads like the Fortune 500; it includes IBM, American Express, and Proctor & Gamble. The National Aeronautics and Space Administration (NASA) estimates it lost $12 million to toll fraud, while the United Nations was victimized to the tune of $1 million.

Even the Drug Enforcement Agency (DEA) was tapped. Its remote access number in Houston, TX, was used by criminals for eighteen months. About $2 million in phone calls were charged to the DEA, many of them to drug-exporting countries.

How did the hackers do it? How did they sneak past the safeguards of such presumably secure institutions?

Committing toll fraud is fairly easy. The only equipment a crook needs to go into business is a computer equipped with a modem and an "autodialer," a widely available device that costs about twenty-nine dollars and can randomly dial 1-800 numbers. Hackers typically set their autodialers to work by pressing some buttons; the computer then inevitably connects with some 800 lines. It records the connections in a printout.

Hackers read the printouts, then instruct their computers to search again. This time, they take one of two tacks. They seek out the code numbers that employees punch in when they're on the road and want to make long-distance calls at the company's expense. Or they try to worm their way into an individual employee's voice mailbox, and then ferret out the "trunk access code"—a typically little-known four-digit number which, when dialed, routes a caller around a phone's security systems, so he or she can make unlimited long-distance calls.

Such strategies can work because thousands of corporations are equipped with telephone "ports" set up to enable people to enter their phone systems remotely. They're equipped with DISA ports— which are those ports designed to allow traveling employees to dial into the system and back out again—and with "RMAT ports"—remote access ports that enable technicians to access and repair phone systems from afar. When hackers penetrate these gateways they sell the access codes they glean for as much as ten thousand dollars. Their victims, meanwhile, get slapped with big, inescapable bills.

The law holds that, if a business owns its own phone equipment, it is responsible for all calls going through that equipment, whether the calls are authorized or not. Several court cases have upheld this provision, and phone companies like AT&T, MCI, and U.S. Sprint scarcely jump to cover the cost of toll fraud. Besides, they'd argue, customers control the security of their own equipment.

These businesses all monitor international calling traffic, and alert customers when they note unusual calling patterns. But they insist on close to full payment for fraudulently made calls. MCI, for instance, offers a 30-percent discount to first-time victims of toll fraud, and AT&T gives at best a partial discount to victimized clients.

Richard T. Hope, senior attorney for AT&T, has defended this policy: "The customer alone knows what calls are authorized or unauthorized." And he is right: Customers can distinguish legitimate calls from bogus ones. The problem is that, too often, they can't do so until it's already too late.

How To Prevent Hackers From Infiltrating Your Computer System

James Wade writes that safeguards needed to protect computer and telecommunications systems must be risk-oriented and based on realistic cost-benefit analyses. To provide a seamless protection, "safeguards must be easy to use and provide a provable level of trust. . . . On one hand, security must become more technical in its design; at the same time, it must be easier to implement by users throughout the enterprise." He reminds us that the half-life of computer technology is now estimated at about a year, which means that new technological advances will make previous advances obsolete in about one year's time. Unfortunately, hackers keep pace with technological advances, too, so what can you do to protect yourself and your business?

Develop a written computer security policy and educate your employees on the potential for computer fraud. The policy should at the very least cover the topics of access, physical security, backup measures, record-keeping, storage procedures, and copying programs and disks. Make sure all employees understand and follow the security procedures.

Ask employees to sign a confidentiality and proprietary information agreement that's been approved by the corporate attorney.

Limit access to computer facilities.   The identification of all nonem-
ployees and their reason for needing entry should be verified, and
only employees whose work requires they enter the facilities should
be allowed access.

*Install a software program that continually checks for viruses and alerts you when such
an alien program is spotted.*

Consider installing an encryption system that enables you to send encoded messages.
Message recipients can decipher the code, as long as they have specific software.

Guard passwords with your life!   Never publish—or even write down—a
computer password. (It's not unusual for con artists to go through
garbage cans for such important information.) Change computer
passwords regularly.

Group your computers in one spot, preferably in the middle of your building.   The
interference from the building's phone lines and your computers'
combined electromagnetic "noise" will make eavesdropping from
a distance difficult.

*At least once a year, hire an outside consulting firm to audit your computer security
system.*

How To Protect Your Business From Toll Fraud

*Don't install risky features in your telecommunications system that create vulnerabili-
ties unnecessarily.*

If possible, refrain from installing a DISA port.   Instead of offering this
phone system feature, which enables employees out of the office to
dial in and then out again, instruct employees to use telephone
calling cards when they want to make long-distance calls at the
company's expense.

*If you must maintain a DISA port, restrict access to it and instruct employees to guard
their authorization codes the same way they would computer passwords.*

Create long, random passwords or access numbers, and change them frequently.
Don't use the default passwords or access numbers.

Never publish the 800 numbers employees use to access your DISA port.

Delete DISA authorizations for employees who've left your company.

Make sure that no one can dial into your voice mail system and then dial out again.

Establish a procedure to regularly remove any voice mailboxes that are not currently in service.

If possible, refrain from setting up an RMAT port, which enables technicians to enter and repair your system remotely. Although your vendor may squawk, there are viable alternatives, such as use of temporary access codes created by the in-house system manager, or the use of a smart modem.

If appropriate, install a block on your phone system that disables users from making international calls at your expense.

Closely monitor computer-generated call detail reports that itemize calls made from your system.

Consider buying toll fraud protection, which is available from most phone companies. Keep in mind that it's not inexpensive, and the insurance just covers the fraudulent phone charges, not any business losses. And it's not meant to take the place of appropriate security measures.

Consider purchasing a software program that "flags" any signs of hacking. Ask your telecommunications vendor and long-distance carrier for specific referrals, and check out any supplier carefully; because this is a new industry, you can count on finding fly-by-night vendors and others who will promise more than they can deliver.

What To Do If You're Victimized

If you've been hit by toll fraud, temporarily deactivate your company's 800 lines, then contact your attorney, the police, your local district attorney's office, and your phone company.

If your phone company refuses to cover any of the fraudulently made toll calls, think twice before suing. The courts have upheld the rulings that companies that own their own phone equipment are responsible for all calls made on their systems.

If a hacker has cracked your security system, contact your attorney, the police, and the district attorney.

CONCLUSION

While I was writing this conclusion, I received the following postcard from U. S. Credit Systems, Inc., in my mailbox.

IMPORTANT NOTICE

THIS NOTICE INFORMS YOU THAT *YOU ARE APPROVED* FOR A *U.S. CHARGE*[SM] **CREDIT CARD** WITH THESE CARD MEMBER BENEFITS:

- ☑ **$2,500 Immediate Line of Credit - GUARANTEED!**
- ☑ **Personally Embossed *U.S. CHARGE*[SM] CREDIT CARD**
- ☑ **Get your own Major Bankcard regardless of your credit situation!**
  (This card honored worldwide at over 5 million locations)
- ☑ **NO CREDIT CHECK and NO INTEREST CHARGES!**
- ☑ **Cash Advance Program**
- ☑ **Debt Consolidation for Personal Bills**

GUARANTEED ACCEPTANCE

YOU ARE APPROVED - You cannot be turned down! (if 18 or older)
CALL TODAY and talk with one of our New Account Representatives about your New Credit Card and Card Member Benefits.

TOLL FREE   **1-800-737-1000**   TOLL FREE

Approved Accounts Department
When calling, please refer to your Approval Code on the reverse side.

I called the 800 number on the card and the operator confirmed the information shown. I then called the Better Business Bureau in Phoenix, AZ. They reported numerous complaints about the company, including no refunds, slow refunds, and harassing phone calls, just to list a few. Although it had responded to some of the BBB's complaints, the business "doesn't meet Better Business Bureau standards," according to the spokesperson with whom I spoke.

I phoned the general manager of U. S. Credit Systems, Inc., Shannon Qualley. He reported to me that U.S. Credit had three hundred seventy thousand card holders and that the six-year-old company was mailing eight thousand cards per week. Qualley explained to me his understanding of what the postcard actually says. His remarks and my comments are on the right side of Figure 1.

A book about confidence games would have to be at least one thousand pages to thoroughly cover all the scams in existence. I've attempted to inform you of the most common ones. And, I'm sure that, as this book went to press, and even as you're reading along, new scams are being devised and executed. Hopefully, you'll be more aware and alert to them after having read this book.

Each and every day of our lives we are driven to make purchasing choices and asked to assess value. I hope that *Easy Money* will make you a little more cautious, a little more careful in your buying and investing decisions, and a little more skeptical about the people with whom you do business and any others to whom you may give your hard-earned money.

Fortunately for the potential victim, all of the con artists' schemes have a common thread: the promise of something for nothing, a deal too good to believe, immediate relief for an insurmountable problem, or the confidence that one person can solve your problem—whatever that problem may be. I hope that you see the foolishness of the "quick buck," the easy answer, and the absurdity of instant solutions to the problems life presents.

The confidence man and woman could become as rare as the California condor if people would simply follow a few basic rules:

Never forget: If it appears too good to believe, don't believe it.
Be suspicious of all strangers.
Question all business transactions.
Thoroughly check out everyone with whom you do business.

Card Information	General Manager's Remarks and My Comments

IMPORTANT NOTICE
THIS NOTICE INFORMS YOU
THAT *YOU ARE APPROVED*
FOR A U.S. CHARGE^{SM}
CREDIT CARD WITH THESE
CARD MEMBER BENEFITS:

$2,500 Immediate Line of Credit—GUARANTEED!	After you purchase $500 worth of merchandise in their catalog
Personally Embossed U.S. CHARGE^{SM} CREDIT CARD	After you pay $33.60 + $8.40
Get your own Major Bankcard regardless of your credit situation! (This card honored worldwide at over 5 million locations)	After you send a check for an amount equal to your credit limit
NO CREDIT CHECK and NO INTEREST CHARGES!	Only on the U.S. Charge^{SM} Credit Card
Cash Advance Program	Only available if you get major credit card with a cash deposit made to secure advance
Debt Consolidation for Personal Bills	Send U.S. Charge^{SM} your money each month and they pay your bills for you. (Of course, if they fail to pay your bills, you still owe the payment.)
GUARANTEED ACCEPTANCE YOU ARE APPROVED—You cannot be turned down! (if 18 or older) Call today and talk with one of our New Account Representatives about your New Credit Card and Card Member Benefits.	For the U.S. Charge^{SM} Credit Card You receive a $100 discount certificate good toward your first purchase in their catalog. (If the prices in their catalog are inflated, you gain nothing.)
TOLL FREE 1–800–737–1000 TOLL FREE Approved Accounts Department When calling, please refer to your Approval Code on the reverse side.	(Three people called and used the same "approval code" without any of the Account Representatives asking any questions.)

Figure 1

Verify every investment or business opportunity with independent experts.

Don't contribute money to any cause without knowing exactly where the money is going.

Jealously guard all personal information such as your Social Security number, bank account information, credit card information, your driver's license number, your phone number, and even your birth date.

Don't pay for anything up front unless you've dealt with the firm before and know it to be reputable. Wait until a product or service is delivered before issuing payment.

If you're lonely, join a legitimate social organization or association in which you have an interest.

Never gamble with someone you don't know well.

Have your attorney or other trusted business professional read every contract before you sign it.

Don't participate in any illegal schemes.

Remember: Nothing takes the place of hard work, good planning, caution, and practical solutions. Quick fixes usually result in disastrous consequences. Millions of marks can attest to that fact.

Unfortunately, as long as there are people who are desperate, trusting, lonely, greedy, naive, sick, or senile, there will be con artists. Predators and parasites abound in the animal kingdom, and the human race contains some of the worst. The con artist pretends to be your friend, confidant, or long-lost relative. He may even be your doctor, lawyer, accountant, minister, or another whom you trust. Once he wins your trust he may take you for everything you're worth. Like the lion eating his prey, the confidence man or woman enjoys the chase, the kill, and the feast.

I've dealt with illegal con games in *Easy Money*, but there are what one might call "legal cons," too. *Caveat emptor,* the principle that someone buying something does so at his or her own peril (commonly known as "buyer beware"), should be remembered whenever you're thinking about handing over your hard-earned money to anyone. When you board an airplane after having written a check for one thousand dollars to travel from Los Angeles to Miami, and the passenger next to you paid only two hundred twelve dollars for the same flight, you often feel conned. If a passenger is unable to make the flight because of some unforeseen event and can't get a refund, it feels just like being cheated. When staying at a hotel that adds seventy-five cents per telephone call and then doubles the price of each call, the traveler feels ripped-off. Bait-and-switch schemes are commonplace, even in the most reputable retail stores. There's often a very fine line between what's illegal and what's unethical. A buyer can never really let down his or her guard.

After researching *Easy Money* I realized how many times I had been conned over the years. I feel a little foolish now that I know how the swindles that I bought into actually worked. I feel a little angry that people took advantage of my ignorance, naïveté, and greed. I feel hurt that people whom I trusted violated that trust. After dealing with those feelings I have an additional feeling—one of strength; the kind of inner strength that usually accompanies accomplishment. It felt great to free myself from nicotine addiction. It felt terrific to win in business where so many before me had failed. And it's a tremendous feeling to know that a swindler can no longer take advantage of me.

Knowledge is strength. If by writing *Easy Money* I have saved one person's life savings, one person's home, or one person's mental or physical health, then I will have achieved my goal. If only one con artist is taken off the street, I will be successful. If you are able to avoid being swindled because you recognized a con game before "donating" your money to what is truly a lost cause, then you'll understand the terrific sensation of power you can have over one of the lowest forms of life on this planet: the confidence artist.

GLOSSARY

addict A victim who repeatedly is taken in by a con artist.

advance fee scam Any form of con in which a swindler falsely promises his victim that he will get a bank loan or credit card provided he or she pays a "small" fee for these services up-front.

advertising solicitation scheme A scam in which the con artists convince businesses to place costly ads in nonexistent or misrepresented publications. The schemes often involve solicitations which look very much like invoices.

autograph A con game in which the victim is cajoled into signing a slip of paper that is later changed into a negotiable check.

automatic debit scam When a con artist makes unauthorized withdrawals from a victim's checking account.

bail bond con In this scam, the con artist phones his victim in the middle of the night, posing as a neighbor's friend. The con says that the neighbor has been unjustly tossed into jail and needs someone to post bail. Then he visits his victim's home and picks up the money.

bait-and-switch A customer tries to buy a product advertised at a special or sale price, but the product is not available. The customer is pressured into buying another, usually more expensive, product instead.

bank examiner scheme In this classic con, the con man impersonates a bank examiner or law enforcement official such as a policeman. Informing his victim that a bank teller is suspected of stealing money from his or her bank, he then urges the victim to help catch the thief by withdrawing a certain amount of cash and temporarily giving it to the "police." Often, the bunco artist instructs his victim to handle bills with gloves to avoid fingerprinting them. Always, he keeps the cash.

bankruptcy fraud When a business uses the federal bankruptcy laws to defraud creditors, such as creating a phony company in order to establish credit or buying an established business for little money down with the intention of shutting it down. It frequently involves filing for bankruptcy after buying merchandise on credit, subsequently selling the merchandise in secret, and hiding the profits of the sale.

big con Any confidence game in which the victim is sent to get funds, usually from his bank account. Big cons are generally more complex than "short cons," in which the victim is bilked only of the money he has on his person. Also known as a Long Con.

big store A place of business that's been created to fool a mark into thinking it's a legitimate business.

blind pool penny stock scam An investment scam in which the victim is persuaded to invest in a penny stock company "blindly"—that is, without any notion as to how he'll make a profit. The company's bogus promoter buys the stock at a fraction of what the public pays. He constantly manipulates the stock price with boiler-room sales, and then, when the stock reaches its peak, he sells out. The price collapses and the victim is left with worthless stock.

block hustle A con that involves a hustler covertly hawking "stolen goods" on the street for a fraction of their value. The con artist may persuade his victim not to open the box containing the goods until the victim has privacy. The box, of course, contains worthless items such as bricks or newspapers.

blow-off Getting a mark to leave after he's been conned, hopefully without arousing his suspicion.

boiler room   A telemarketing enterprise that uses high-pressure sales tactics over the phone. It is often operated out of inexpensive, low-rent headquarters. Often false and misleading information is provided in order to solicit business.

boodle   A phony bankroll, usually made up of small bills, that the con artist uses to deceive a victim.

bunco (also bunk or bunko)   See *confidence game.*

c or the c   Abbreviated form of con or confidence game.

call-sell operator   One who sells calls, frequently to poor immigrants, using stolen phone access codes or stolen credit calling card numbers.

card activation system   A security procedure instituted by credit card issuers. Credit cards cannot be used until the cardholder contacts the issuer and verifies his or her identity, usually with a Social Security number.

chain letter   See *Ponzi scheme.*

check kiting   An embezzlement scam that hustlers play on banks. The con man opens a checking account at Bank A by giving the teller a check written on an empty bank account at Bank B. Then, the next day, he deposits into his account at Bank B a check written on his account at Bank A. He continues to float, or "kite," checks in this manner for several days. His bank accounts swell at no cost to him, and then, suddenly, he withdraws the cash from both accounts and hits the road.

chump   See *mark.*

computer virus   A computer program specifically created to alter or destroy data.

con mob   All of the hustlers involved in a particular confidence game.

confederate   See *shill.*

confidence game   A swindle or deceptive scheme in which fraud is perpetrated upon a victim after the perpetrator wins the victim's confidence. The victim is led to believe that he or she will profit—sometimes illegally—from the relationship. Also known as bunco and flimflam.

counterfeit product   An exact replica of a product, including the genuine article's brand name and logo.

coupon fraud   The fraudulent use of legitimate coupons originally intended to enable consumers to obtain a discount or free product or service. Coupon fraud may be committed by making and using counterfeit coupons, unauthorized agents securing and selling coupons, or redeeming coupons for merchandise never purchased.

cracking   Using a computer affixed with a modem to infiltrate another party's electronic system for criminal purposes. Not to be confused with hacking, a more general term used to describe the passion of often innocent, frequently antiauthoritarian computer aficionados.

credit repair scheme   Any scheme where swindlers promise to clean up the credit records of individuals with poor credit for a fee. These schemes often involve creating a new identity for the victim.

damage claim artist   A con artist who pretends to be injured, threatens to sue, and then accepts an out-of-court settlement in lieu of going to court to recover damages.

digital signature   A computer code that enables the purchaser of a software program to tell if the program has been tampered with.

dirt-pile scams   The mark is given the opportunity to invest in a gold mining operation by purchasing a quantity of unprocessed dirt from the mine. Although the dirt is guaranteed to contain enough gold to cover the cost of the investment, in reality, the investment is virtually worthless. Central to the scam: The mark is told that the return on investment takes from one to three years. This gives the promoters time to get money from lots of investors before anyone gets suspicious.

diverter fraud   A fraud that involves reselling drugs in order to bilk the insurance company. A healthy patient fills a prescription at a crooked pharmacy, then sells the prescription back to the pharmacy at a small fraction of the cost. The pharmacist then resells the prescription.

dummy supply company   A nonexistent vendor that invents purchase order records and then receives the payments.

dumpster diver   An individual who delves into trash in hopes of recovering and using valuable information such as computer passwords, credit card receipts, etc.

egg See *mark.*

the electric bar A con worked at a tavern with a magnetized plate and dice with metal spots configured to turn up the desired numbers each time they're rolled and the electrical current is on.

embezzlement Taking or converting (usually company) money or property for one's personal use or benefit in violation of a trust.

file segregation Creating a new identity for a person with poor credit so that he or she appears to have a clean credit history.

flimflam See *confidence game.*

foreclosure forestallment scam When a con man posing as a "financial counselor" promises to postpone foreclosure on a victim's home for an up-front fee.

foreign bank investment scam A con (usually telemarketing) in which swindlers falsely promise victims huge profits from investments in overseas banks.

franchise fraud Any scam in which a franchiser defrauds a franchisee by disappearing with the investment money, going out of business, misrepresenting the amount of training or field support, or shows in some other way that he dealt in bad faith.

friendship swindle A scam that starts when a con artist befriends a lonely old person, ostensibly for altruistic reasons. The con endears himself to the senior by spending time with him or her and then, after a while, begins to borrow large sums of money from his aging "friend."

the give away A con game that revolves around a swindler selling cheap merchandise, then fully refunding his victims and, finally, selling worthless goods at an inflated price before escaping.

gold brick con An old-time confidence game in which the swindler disguises a normal brick as a gold one and sells it to a victim.

green-goods racket A scam in which a victim pays real money for what he believes is perfectly made counterfeit cash.

grifter A criminal who lives by his wits without using violence. Another name for a skilled con artist.

hacking When a person who is intensely interested in computers tries to break into computer systems. Unlike computer cracking, hacking is not always done for criminal intent but for the sheer challenge of trying to break in.

home diversion game A scam that starts when two con men visit the home of their victim, usually an old person. One con artfully distracts the victim as the other scours the house, searching for jewelry or cash to steal.

hot seat A con game in which the victim is convinced he's been hired to deliver a bundle of cash, and is then persuaded to post a deposit to demonstrate his good intentions. The bundle of cash turns out to be filled with shredded paper.

house of cards See *Ponzi scheme.*

insideman One member of a group of con men who receives the mark brought in by the outsideman.

Jamaica switch In this con game, the victim is asked to hold a bundle of cash for a "visiting foreigner" while the foreigner, who is really a swindler, goes off to conduct some business. The victim is required to post a small deposit as earnest money. He realizes that he's been had when the bunco artist never returns, and he opens the "bankroll" to find that it's been switched for a wad of ripped-up newspaper.

knockoff product Almost-identical replicas of products. Unlike a counterfeit product, a knockoff intentionally changes the brand name or logo of the genuine article.

loan broker scam See *advance fee scam.*

mail fraud Any scheme to defraud that uses the mail as an important element. The entire intent of the scam could be to defraud people of their money, or the information presented about the products advertised could be misrepresented or misleading to the recipients.

mark A term for the target or the victim of a confidence game. Also referred to by con men as the egg, the chump, or the sucker.

mooch A potential victim, especially of telephone swindlers.

Multiple Employer Welfare Arrangement (MEWA) Several small employers pool their resources and use combined dollars to insure health coverage for workers. Although originally created to help small businesses get health insurance, many have become fraudulent and have refused to pay the claims of policyholders.

the mush   A con game played at ballparks or racetracks on a rainy day. The swindler takes bets on the sporting event, and then raises his umbrella (his mush) and vanishes into the crowd.

need help scams   The scam artist tells strangers that his wife is sick, his car has broken down, or other tales of woe. The swindler collects cash, then disappears.

never received issue (NRI)   A credit card scam in which a card is intercepted and stolen before it ever gets to the rightful cardholder.

obituary hoax   In this scam, a con artist pores over a newspaper's death notices, then visits the home of the bereaved. He may demand payment on a debt owed by the dead person, or he may try to deliver a C.O.D. package that is worth far less than the cost of delivery.

outsideman   Also known as a roper or a steerer. An outsideman locates a likely victim and brings him into the con game.

paper accident   A "car accident" created on paper by con artists hoping to bilk an insurance carrier. Hustlers, in manufacturing a paper accident, often forge wreck photos, police reports, and repair estimates. In some cases, they even create "paper vehicles" by providing vehicle identification numbers of cars that don't exist.

paper firm   A fictitious company—often an insurance company—created to defraud businesses. It exists only on paper.

paper pirates   Fraudulent telemarketers who call businesses, pitching office products that sound inexpensive but are, in reality, shoddy and overpriced. Also known as toner phoners.

the payoff   An intricate, classic con game. A wealthy mark is made to believe that he'll be betting on a fixed horse race in order to swindle a huge racing syndicate. At first the mark bets with money given to him by the con men. His trust bolstered, he is then encouraged to raise all the betting money he can. The cons then pocket the cash and take off.

PBX fraud   See *phone phreaking*.

phone phreaking   Using computers to infiltrate and tamper with phone systems, usually to place costly calls that are charged to the company's bill. Also called PBX fraud.

phony invoice scheme   Swindlers send legitimate-looking bills for undelivered goods or services to businesses.

pigeon drop   A classic street swindle that starts when a hustler meets a victim and then strolls along with him, only to "discover" a stray cache of money. The con man convinces the victim that they should take the cash to a lawyer who can hold the money until it can be legally distributed. The lawyer (who is, of course, a cohort of the con) convinces the victim to put up earnest money while the cash is being held. The victim never sees the earnest money again or his half of the funds that were discovered.

plant   See *shill.*

playing the doctor   Street slang for executing diverter fraud, a scam involving a pharmacist who resells drugs. See *diverter fraud.*

Ponzi scheme   An investment racket in which the scam operator collects investment money and then pays his clients "interest" by skimming funds from the deposits made by later investors. Many victims actually make early profits in Ponzi scams, but they inevitably get bilked if they stay in the scheme because the operator ultimately runs off with their investments. Also known as a pyramid scheme, house of cards, chain letter, and snowballs.

premium diversion fraud   Diverting insurance premiums paid by policyholders so that the money will not be available to pay claims later.

pyramid scheme   See *Ponzi scheme.*

the rag   Like the payoff, this con game involves hustlers ripping off a rich person by leading him to believe that he'll reap a huge profit at the expense of a big business. The grifters claim that they represent a legitimate stock brokerage aiming to financially break a phony brokerage. They help their victim to profit on several initial investments and then, once they've gained his confidence, they fleece him.

reinsurance scam   Undercapitalized reinsurance companies—often outside the United States—tout bogus or inflated assets. The insurance companies using the firms, having decreased their reserves accordingly, are often unable to meet the legitimate demands for claims and are increasingly being forced out of business.

reload scam Consumers who've fallen for prize offers on postcards are called back by fraudulent telemarketers and given a second chance to be suckered in again.

roper See *outsideman.*

running the buckets A scam pulled by crooked house painters. The cons use two or three buckets of paint in their work, then run several others through a vat of pigment so that it looks like twenty or so buckets have been used to complete the job. The victim ends up paying for more paint than was actually used.

the send The point in a con game at which the victim is sent home or to the bank for money.

shill In partnership with the con artist, a shill is someone who acts as a customer to win the confidence of a potential victim. The victim sees the shill "win" or make a profit and gains confidence in the con artist's proposal. Also called a plant or confederate.

short con A con in which the victim is taken for only the money he is carrying at the time.

shoulder surfer A criminal who steals victims' phone calling card numbers by loitering near phone booths and peering over callers' shoulders. Shoulder surfers usually haunt airports, hotels, and train stations, where banks of phones are prevalent. The card numbers are often sold.

shake with the button A quick, old-time scam in which the mark and the con artist are arrested for gambling on the street and "shaken down" by a phony cop, who is a cohort of the con man. The mark is allowed to leave.

snowballs See *Ponzi scheme.*

soap game This archaic scam involves cons who hawk bars of soap that are supposedly wrapped in twenty-dollar bills. People fall for the ploy because, typically, the crowd is sprinkled with shills who actually do get bills with their soap.

social engineering   When a computer cracker attains a secret password by talking to someone. For instance, a "social engineer" might phone a company's secretary and, posing as an executive, says he's forgotten his password in order to gain access to the computer system.

Spanish prisoner   An involved con game in which a victim is convinced that a prisoner will reveal his hidden treasure to the victim once the victim secures legal aid for the person in jail.

steerer   See *outsideman.*

sting   When a con artist takes his victim's money.

straw man   Term used for someone who profits by posing as someone he's not, usually in a real estate transaction. For example, someone who's paid by a con to pose as a buyer or seller in a property deal but who really has no interest in the property other than what he's being paid to participate. The straw man may or may not be in on the con game.

suckers list   Used by telemarketers, these are lists of people who've been conned one or more times.

sweetheart scam   When a con artist romances his victim in order to obtain the victim's money or other assets.

switch   When a con artist "innocently" guides his intended victim into a discussion of the mechanism of the scam to make the victim think it was his or her idea all along. Also, to substitute one item for another, such as a phony item for a legitimate one.

the tat   A gambling swindle used in nightclubs. The con asks his victim to play a dice game such as craps with him. The victim rolls a regular die, but the con uses a "tat," or a crooked die, that always lands on the number the con wants it to.

technical cracking   Using software and computer savvy to infiltrate another party's electronic system. Often, technical crackers employ a "dictionary attack." They create a dictionary of possible passwords and then try those words on the system they are seeking to infiltrate.

teleblackmail   Blackmail of innocent employees who've been conned by fraudulent telemarketers, often the toner phoners. The telemarketers blackmail the employees who unsuspectedly purchased supplies at inflated prices by sending them gifts and threatening to tell their bosses that they bought expensive office supplies and accepted extravagant gifts from a vendor.

three-card monte   A card game con in which tricksters ask the victims to select a queen from a trio of cards that usually includes two aces. The victim is able to "find the lady" easily at first, because the cons "unwittingly" bend the corner of the queen card for him. But the victim's luck quickly goes sour as the cons mislead him by bending the corners of the aces.

toll fraud   Unauthorized use of long-distance services by a party not authorized by a company or one of its staff.

toner phoners   Similar to paper pirates, these swindlers use the phone to peddle poor-quality copy machine ink, or toner, to businesses at inflated prices.

touch   The money taken or "scored" from a victim.

Travelers   Groups of Scottish-, Irish-, and English-Americans living as clans in the southern United States who perpetrate home repair fraud as they travel across the U.S.

WATS line hustling   A generic term sometimes used by the police to describe the activities of high-pressure telemarketers who contact their victims by phone from huge boiler rooms lined with banks of telephones.

the wire   An archaic betting con in which a mark thinks he can get racing results prior to placing a bet. Often, a con artist, posing as a Western Union official, tells the victim he can stall on sending the results of a given horse race to the bookmaker. The victim, believing he can place a bet after the race was run, shells out money to the con, whom he never sees again.

work-at-home scam   The perpetrator of this type of scheme offers victims easy, quick money for a limited amount of work done in the home. These scams, such as stuffing envelopes or assembly work, usually require that the victim pay a fee up front to learn the operation.

RESOURCES

Alliance Against Fraud in Telemarketing (AAFT)
c/o National Consumers League
815 15th Street NW, Suite 928N
Washington, DC 20005
202–639–8140

A program of the National Consumers League, its membership includes consumer groups, trade associations, unions, and governmental agencies that work to provide education to the public and prevent telemarketing fraud. Provides information on fraud practices, distributes education materials, and develops public service announcements to alert consumers to telemarketing fraud. A brochure, *Swindlers Are Calling*, is available.

American Association of Fund Raising Counsel (AAFRC)
25 W. 43rd Street, Suite 1519
New York, NY 10036
212–354–5799

Represents fund-raising counseling firms engaged in consulting on management and planning of campaigns for all types of nonprofit organizations. Maintains committees dealing with professional ethics and public service.

American Association of Retired Persons (AARP)
601 E Street NW
Washington, DC 20049
202–434–2277

Membership organization of persons fifty years of age or older, working or retired. AARP seeks to promote quality of life for older people, targeting the areas of health care, women's initiative, worker equity, and minority affairs. Also sponsors community service programs on crime prevention, defensive driving, and tax aid. Publications include books on housing, health, exercise, retirement planning, money management, and travel and leisure.

American Bankers Association (ABA)
1120 Connecticut Avenue NW
Washington, DC 20036
202–663–5000

Seeks to enhance the role of commercial banks as preeminent providers of financial services through communications, research, legal action, lobbying, and education and training programs.

American Insurance Association (AIA)
1130 Connecticut Avenue NW, Suite 1000
Washington, DC 20036
202–828–7100

Professional association of property and casualty insurance companies that serves as a clearinghouse for information on the insurance business for both consumers and insurance professionals.

American Medical Association (AMA)
515 State Street
Chicago, IL 60610
312–464–4818

National professional association of physicians. Works to promote high-quality medical practice through dissemination of information and the activities of its medical ethics committee.

American Society of Travel Agents (ASTA)
1101 King Street
Alexandria, VA 22314
703–739–2782

Professional association of travel agents and others in the travel industry. Among other activities, they seek to promote professional and ethical conduct in the travel agency industry and facilitate consumer protection and safety when traveling.

American Telemarketing Association (ATA)
444 N. Larchmont Boulevard, Suite 200
Los Angeles, CA 90004
213-463-2330
800-441-3335

Provides services and information to businesses that use telephone sales to market products. Seeks to dispel public perception of telephone marketing as "junk calls."

Bankcard Holders of America (BHA)
560 Herndon Parkway, Suite 120
Herndon, VA 22070
703-481-1110

A membership organization of bank and credit card holders that works to educate the public about the wise and careful use of credit. Conducts educational programs and surveys, monitors economic trends, and makes public service announcements promoting credit awareness.

Call for Action (CFA)
3400 Idaho Avenue NW, Suite 101
Washington, DC 20016
202-537-0585
TDD 202-537-1551

A public service program involving 800 volunteers from the broadcasting industry that provides consumers with free, confidential information and assistance in solving their consumer problems. The Intercity Network office provides help to consumers in cities where no volunteers are available and handles mail-order purchase problems. Sponsors "Ask the Expert," a consumer education program that makes professionals such as doctors, pharmacists, lawyers, and financial advisers available to answer questions free of charge.

Commodity Futures Trading Commission (CFTC)
2033 K Street NW
Washington, DC 20581
202-254-6387

The CFTC regulates trading on the thirteen U.S. futures exchanges. Contact the Office of Communication and Education Services of the CFTC in Washington, DC, or call 202-254-8630 for more information.

Consumer Federation of America (CFA)
1424 16th Street NW, Suite 604
Washington, DC 20036
202-387-6121

An organization of consumer groups and protection agencies that disseminates information on consumer issues and serves as an advocate for consumer rights.

Consumer Product Safety Commission
5401 Westbard Avenue
Bethesda, MD 20207
301-492-6580
Consumer Product Safety Hotline 800-638-CPSC
TDD 800-638-8270
In Maryland, TDD 800-492-8104

An independent federal regulatory agency that seeks to protect consumers from dangerous products. The agency maintains a clearinghouse of information on product-related injury and conducts outreach programs for consumers, industry, and local governments. Information is available from the Office of Information and Public Affairs.

Consumer Sourcebook
Robert Wilson, Editor
Gale Research, Inc.

A subject guide to approximately 7000 federal, state, and local government agencies and offices; national, regional, and grassroots associations and organizations; and information centers, clearinghouses, and related consumer resources. Most larger libraries have this book in their reference collections.

Council of Better Business Bureaus (CBBB)
4200 Wilson Boulevard, Suite 800
Arlington, VA 22203
703-276-0100

The CBBB is supported by local Better Business Bureaus and their membership of more than 240,000 businesses. It serves as a spokesperson for business in the consumer field, supports consumer education programs, and works to arbitrate consumer complaints. Local bureaus handle over 11 million public contacts annually without charge. CBBB sponsors Auto Line, a national mediation and arbitration service between car owners with complaints and participating automobile companies. Look for your local Better Business Bureau office listed in the white pages of your telephone book.

Department of Housing and Urban Development (HUD)
Interstate Land Sales and Registration Division
451 7th Street SW
Washington, DC 20410
202–708–0980

Helps determine consumer rights regarding housing under the Full Disclosure Act of 1968. The Act generally applies to developers selling or leasing 100 or more unimproved lots through interstate commerce, who must register their subdivisions with HUD. For more information, contact the Office of Public Affairs at HUD. To report fraudulent activities, call the HUD Hotline at 800–347–3735, or TDD 202–708–2451. For the nearest regional office, check the white pages of your telephone book under "U. S. Government."

Direct Selling Association (DSA)
1776 K Street NW, Suite 600
Washington, DC 20006
202–293–5760

Association of multilevel marketers and distributors who sell products door-to-door, by appointment and through home-party plans. The DSA sponsors the Direct Selling Education Foundation, which works to protect the public interest in the marketplace. The foundation promotes ethical standards, consumer knowledge, and satisfaction through its educational programs.

Federal Bureau of Investigation (FBI)
United States Department of Justice
10th Street & Pennsylvania Avenue NW
Washington, DC 20535
202–324–3000

The law enforcement arm of the U.S. Justice Department, the FBI investigates all federal crimes except those assigned to other agencies. For the nearest office, check the white pages of your telephone book under "U.S. Government."

Federal Trade Commission (FTC)
Bureau of Consumer Protection
6th and Pennsylvania Avenue NW
Washington, DC 20580
202–326–2222

Consumer protection is one of the major purposes of the FTC, which actively seeks to prevent unfair and deceptive advertising and marketing practices, enforces the Consumer Credit Protection Act, and serves as an advocate for consumer concerns before courts and legislative bodies. Inquiries concerning consumer protection and complaints should be directed to the nearest regional office. For the nearest office, check the white pages of your telephone book under "U.S. Government."

Food and Drug Administration (FDA)
Consumer Affairs and Information
5600 Fishers Lane
Rockville, MD 20857
301–443–5006

The FDA provides information to the public through a network of consumer phones that can be reached in any of its 32 regional offices. Look for your local FDA office listed in the white pages of your telephone book under "U.S. Government."

Fraud & Theft Information Bureau
217 N. Seacrest Boulevard, Box 400
Boynton Beach, Florida 33425
407–737–7500

Part of the National Association of Credit Card Merchants, it publishes the *Bank Identification Number (BIN) Directory* for merchants, along with other fraud-control publications.

Health and Human Services Hotline
HHS OIG Hotline
P. O. Box 17303
Baltimore, MD 21203–7303
800–368–5779
In Maryland 800–638–3986

Receives complaints concerning fraud involving programs (such as Medicare) administered by the Department of Health and Human Services.

Internal Revenue Service (IRS)
Department of the Treasury
1111 Constitution Avenue NW
Washington, DC 20224
202–622–5000

Consumers may file complaints against deceptive charitable organizations with the IRS. For a local or regional office near you, check the white pages of your telephone book under the heading "U.S. Government."

Immigration and Naturalization Service (INS)
425 I Street NW

Washington, DC 20536
202–514–4316

Provides information regarding immigration and naturalization to the public while enforcing immigration laws. For the district office nearest you, look under "U.S. Government" in the white pages of your telephone directory.

International Anti-Counterfeiting Coalition, Inc. (IACC)
818 Connecticut Avenue NW, 12th Floor
Washington, DC 20006
202–223–5728

IACC membership includes American, European, and Asian corporations and associations. It works to eliminate counterfeiting of a wide variety of merchandise, disseminates information to the public concerning the problems caused by purchasing counterfeit products, advocates strong law enforcement and conducts enforcement programs in the U.S., Thailand, and Italy.

International Franchise Association (IFA)
1350 New York Avenue NW, Suite 900
Washington, DC 20005
202–628–8000

Members include firms in 58 countries involved in franchise businesses. Holds annual symposia, workshops, and trade shows on various aspects of the franchise business. Publishes *Franchise Opportunities Guide.*

International Trade Commission
500 E Street SW
Washington, DC 20436
202-205-1819

Details procedures to follow in obtaining an exclusion order against foreign product counterfeiting.

National Association of Consumer Agency Administrators (NACAA)
1010 Vermont Avenue NW, Suite 514
Washington, DC 20005
202–347–7395

Organization of state, county, and local governmental consumer protection agencies; federal agencies, universities, and foreign consumer agencies. The NACAA works to enhance consumer services, conducts seminars and public policy forums to promote consumer interests, and maintains a clearinghouse of information for consumer education.

National Association of Home Builders of the U.S. (NAHB)
15th and M Streets NW
Washington, DC 20005
202-822-0200

Professional association of single and multifamily home builders, commercial builders, and others associated with the building industry. Sponsors seminars and workshops on a variety of subjects related to the building industry.

National Association of Realtors (NAR)
430 Michigan Avenue
Chicago, IL 60611-4087
312-329-8200

The NAR is a federation of 50 state associations and 1848 local real estate boards that promotes education and high professional standards in the real estate field.

National Association of Securities Dealers (NASD)
1735 K Street NW
Washington, DC 20006
202-728-8000

The self-regulatory agency for NASDAQ (National Association of Securities Dealers Automated Quotations) and over-the-counter markets.

National Charities Information Bureau (NCIB)
19 Union Square West, 6th Floor
New York, NY 10003-3395
212-929-6300

An organization founded in 1918 that provides a reporting and advisory service about national and international nonprofit organizations that solicit contributions from the public. The NCIB promotes high ethical standards in the field of philanthropy and provides donors with independent reports on the purposes, programs, and stability of nonprofit groups. Publications include: *Wise Giving Guide, The 1-2-3 of Evaluation,* and *Charitable Giving: What Contributors Want to Know.*

National Consumer Fraud Task Force (NCFTF)
1500 W. 23rd Street
Sunset Island, No. 3
Miami Beach, FL 33140
305-532-2607

The NCFTF attempts to shut down career, counseling, and marketing operations that promise job seekers access to hidden job markets for advance fees. Offers consultation to victims of fraudulent employment firms, and encourages public awareness of these types of fraudulent companies.

National Consumers League (NCL)
815 15th Street NW, Suite 928N
Washington, DC 20005
202–639–8140

Encourages public participation in governmental and industry decision-making. The NCL conducts research, educational, and advocacy programs on consumer and worker issues, including: insurance, credit, health, telemarketing fraud, and product safety and standards. Publishes numerous consumer guides, fact sheets, and other educational materials.

National Council Against Health Fraud (NCAHF)
P.O. Box 1276
Loma Linda, CA 92354
714–824–4690

An organization of health and legal professionals that seeks to educate the public on fraud and quackery in health care. The NCAHF offers advice to consumers, provides expert witnesses for health fraud trials, and assists law enforcement officials with health fraud cases.

National Fraud Information Center (NFIC)
A Project of the National Consumers League
800–876–7060

A consumer service project of the National Consumers League, the NFIC offers information on current major frauds and counselors to assist those who have been defrauded with filing complaints.

National Futures Association (NFA)
200 West Madison Street, Suite 1600
Chicago, IL 60606
312–781–1300
800–621–3570
800–572–9400 (in Illinois)

Industry association for brokers and others involved in the trading of futures on the commodity market. Works to provide more effective industry self-regulation, member qualification screening, and monitors and enforces customer protection rules and uniform business standards. The NFA also arbitrates customer disputes. They publish a free annual review, along with numerous information pamphlets and guides.

National Health Care Anti-Fraud Association (NHCAA)
1255 23rd Street NW, Suite 850
Washington, DC 20037
202–659–5955

Network of private insurance companies and public and private agencies that work against health insurance fraud and share information on claims.

National Insurance Consumer Organization (NICO)
121 N. Payne Street
Alexandria, VA 22314
703–549–8050

A public-interest organization that works to educate consumers on all aspects of buying insurance. NICO provides consumer advocacy on public policy issues and works for reform of unfair practices and abuses in the insurance industry. Publications include *Buyer's Guide to Insurance: What the Companies Won't Tell You,* and a variety of other informative books, pamphlets, and consumer guides.

National Insurance Consumer Helpline
800–942–4242

National Office Machine Dealers Association (NOMDA)
12411 Wornall Road
Kansas City, MO 64145
816–941–3100

This association of retailers and suppliers of office machines offers seminars and conducts research. Provides information on returning unordered supplies and other related business fraud.

National Office Products Association (NOPA)
301 N. Fairfax Street
Alexandria, VA 22314
703–549–9040

Industry association of manufacturers, manufacturers' representatives, wholesalers, and retailers dealing in office products, furniture, and machines. NOPA sponsors seminars, conducts research, and publishes an annual directory of its membership that includes a buyer's guide covering 156 product categories.

North American Securities Administrators Association (NASAA)
1 Massachusetts Avenue, NW, Suite 310
Washington, DC 20001
202–737–0900

Organization of state and provincial officials involved in enforcing securities sales laws.

Patent and Trademark Office
2011 Crystal Drive
Arlington, VA 22202
703–305–8341

The Patent and Trademark Office maintains and records patents and trademarks for products and product names. In addition, it provides information to individuals and businesses involved in litigation concerning infringement of patent and trademark rights.

Philanthropic Advisory Service
Council of Better Business Bureaus, Inc.
4200 Wilson Boulevard
Arlington, VA 22203
703–276–0100

Provides information about national fund-raising organizations. Complaints about national charities may be directed to the Philanthropic Advisory Service.

Securities and Exchange Commission
450 Fifth Street NW
Washington, DC 20549
202–272–7440

Administers federal securities laws that seek to provide protection for investors to ensure that securities markets are fair and honest. Regulates public offers and sales of securities. Answers questions about securities dealings; verifies registration of securities dealers and firms. The Publications Unit offers materials to assist potential investors. Has nine regional and branch offices; check in the white pages (under "U.S. Government") or call the Washington, DC, office for the branch in your area.

U.S. Copyright Office
Library of Congress
Washington, DC 20559
202–707–3000

The Copyright Office provides information about copyrights, copyright law, and registration procedures.

U.S. Customs Service
Department of the Treasury
1301 Constitution Avenue NW
Washington, DC 20229
202–927–2095

The Customs Service investigates fraudulent import practices, violations of copyright, trademark and patent laws, and marking requirements for imported merchandise. In addition, Customs enforces requirements dealing with product and consumer safety as they relate to imported goods.

U.S. Department of Commerce (DOC)
14th Street between Constitution Avenue and E Street NW
Washington, DC 20230
202–377–2000

The Department of Commerce oversees all commerce within the U.S., trade with foreign countries, and administers a wide variety of programs related to trade through its divisions.

U.S. Postal Service
475 L'Enfant Plaza SW
Washington, DC 20260-0010
Attn: Chief Postal Inspector
     Fraud Section
202–268–2000
Postal Crime Hotline: 800–654–8896
Washington, DC and vicinity residents: 202–484–5480

Investigates reports of violations of federal postal laws, including bogus mail-order investment schemes, phony invoices, solicitations disguised as invoices, and any scheme that includes documents sent through the U.S. mail. Contact your local post office for help concerning mail fraud, or call the Postal Crime Hotline.

U.S. Social Security Administration
Department of Health and Human Services
6401 Security Boulevard
Baltimore, MD 21235
410–965–7700

The Social Security Administration conducts investigations into fraudulent activities involving Social Security funds or recipients. Their toll-free hotline is 800–772–1213.

Weiss Research, Inc.
P.O. Box 2923
West Palm Beach, FL 33402
407–684–8100
Sales: 800–289–9222

Publishes *Insurance Safety Directory: A Complete Guide to Life, Health and Annuity Companies With Their Safety Ratings,* a guide for consumers and investors that lists insurance companies and ranks them according to the financial strength and stability of the company. Companies with a B+ or higher rating are listed in a consumer guide section in the directory, which is available in many libraries. Provides consumers with the only ranking of the nation's 72 Blue Cross and Blue Shield plans.

Specific addresses for the following may be found in the City, County, and State Government listings in the white pages of your telephone directory:

District Attorney's Office
State Attorney General's Office

Both the District Attorney's Office and the State Attorney General's Office investigate and prosecute fraud cases.

Social and Health Services
Social Services
Welfare Office

Report fraud and abuse of financial assistance programs, medical assistance programs, and food stamps to these local, county, and state agencies. They are known by a variety of names depending on the locality.

State Securities Commission
State Securities Department
Department of Corporations

All of the above regulate offers and sales of securities by companies in the state. You may need to contact your state capital's information bureau for more information.

INDEX